DEREK PRIME & ALISTAIR BEGG

On Being *a*
Pastor

Understanding
Our Calling and Work

MOODY PUBLISHERS
CHICAGO

All Scripture quotations, unless otherwise indicated, are taken from the *Holy Bible, New International Version*®. NIV®. Copyright © 1973, 1978, 1984 by International Bible Society. Used by permission of Zondervan Publishing House. All rights reserved.

Scripture quotations marked KJV are taken from the King James Version.

Library of Congress Cataloging-in-Publication Data

Prime, Derek
    On being a pastor : understanding our calling and work / Derek Prime and Alistair Begg.
        p. cm.
    ISBN 0-8024-3120-8
    1. Pastoral theology. I. Begg, Alistair. II. Title.

BV4011.3.P75 2004
253'.2—dc22

2004000012

1 3 5 7 9 10 8 6 4 2

Printed in the United States of America

*To the rising generation of pastors
and teachers and those who through
the grace of God will be called
to follow in their footsteps.*

CONTENTS

FOREWORD

The Christian pastor holds the greatest office of human responsibility in all creation. He is called to preach the Word, to teach the truth to God's people, to lead God's people in worship, to tend the flock as a caring shepherd, and to mobilize the church for Christian witness and service. The pastor's role also includes an entire complex of administrative and leadership tasks. Souls are entrusted to his care, the truth is entrusted to his stewardship, and eternal realities hang in the balance. Who can fulfill this job description?

Of course, the answer is that no man can fulfill this calling. The Christian pastor must continually acknowledge his absolute dependence upon the grace and mercy of God. As the apostle Paul instructs us, we are but earthen vessels employed for God's glory. On his own, no man is up to this task.

Derek Prime and Alistair Begg are two seasoned pastors armed with biblical truth, theological conviction, and practical insight. In *On Being a Pastor,* these faithful ministers share their hard-earned wisdom, combining personal testimony with solid theologically grounded reflections. This is a book every pastor should read.

Reading this fascinating book is like sitting down with two good mature and proven pastors who speak to their fellow pastors as warm friends. These men know what the pastorate is all about. They are preachers of renown and international reputation. Yet, they welcome us into their conversation as encouraging friends, ready to speak honestly about the pastor's calling and responsibility. They do not dodge the hard issues, and their honesty is both bracing and encouraging.

This book belongs in the hands of every pastor and theological student preparing for the ministry. There is a wealth of wisdom in these pages, and a real education between these two covers. This book will call every pastor to a higher standard of service—and an even greater joy in this great calling.

R. Albert Mohler Jr., President
The Southern Baptist Theological Seminary

AUTHORS' NOTE

We need to begin with a word of explanation. This book was originally written by Derek when he had been a pastor for thirty years and was about to conclude his ministry at Charlotte Chapel in Edinburgh. In God's goodness that original edition of 1989 was reprinted and widely used. In contemplating the suggestion that it should be reissued, two convictions emerged. First, it was felt that it would benefit from some revision by Derek, because while biblical principles remain constant, the situations to which they have to be applied change; and, second, since the book has been read and used in the USA, that it would benefit from the input of an American church's pastor—that of Alistair. It has been a great pleasure to work together again, as Alistair began his ministry as Derek's assistant in Edinburgh. Throughout the book therefore we write as *we,* and where our circumstances prompt a different application of the same principles we preface our individual contributions by the initials DP or AB.

INTRODUCTION

W e doubt if we would have written this book had we not been encouraged to do so. It seems presumptuous even to appear to be telling other pastors and teachers what they should do—and that has not been our intention. For that reason we have tried as often as possible to use the pronoun "we" rather than "you."

Our aim has been to review the ministry of pastors and teachers in the Church and, in cases where it may help, share our own experience and practice, not as a model but as a possible guide and starting point, no matter how amended or adapted, for those who are at the beginning of their ministry or others who may benefit from the stimulus of comparing their own way of doing things with someone else's.

We believe in the pastoral ministry. Changes in the life of the contemporary Church have produced a crisis of identity for many pastors and teachers. There has been a justifiable reaction against what has been commonly termed "the one-man ministry" —justifiable in that no one possesses all the gifts of ministry, and the traditional distinction between "clergy" and "laity" is neither biblical nor helpful. But—as so often happens—the pendulum can swing too far the other way, and the gifts of the Spirit and the priesthood of all believers may be interpreted to mean that all are equally equipped to minister, to the neglect of the proper place that should be given to the gifts of pastoral care and teaching. The development of team ministries means that pastors and teachers may have their twin tasks separated, so that they are expected to fulfill one more than the other, and sometimes even to relinquish one vital part of their ministry altogether.

Behind this book there are five basic convictions. First, Christ's special gift to His Church is the gift of pastors and teachers, a conviction based upon understanding Ephesians 4:11 to mean that He endows individuals with both gifts. They may or may not be set apart by God's people to give all of their time to these tasks. Where church financial resources are not available, some will support themselves partly or completely by the contemporary equivalent of "tent-making."

Second, the pastor and teacher is an elder among other elders in the local church, irrespective of whether or not the term *elder* is used to describe church leaders.

Third, the work of the elders—by whatever name they are described—needs to be encouraged and developed. There is no better team ministry than that of an eldership raised up by the Holy Spirit in a local church fellowship.

Fourth, whatever the pattern is for shared leadership in the local church, there must be a leader among leaders. It is common for the leading teaching elder—the pastor or minister—to be also the presiding elder. This does not have to be the case, but it proves the best arrangement in most churches.

Finally, both the pastor and teacher himself and the church fellowship of which he is a part need to be clear as to his function and place in the body of Christ. His principal task is to edify the church by spiritual feeding. We cannot overestimate the importance of the edification of God's people through regular and systematic teaching and preaching of His Word. A seminal Scripture for thought is Acts 9:31 where Luke explains that, after Saul's conversion, "the church throughout Judea, Galilee and Samaria enjoyed a time of peace. It was strengthened; and encouraged by the Holy Spirit, it grew in numbers, living in the fear of the Lord." The implication is that as the church was strengthened spiritually, so it grew numerically. Since the Church grows and flourishes as the Word of God has free course and is honored, any uncertainty as to the place of pastors and teachers in the Church militates against the spiritual stability, discipline, prosperity, and growth of Christ's people. It is not surprising that Satan uses confusion concerning their place in the Church as a subtle ploy to harm her.

CHAPTER 1

THE CALL
AND THE CALLING

DEFINING OUR TERMS

The ministry of undershepherds and teachers is not simply a job. Rather it is a vocation, the answering of a specific call from God. It is the highest calling in Christian service. As a young man, F. B. Meyer shared his call to the ministry in a letter to a friend:

> For friendship's sake I do not like to conceal from you, or in fact from any one else, the decision to which I have come. So to be frank, I have decided my future course, and am going, with help from above, to be a minister of the Gospel. Now I can imagine your astonishment, but it is a fact. I need only add that it appears to me to be the noblest aim in life to live entirely devoted to the one object of bringing others to know Him who has accomplished so much for us. When weighed against the hereafter, earth and its careers sink into insignificance.[1]

Six months after his conversion, John Stott, still only seventeen, "was sure of his future calling to the ordained ministry of the Church of England." When he was completing his university course, his parents were unhappy at his pursuing his call. In a letter to his father, he gave the reasons for his decision, the first of which was, "*Obedience to my call.* Whatever you may think of it, I have had a definite and irresistible call from God to serve Him in the Church. During the last three years I have become increasingly conscious of this call, and my life now could be summed up in the words 'separated unto the gospel of God.' There is no higher service; I ask no other."[2] To make such claims about God's call we must define our terms. By call we mean the unmistakable conviction an individual possesses that God wants him to do a specific task.

The task in view is that defined by the New Testament as being a pastor and teacher. God calls men to shepherd God's flock and to care for its well-being, to show God's people by example and instruction how they should live lives worthy of God their Savior. Sometimes pastors and teachers may be described as elders, bishops, or overseers, but whatever their description and title, an essential qualification is that they should be "able to teach" (1 Timothy 3:2).

They are all called to take their share in the direction of the affairs of the local church, but not all are called to give the whole of their time to the work of shepherding and teaching (1 Timothy 5:17). We have both in view, but our particular focus is upon those set apart to give the whole of their time to this calling. However we view a pastor, or minister, or leader among leaders, within a Christian fellowship, we should think of him in terms of the New Testament elder, and as an elder among elders. We are thinking not so much of an office that may be held but of the exercise of a spiritual gift. The church has often tended to be office-oriented instead of gift-oriented, and the right balance needs to be struck.

THE IRRESISTIBLE NATURE OF THE CALL

Advice frequently given is, "If you can avoid entering the ministry, do so! If you can do something else, do it!" This is sound counsel. If it is right for a man to give himself completely to the ministry of the gospel, he will feel that it is the only thing he can do. John Ryle, a nineteenth-century bishop of Liverpool, had no early sense of call, and when he shared his decision to enter the ministry it came as a complete surprise to everyone. His explanation was, "I felt shut up to do it and saw no other course of life open to me." And thus it has ever been.

Such advice makes good sense about any employment. Where possible we should enjoy what we do in life and engage in it with enthusiasm. Few make any impact for good upon others if they work halfheartedly. The ministry demands much of a man and his family. Before entering upon it, therefore, he needs to count the cost. Our Lord's words about the importance of a man not looking back once he has put his hand to the plow have particular relevance to pastors and teachers. Many have begun and then, sadly, stopped.

More important still, behind this advice there is the basic truth that God always gives a clear call to those whom He has chosen for the ministry, so that when that call comes they can do nothing other than respond to it. They will not be able to say no to it. It follows that if someone thinks he may be called to the ministry but is not absolutely certain, then he should wait until he is sure. God does not give uncertain calls. As Dr. Martyn Lloyd-Jones expressed it, "It was God's hand that laid hold of me, and drew me out, and separated me to this work."[3]

In focusing upon the call of pastors and teachers, we are not suggesting that God's call does not come equally to others for different tasks. Nevertheless, the call to shepherd God's people and to teach them His Word is a special calling because of its strategic and unique importance for the spiritual well-being of Christ's flock.

The Call in the Context of God's Calling of All Christians

The words *call* and *calling* are used in a number of ways in the New Testament, and the call to the ministry is not the first call from God an individual receives. First Corinthians 1:1–9 provides a typical example. The primary call is to fellowship with God's Son Jesus Christ (verse 9)—a call to union with Christ and all its glorious benefits. The second call is to holiness (verse 2). Calling and justification bring the inevitable consequence and privilege of sanctification. The third call is to service, and frequently to specific service. In Paul's case, his primary service was to be an apostle (verse 1). God's call to be a shepherd and teacher is a specific call.

Old Testament Examples

The prophets' experience exemplifies the manner in which God works in commissioning His servants. The Old Testament prophets found God's call irresistible, much as sometimes they shrank from its implications. The call came in a variety of ways and circumstances, but it was essentially the same. For Moses it came forty years after his failure to wait God's time as he foolishly took matters into his own hands by physically defending a fellow Hebrew. At the time of his call he was carrying out his daily occupation of caring for sheep in the desert (Exodus 3). He was immediately aware of God's holiness (verse 5), and he was so overwhelmed at the implications of God's call that he asked, "Who am I, that I should go . . . ?" (verse 11).

Isaiah's call came when he visited the temple during a period of national crisis (Isaiah 6:1). He, too, was acutely conscious of God's inexpressible holiness. But in hearing God ask, "Whom shall I send? And who will go for us?" he could do no other than say, "Here am I. Send me!" (verse 8). Jeremiah was told that before he was formed in the womb God both knew him and set him apart for the work of a prophet (Jeremiah 1:5). This staggering truth did not stop

Jeremiah from responding, "Ah, Sovereign LORD . . . I do not know how to speak" (verse 6). But the call was irresistible.

Apostolic Example

The apostles are the principal examples of those called to be shepherds and teachers. Ministers are not apostles, but apostles were ministers—they were shepherds and teachers. The apostle Peter's manner of addressing the leaders of the churches in Asia Minor in his first letter is significant: "To the elders among you, I appeal as a fellow elder . . ." (5:1). What the apostles did in the Acts of the Apostles, when they took steps to ensure that they gave priority to prayer and the ministry of the Word (6:2), ministers today ought to do, for their priorities are identical.

The gospel writers describe how the apostles each received a distinct personal call from our Lord Jesus Christ to the ministry for which He was to prepare them. The same was true for the apostle Paul, whose call came after the others'. From the moment of his conversion Paul was aware of God's call. When Ananias was somewhat hesitant to go to Paul at the announcement of Paul's conversion, the Lord reassured him, "Go! This man is my chosen instrument to carry my name before the Gentiles and their kings and before the people of Israel" (Acts 9:15). Referring later to his conversion, Paul elaborates upon this and relates that when he asked, "Who are you, Lord?" the Lord replied,

> *I am Jesus, whom you are persecuting. . . . Now get up and stand on your feet. I have appeared to you to appoint you as a servant and as a witness of what you have seen of me and what I will show you. I will rescue you from your own people and from the Gentiles. I am sending you to them to open their eyes and turn them from darkness to light, and from the power of Satan to God, so that they may receive forgiveness of sins and a place among those who are sanctified by faith in me.* (Acts 26:15–18)

It was with the conviction of this call that Paul worked and wrote, so that he begins the passage we have referred to in 1 Corinthians 1 with the words, "Paul, called to be an apostle of Christ Jesus by the will of God" (verse 1)—a conviction consistently echoed in his other letters (cf. Romans 1:1; 2 Corinthians 1:1; Galatians 1:1; Ephesians 1:1; Colossians 1:1; 1 Timothy 1:1; 2 Timothy 1:1; Titus 1:1).

THE DEVELOPMENT OF THE SENSE OF CALL

The call to shepherding and teaching comes in a variety of ways—and history shows this has always been the case. The key factor is that it is God the Holy Spirit who issues the call. The call comes about through sensitivity to God's dealings with us as we pray, through reading the Scriptures, and through listening to the preaching of God's Word, and often it is reinforced as we discover how God's call has come to others both at the present time and in the past.

The call usually begins with a desire to care for the spiritual well-being of others and to preach God's Word. Circumstances may put us in the position where we feel that we must do something to help people. Alan Stibbs was an extremely able expositor and teacher. His testimony to the way in which he developed his gifts was that although the Scripture Union group at his school in England was well attended, there was no one who would undertake the leadership of the group. So for two years between the age of sixteen and eighteen, he carried this responsibility alone. And so it was that three times a week he had to stand before his school contemporaries and seek to show them that, from a Bible passage fixed by others, God had something to say to him and them. Let him give his own testimony from this point:

> During the same period, when I was seventeen, I "discovered," and was arrested by, 1 Corinthians xiv. Here I found an injunction to

covet spiritual gifts, especially to prophesy (see verses 1, 12, 19). In the light of other statements in the chapter I understood prophesying to mean, not foretelling the future, nor receiving new revelations from heaven, but expounding revealed truth in a manner both intelligible and helpful to the hearer. Such an exposition should be related to men's condition, and should be expressed in words that they can understand. Its aim should be to bring to the hearers instruction, challenge and encouragement (verse 3).

So I began as a schoolboy of seventeen to pray for this gift, and—on each occasion when I expounded God's Word—to pray for the grace worthily to exercise the gift to the glory of God and the blessing of men. Such prayers I have continued often to pray since; and I can humbly testify that God has answered my prayers.[4]

Our circumstances may be entirely different, but the desire to assist others by means of the Scriptures will be present. It may not be put into words and shared initially with others, because we may feel that it is rather presumptuous to have such thoughts. Reserve is not out of place. But where there is a genuine call, the desire to serve in these specific ways will grow and become dominant. The early Church obviously expected individuals to be drawn to pastoral and teaching responsibilities, and to recognize God's call, since one of the "trustworthy sayings" that they regularly quoted to one another was, "If anyone sets his heart on being an overseer, he desires a noble task" (1 Timothy 3:1). Although it can be sheer presumption to have such a desire, it will equally be simple obedience on the part of those called by our Lord Jesus Christ.

If genuine, the desire to be a shepherd and teacher will be nurtured. There will be a desire for preparation and training, since one of the evidences of a call is the possession of the qualifications for it. An obvious example is the knowledge of the Scriptures, and anyone with a call from God will make the most of every opportunity to study them. Opportunities for sharing in the care of others and of teaching and preaching will be seized. These tasks will never be irksome, but sheer joy. As opportunities are taken, people will become aware of the gifts of pastoral care and preaching and will comment on them. Such encouragements will fire the desire to pursue God's call all the more.

Most important of all, the spiritual leaders of the church to which a Christian belongs may take the initiative in raising the issue of the call to the ministry, particularly if, as they ought, they regularly ask God for sensitivity to the gifts Christ gives to His body.

We may not always be aware at first as to whether God's call is to give all or part of our time to shepherding and teaching—for there is a place for both. That ought not to be a major preoccupation, in that such uncertainty simply indicates that the time is not yet right for action. At the appropriate stage God will make it plain.

Sometimes the call may come to its climax through the invitation of a church to become its pastor. As an occasional or regular ministry is exercised within a church, God the Holy Spirit may give the leadership and membership an unmistakable conviction as to God's call, which they then publicly recognize and obey by their invitation.

The confirmation of the call to the ministry is of vital importance. It is not enough to feel that we may possibly have a call to the ministry. Such uncertainty leads to tragic mistakes. It has been traditional to speak of the double call to the ministry: There is first the inward call an individual becomes personally aware of; there is, second, the outward call of God's people as they recognize the calling and gifts an individual has for the ministry. Acts 13 provides a powerful example of the latter in the call of Paul and Barnabas to Gentile missionary work. As the church met together for the worship of God and for prayer, the Holy Spirit instructed the church to set them apart for the work to which He had called them (Acts 13:2). In one verse Luke writes of the church sending them off, and in the next of the Holy Spirit (verses 3, 4).

If formal training is part of the preparation for the ministry, then the call should also be put to the test by those responsible for the training. This is a good double check of the outward call of God's people, but it ought never to replace the confirmation of the individual's call by the company of God's people to which he belongs. No church is better able to confirm a call to the ministry than a man's home church—it is the natural and appropriate proving ground. He should submit himself, therefore, to the spiritual leadership of his church fellowship, asking them to test his call. Situations exist where someone may not have the advantage of belonging to a church fellowship where his call can be properly tested. In such circumstances, besides the tests any training establishment may apply, it is important that he should willingly submit himself to the judgment of Christians who know him well and who may be relied upon to be completely honest in stating their convictions.

Sometimes a man's call may be immediately obvious to his own church fellowship and leadership. The outward call then straightaway matches the individual's inner call. On other occasions time may be required to allow the gifts of shepherding and teaching to emerge more clearly. It may be appropriate for the spiritual leadership to consider how they may deliberately provide scope for the exercise and development of the gifts appropriate for a call to the ministry. Ideally the church leadership should be able to share with the membership the possible call a member has, and to say that they will provide him with opportunities of ministry within the church fellowship with the specific aim of testing his call. Members will then not be surprised to see him asked to preach or to help in pastoral work or in the conduct of worship.

When inner and outward call match and come together, then is the time to proceed further. According to an individual's circumstances, formal training may be the next step. For others it will be a matter of waiting for a call to a church. But the testing of the call we have suggested is imperative and must not be bypassed. Mistakes made at this stage will be disastrous for the person concerned and—more important still—for the well-being of God's flock.

Writing in his diary on February 15, 1835, Robert Murray M'Cheyne wrote, "To-morrow I undergo my trials before the Presbytery. May God give me courage in the hour of need. What should I fear? If God see meet to put me into the ministry, who shall keep me back? If I be not meet, why should I thrust forward? To Thy service I desire to dedicate myself over and over again."

What could be worse for a church fellowship than to have someone attempting to be a shepherd and teacher without God's call? It is important, too, because throughout a man's ministry the enemy of souls will contest his call, especially when the going is tough. Tremendous strength comes from reviewing the manner in which God confirmed our call through the unanimous understanding He gave others of His will concerning us. That was clearly the point of Paul's reminders to Timothy of the way in which God's call to Timothy to be a shepherd and teacher had been confirmed (1 Timothy 1:18; 4:14).

DP My own conviction concerning the call to the ministry was present soon after my conversion in my teens. It surfaced when it was my turn to give the talk at the young people's meeting of the church through whose witness I had been brought to Christ. The pastor was present, and afterward he turned to me and asked, "Derek, have you ever thought of the ministry?" At the age of sixteen I had thought that to have such a desire so early was rather presumptuous, and yet it was wonderful to me that it was not I who raised the subject but my pastor. His question strengthened my desire to take things further. Throughout my national service and my time at university, the conviction did not leave me. Rather it grew as opportunities for ministry arose both in the forces and in the Christian Union.

In my last year at university I wrote to the elders of

my home church and asked for their honest conviction as to my call. Their considered response was that they were sure about it, but they were not clear as to the timing, and they thought that my work initially might be with young people.

Coming from a non-Christian background, my parents opposed my going into the ministry, even though they consented to my switching to theology in my third year at university. And so I taught first history and then religious knowledge for three and a half years in a boys' grammar school. During this time opportunities for preaching multiplied, and I became an elder of the church where I had been converted. To my surprise, during a pastoral vacancy, one of the elders intimated to me after a church prayer meeting that he and the other elders had come to the conclusion that it was God's will that I should become pastor of the church, and that they would share that conviction with the church if I felt an answering conviction.

There have been many occasions when being a pastor has proved difficult, and the enemy of souls has whispered, "Are you sure you did the right thing? Should you be in the ministry at all?" I have gained immeasurable strength from remembering that my decision to obey God's call was confirmed initially by the elders as I submitted myself to their direction, and then underlined by the clear call of God's people in a situation in which I had no hand. I would wish that kind of confirmation to be the experience of every shepherd and teacher, because it provides undoubted sustaining power.

AB When I think of being called to pastoral ministry I begin with Sunday afternoons in our home in Glasgow.

My parents routinely welcomed pastors and missionaries to our home for lunch and tea. I have vivid recollections of these "ancient men," who were probably in their forties, saying to me: "Maybe one day, son, you'll grow up to be a minister." It was only years later that I recalled these statements. I think it would be true to say that they returned to haunt me.

As a teenager I had begun to speak at Christian coffee bars, which were a feature of the sixties. I was also a Bible class leader for a group of ten-year-old boys. Each opportunity proved difficult and yet delightful, and the feedback I received was encouraging. However, it did not create within me a desire for pastoral ministry. In fact it never occurred to me. I was committed to the idea of becoming a lawyer. Too much Perry Mason had fueled my aspirations for courtroom drama. But it was not to be.

God used failure and disappointment to redirect my life. Even when I was a student at the London Bible College I was thinking about student work or some area of evangelism but not the role of pastor-teacher. I can still recall the occasion when the hammer dropped. I was eating lunch with a number of friends and one member of the faculty. The previous weekend I had been speaking at a youth retreat on the south coast of England. When I mentioned that I was increasingly disenchanted by the experience of making friends on Friday evening only to say good-bye on Sunday with no prospect of seeing them again or of following their progress, the faculty member looked at me from across the table and said: "Alistair, I can tell you why you feel that way. God has given you a pastor's heart." One of my friends laughed, and I wasn't sure how to respond.

I was twenty-three years old, about to graduate and be married, and I could see no prospect of a church being brave enough to take on a project like me. The opportunity to become the "assistant to the pastor" at Charlotte Chapel was then a crucial step in my call. It was in that context that the elders and congregation evaluated me and offered an objective affirmation of the growing sense of being "shut up to the ministry" that was in my heart. The occasion of my ordination to the gospel ministry in October 1976 was the final piece in the jigsaw puzzle of my call. For the past twenty-seven years I have enjoyed the immense privilege of pastoral ministry without ever seriously questioning whether I should, or even could, have done anything else with my life.

Paul and Barnabas found themselves in acutely difficult circumstances as they evangelized in the Gentile world. We can imagine Paul or Barnabas asking themselves, "Did we commission ourselves? If so, we deserve problems! But no! God called us, and He confirmed it by the corporate wisdom, judgment, and convictions of others" (see Acts 13:1–3).

If in doubt of a call, do not proceed—that counsel must always be given. It may be that the call is uncertain because it is not really present, or because the time is not yet right. We must proceed only when we can do so with certainty. Too much is at stake—for ourselves and for others—to do otherwise.

THE BEST KIND OF TRAINING

Anyone who is sure of God's call will be concerned to achieve the best kind of preparation. Experience shows that God does not deal with everyone in the same way in the matter of training. What is also clear is that the best training a person can receive—sometimes almost unconsciously—is that within his own home church where he serves and proves himself.

Straightforward university training in theology is God's way for some. Such training can sometimes be spiritually arid, and the Christian fellowship and spiritual stimulus of other students is then especially important. While not the right preparation for many, it is plainly God's purpose for some. For others the preferable course will be the training provided by theological seminaries or Bible colleges. Where there is a commitment to a particular denomination, there will be a training institution where the individual is expected to train.

But these are not the only options. It is possible to study by means of correspondence or distance learning courses, linked sometimes with brief periods of full-time study throughout the year. There is much to be said for this arrangement when a person is older and has family responsibilities, especially if through earlier training he has already acquired habits of disciplined study. A further possibility is to serve as an assistant or intern—during which time a call can be well tested—and mornings can be made free to study for a seminary or college course, a plan of directed reading, or a university diploma or degree.

Dogmatism is out of place about the best means of preparation for the ministry. Differing personal circumstances demand flexible approaches to the subject. What is crucial is that no one should make the decision on his own about training, but in consultation with those who are over him in the Lord and who are in a position to provide guidance.

THE MINISTER'S CALLING

It is appropriate to move from a minister's call to a minister's calling. The word *minister* is an appropriate place to begin: He is above all one who ministers—in other words he is a servant. One of the paradoxes of Christian leadership is that the leader is not a boss but a servant—someone who follows in the footsteps of Him who washed His disciples' feet. This is a good reason for placing the emphasis upon the gifts of ministry rather than the office of a minister.

The Corinthian Christians fell into the snare of making too much of the servants God gave them—men like Paul, Apollos, and Cephas—and giving their allegiance to them rather than to Christ Himself. Paul counters that harmful tendency by asking a pertinent question, "What, after all, is Apollos? And what is Paul?" with an equally pointed answer, "Only servants, through whom you came to believe—as the Lord has assigned to each his task" (1 Corinthians 3:5). Contemporary use has given the word *minister* a rather respectable sound, so that it implies station and office. But not so in the New Testament, for it properly implies lowly service—in fact, like that of a table waiter! James Haldane, who, together with his brother Robert, had great spiritual influence in Scotland in the late eighteenth and early nineteenth centuries, was described by an Edinburgh pastor in terms that are an example to all Christ's undershepherds: "James Haldane is . . . willing to become the servant of all, provided he be but useful." Service, not dominion, is a minister's calling.

The preeminent picture of the Lord Jesus in the Scriptures is that of the Servant of the Lord, and it is in His footsteps that we who minister are to follow, since it is in His footsteps we are to teach God's people to walk also (1 Peter 2:21).

A succinct description of a minister's calling is given in Ephesians 4:11. Paul explains that the ascended Lord Jesus "gave some to be apostles, some to be prophets, some to be evangelists, and some to be pastors and teachers," a passage paralleled in 1 Corinthians 12:28. The gift of pastors and teachers in Ephesians 4 is directly linked with the Church's growth. "Pastor" can equally well be translated "shepherd." The gift of pastors and teachers is described in the context of God's ultimate purpose of personal maturity in Christ for redeemed mankind: "to prepare God's people for works of service, so that the body of Christ may be built up until we all reach unity in the faith and in the knowledge of the Son of God and become mature, attaining to the whole measure of the fullness of Christ" (4:12–13). Our Lord Jesus Christ Himself is the Chief Shepherd and Chief Teacher, but He commissions individuals to fulfill these functions on His behalf (cf. John 21:15–17). Pastors and teachers carry on Christ's ministry to the Church.

The term "pastor and teacher" denotes one office in Ephesians 4:11, and shepherding and teaching are twin tasks. Some have tried to separate them in that they feel that their call is just to teach and not to shepherd. But the shepherding aspect of the ministry keeps us in touch with reality—with genuine issues and problems—as we teach the Word of God. To teach the Scriptures effectively we must apply them, and, with the Spirit's help, we can do this only as we are in touch with things as they really are in the lives of men and women. We have to determine sometimes the order of their priority in our work, in that some may be called more to pastoral work, and others more to teaching. But both are priorities, and they need to be kept together.

A minister—the servant of Christ and of His people—is first of all a shepherd. This description demands that we should know our flock well, so that we appreciate where they are in their understanding (whether, in terms of John 21, they are lambs or mature sheep). We are to get alongside the members of the flock so that we may encourage, comfort, urge, or warn them, as may be appropriate at any given moment (Acts 20:31; 1 Thessalonians 2:12). Each function proves necessary at different times, and our object in exercising them is to help people to live lives worthy of God who has called them into His kingdom and glory (1 Thessalonians 2:12).

A minister—the servant of Christ and of His people—is, second, a teacher. Keeping in view the picture of a shepherd, sheep require good pasture—the pasture of God's Word—presented in such a balanced, spiritual, and heartwarming way that the sheep are nourished and encouraged in their commitment to Christ and their growth to maturity. Good shepherding provides the best pasture by means of sound instruction.

The New Testament employs a number of other descriptions and pictures that amplify these two basic descriptions in Ephesians 4. A minister is to be like a father in the encouragement he gives to his children to aim at the best and the highest (1 Thessalonians 2:11–12). He is to be like a mother with her young children in terms of his gentleness with God's people (verse 7). He is to love them so much that he will be willing not only to share the gospel with them in all its fullness, but also his life as well (verse 8). He will be ready for them to be a burden to him, but he will never want to be a burden to them (verse 9). He will also see himself as something of a watchman or a guardian (Acts 20:28; Jude 3). There are always "savage wolves" wanting to come in among the flock who will not spare it if they can do harm (Acts 20:29).

THE CONTINUING PROOFS OF A CALL

There are obvious signs of the genuineness of our call. First, we will recognize that all our gifts belong not to ourselves but to Christ and His people, and we will want to use them faithfully to administer God's grace in its various forms (1 Peter 4:10–11). We will appreciate that our gifts are God-given and therefore a trust.

Second, when we speak, we will do so as those uttering the very words of God (1 Peter 4:11), as those approved of God to be entrusted with the gospel (1 Thessalonians 2:4). We will not want to impress our opinions upon people but to release God's Word in their lives. We will not be mindful of our own authority; our God-given sense of call will authenticate our ministry.

Third, we will not try to please men but God (1 Thessalonians 2:4), which means we will not look for human praise. We will not despise either the praise or the appreciation of God's people, but they will never be what we seek or the criterion of what we should do. It is a great blessing if God gives us this understanding from the commencement of our ministry. Dr. W. E. Sangster's first charge was the pastoral care of two churches in North Wales, one called St. John's, old-established and predominantly Welsh, and the other called Rhos, new and predominantly English. In the welcome meeting at Rhos, the members were anxious to tell their new and young minister what was what, and each department leader proceeded to tell him what was expected of him, and "stressed the importance of his own department, and made it clear that the kingdom of heaven was at hand only if the minister devoted his chief energy to that department. The long series of speeches and the carping atmosphere made an adequate reply impossible." Paul Sangster relates how his father, dignified even at his young age, stood up and said simply, "Thank you for your advice. I will try to please you all, but I shall try most of all to please God." With that he sat down and the meeting was over![5]

Fourth, we shall serve God with the strength He provides, with the determination that in all things He may be praised through our Lord Jesus Christ (1 Peter 4:11). And above all, we will be examples of holiness, righteousness, and blamelessness (1 Thessalonians 2:10), and "example[s] for the believers in speech, in life, in love, in faith and in purity" (1 Timothy 4:12), so that whatever they have learned or received or seen in us they may put into practice with the confidence that the Lord of peace will be with them (Philippians 4:9). That brings us logically to our next subject—the life and character of a minister.

CHAPTER 2

LIFE AND CHARACTER

You may be tempted to bypass this chapter, because you know what it is likely to say. You may excuse this reaction by suggesting that your concern is to get down quickly to the practicalities of the ministry.

But there can be—sadly—a difference between knowledge and action. We need reminding of the most important things even though we know them already (cf. 2 Peter 1:12–15). What is more, nothing is more practical and down-to-earth than the people we are. It is the subtle enemy of our souls who tries to make us think that God's requirements concerning our life and character are either unimportant or altogether too familiar. Robert Murray M'Cheyne— the godly Dundee minister who died when only twenty-nine—puts our subject into proper perspective in two of his most telling statements about a minister's personal life: First, "My people's greatest need is my personal holiness"; and second, "How awful a weapon in the hand of God is a holy minister." It was appropriate for Hensley Henson, a Bishop of Durham, to say in an ordination charge,

"We are pledged to a consecrated life not merely to the pursuit of a profession." Paul rightly appeals to Timothy, the young shepherd and teacher, as a "man of God" (1 Timothy 6:11).

THE PRIORITY OF EXAMPLE

Whatever else a shepherd and teacher provides for God's people, he is to give them an example to follow. God's people require examples if they are to be effectively shepherded and taught. Robert Trail (1642–1716) asked a pertinent question, "Doth not always the spirit of the ministers propagate itself amongst the people? A lively ministry, and lively Christians."[1] John Thornton, a wealthy Christian merchant and benefactor of good causes in England in the early nineteenth century, wrote to Charles Simeon at the beginning of his ministry: "Watch continually over your own spirit, and do all in love; we must grow downwards in humility to soar heavenward. I should recommend your having a watchful eye over yourself, for generally speaking as is the minister so are the people."[2] Following proper examples is part of God's provision to help His people obey the gospel's message (2 Thessalonians 3:6–7).

What is more, the example we are to provide is to be maintained all our life. Paul expressed his concern to the Corinthians that he should never himself be disqualified from the prize after having preached to others that they should strive after it (1 Corinthians 9:26–27).

The New Testament places as great a stress upon character as a qualification for spiritual leadership as upon gifting—in fact, probably more upon character. In the qualifications Paul lists for "overseers" and "deacons" in 1 Timothy 3:1–13 and Titus 1:6–9, the whole emphasis is upon personal qualities, apart from the requirement that the overseer must be "able to teach" (1 Timothy 3:2) and to "encourage others by sound doctrine and refute those who oppose it" (Titus 1:9). The fruit of the Spirit is as important as the gifts of the Spirit in the life of a shepherd and teacher, as for any

Christian. No rivalry exists between the two: Both are important and necessary. But the gifts of the Spirit cannot be exercised in a God-glorifying manner—which is their whole purpose (1 Peter 4:11)—if the character of the user of the gift is not also God-glorifying (cf. 1 Peter 4:7–9). The preacher's gift proves its value to the body of Christ as his character demonstrates the truth of what he declares.

THE KEY EXAMPLE

The key example is our Lord Jesus Christ. A foremost purpose of the apostles' three years of training was that they might receive His unique teaching and observe His example. They both heard and saw how things should be done. Our Lord Jesus drew attention to this purpose and on no occasion more powerfully than after He had taken His disciples by surprise in the Upper Room by washing their feet, when it would seem they had declined to wash one another's feet as they had come into the room. Pointedly He asked them, "Do you understand what I have done for you?" Then He made sure that they did. "You call me 'Teacher' and 'Lord,' and rightly so, for that is what I am. Now that I, your Lord and Teacher, have washed your feet, you also should wash one another's feet. I have set you an example that you should do as I have done for you. I tell you the truth, no servant is greater than his master, nor is a messenger greater than the one who sent him. Now that you know these things, you will be blessed if you do them" (John 13:12–17).

Our Lord Jesus' example is a constant reference point in the New Testament. He is the outstanding example of humility and of not looking to our own interests but to the interests of others (Philippians 2:1–11). He is the example of living not to please ourselves but to please our neighbor for his good, to build him up (Romans 15:2–3). He is the example of how we should accept one another (Romans 15:7). He is the example of generosity in costly self-giving (2 Corinthians 8:9). He is the example of how we should behave when we suffer for doing good (1 Peter 2:21). He is the example of the life of love we are to live (Ephesians 5:2). These are some of the many references to His example.

A PROPER RESPONSE TO CHRIST'S EXAMPLE

All Christians are called to follow Christ's example—that is a basic truth of discipleship. Shepherds and teachers in particular are called to follow that example so that others following them will find themselves following Christ better. Having urged the Philippians to follow after whatever is true, noble, right, pure, lovely, admirable, excellent, and praiseworthy, Paul exhorts them, "Whatever you have learned or received or heard from me, or seen in me—put it into practice. And the God of peace will be with you" (4:9). At first sight Paul's words may seem rather presumptuous or even proud. But they are not. He recognized that one of his primary tasks was to follow Christ so closely and uncompromisingly that he provided a clear example for his fellow believers to follow.

The duty of all Christians is to be an example to one another—by that means we spur one another on to love and good works (Hebrews 10:24). But Christian leaders have an unequaled responsibility in this respect. In most spheres of life people are expected to put into practice what they say to others—but none more than those who profess to follow the Lord of glory. Christian leaders are not perfect, and they are not called upon to pretend that they are. But that does not preclude their providing the example God's people need since Christ's power and grace are available to this end.

When any Christian falls into sin, he hurts others. When a Christian leader falls into sin, he hurts many others. A big tree cannot fall without lots of smaller trees falling with it. This sobering consideration explains why people should never be allowed to rush into leadership responsibilities or be pushed too quickly into them. For this reason, an elder should not be a recent convert "or he may become conceited and fall under the same judgment as the devil"

(1 Timothy 3:6). Similarly, we should not be hasty in laying hands upon a man and giving him leadership responsibilities before the right time (1 Timothy 5:22).

The priority of example is reflected elsewhere in the New Testament. James warns against becoming a teacher without due thought "because you know that we who teach will be judged more strictly" (3:1)—that is to say, according to how far we have been examples of what we ourselves have taught. Peter teaches that elders' principal task is to be "examples to the flock" (1 Peter 5:3). Only then may they anticipate receiving "the crown of glory that will never fade away" (verse 4).

THE PRACTICALITIES OF EXAMPLE SETTING

In what spheres is the spiritual leader—the shepherd and teacher—to be an example? In every sphere! Although different ways of expressing the practicalities of example setting are found in the New Testament, the teaching is identical and consistent. The obvious place to go is Paul's letters to Timothy and Titus, because they are addressed to men whose function it was to shepherd and teach. Paul gives directions concerning their ministry and guidance as to what they were to look for in those prepared by God for Christian leadership.

A foundational statement is 1 Timothy 4:12, where Paul urges Timothy, "Don't let anyone look down on you because you are young, but set an example for the believers in speech, in life, in love, in faith and in purity." The best way to interpret these five requirements is by means of the qualifications Paul laid down for elders and deacons in 1 Timothy 3:1–13 and Titus 1:5–9.

Speech

To function as shepherds and teachers we use our tongues a great deal—in private exhortation, public teaching, and preaching.

It often falls to us to chair the discussions of God's people, whether in leaders' meetings or general church meetings, where the use of our tongues is inevitable. We all sin more readily with our tongues than with any other part of our bodies.

Our speech as shepherds and teachers must be restrained and moderate (1 Timothy 3:2), especially when that of others is the opposite. We should never be quick-tempered or quarrelsome (1 Timothy 3:3; Titus 1:7). Rather our speech should be thoughtful. We should try to think carefully before we speak on issues that are delicate or capable of misunderstanding. Our speech should never be frivolous. That is not to deny the important place of humor and fun. But we must avoid the snare of making fun of things that really matter and that may be debased by foolish speech. What we say should be healing and not bruising. In any conversation or debate we should be like lubricating oil that keeps all the pieces of machinery running smoothly together.

This is a high standard, but nothing less is required of us, because more damage is done to the well-being of individuals and of the whole body of Christ by the tongue than any other member of our body. The positive side is that the tongue also has the potential for the greatest good if well used. To guard our speech we have to guard our hearts, for "out of the overflow of the heart the mouth speaks" (Matthew 12:34). If we would say the right things, we must first think them. When our tongues let us down, it is because we have not first watched over our hearts and thoughts.

Lifestyle

Our lifestyle itself is to be an example for others to follow—a lifestyle, first and foremost, of holiness and uprightness (Titus 1:8). We are to be like God our heavenly Father in holiness. The manner in which He is entirely separate from all that is unholy and unrighteous is to be reflected in our behavior. Shepherds and teachers are not to be professional Christians, doing the right things only when in the public eye. In fulfilling our tasks as shepherds and teachers, we ourselves are to be pursuing our Christian privilege and duty of knowing God better and becoming more like Him. As others observe our conduct, they ought to be able to see that we are upright, in that we do not deviate from what is right; and that we are blameless (Titus 1:7), in that no censure can be placed at our door from our failure to fulfill our responsibilities to our neighbor. Busyness with the concerns of God's people must not be an excuse for neglecting our neighbor—this was the priest's and the Levite's mistake in the familiar story of the Good Samaritan.

As shepherds and teachers we should stand out as those who love what is good (Titus 1:8). Our approach to life is to be essentially positive. We know that we live in God's world, and that all His gifts are good; it is man's abuse of God's gifts that is the problem, not the gifts themselves. Whether it is a matter of sport, or what is on television, we are to love what is good and to set an example in this respect.

Our lifestyle should bear the evidences of our heavenly citizenship (Philippians 3:20), in that it indicates where our treasure is. While on the one hand we are to be marked by the willingness to work hard (2 Thessalonians 3:7–10), it is to be equally clear that the love of money is not our motivation (1 Timothy 3:3), and that we want nothing to do with dishonest gain (Titus 1:7). Although it may be a hard path to follow, we should accept whatever salary God's people choose to give, leaving it to others to act on our behalf.

As well as being examples in our daily work, our home life is to be exemplary. That constitutes a challenge to any parent! Every family has its battles to fight in learning to live together as it ought. Most parents undertake parenthood without having the opportunity to practice beforehand. The home life that provides an example is the home that is well managed (1 Timothy 3:4, 12), where children obey their parents with proper respect (1 Timothy 3:4), so that they are "not open to the charge of being wild and disobedient" (Titus 1:6).

Paul asks the pertinent question of potential shepherds and teachers, "If anyone does not know how to manage his own family, how can he take care of God's church?" (1 Timothy 3:5).

We daily rub shoulders with the world around us—through our neighbors, our daily work, and our recreations—and our behavior is to be such that we are worthy of respect (1 Timothy 3:8) and have a good reputation with outsiders so that we "will not fall into disgrace and into the devil's trap" (1 Timothy 3:7). Godliness in the home is essential to our example. What we are there has more to do with our usefulness to God and to others than we may sometimes appreciate.

Love

Love is the priority virtue, and it must be conspicuously present in the shepherd and teacher's life. It is not an option but an absolute necessity. Besides being the first aspect of the Spirit's fruit, it is the basic virtue from which all the others flow. Rather than being lovers of money, we are to be lovers of God and of people, so that we willingly and spontaneously open our homes to them (1 Timothy 3:2). An essential part of any good reputation we have with outsiders, and respect they may give us, will be on account of the love we exhibit toward them and others (1 Timothy 3:7–8; cf. John 13:34–35; Galatians 6:10).

Love displays itself in gentleness and self-control. It wants to serve others and is never overbearing (1 Timothy 3:2–3; Titus 1:7). We are to set an example of loving all people, and especially those of God's family. We are to love the difficult and the unattractive. They are the ones whom we should be inviting into our homes, and into whose homes we should gladly go when asked. We are to love those who oppose us, not viewing them as enemies but as friends to be won over by love.

The expression of love is the most powerful answer to most relationship problems that arise in a church. If it is clear to all that the shepherd and teacher strives to love everyone equally, and endeavors to have no particular friends but rather to be everyone's friend, then people will willingly accept him as a mediator or a calming influence when human relationships are under stress. A church can never have too great an experience of God's love, and the shepherd and teacher must be at the forefront of its expression.

Faith

It is interesting that here as elsewhere love and faith go hand in hand (1 Timothy 2:15; 6:11; 2 Timothy 2:22). All Christians possess faith, but the shepherd and teacher is to be such an example of it that faith grows in the community of believers to which he belongs.

We are to be examples, first, in our knowledge of the faith, holding "firmly to the trustworthy message as it has been taught" (Titus 1:9). As shepherds and teachers, we need to be constantly building upon the foundations of our faith, to develop our understanding of it and its application to contemporary life. We are to know it so as to be able to teach it (1 Timothy 3:2), for then we "can encourage others by sound doctrine and refute those who oppose it" (Titus 1:9). We must "keep hold of the deep truths of the faith with a clear conscience" (1 Timothy 3:9). We must not be surprised or put out if people question us to make sure we do possess a sure grasp of the foundation truths of the faith (1 Timothy 3:9–10).

We are to be examples, too, of the exercise of faith. Nothing honors our Lord and Savior more than our confidence in Him—and not least confidence by prayer in His name (Philippians 1:19). The principle that "without faith it is impossible to please God" (Hebrews 11:6) is fundamental to effective ministry. Addressing ministers, Charles Spurgeon exhorted them,

> Our work especially requires faith. If we fail in faith, we had better
> not have undertaken it; and unless we obtain faith commensurate

with the service, we shall soon grow weary of it. It is proven by all observation that success in the Lord's service is very generally in proportion to faith. It certainly is not in proportion to ability, nor does it always run parallel with a display of zeal; but it is invariably according to the measure of faith, for this is a law of the Kingdom without exception, "According to your faith be it unto you." It is essential, then, that we should have faith if we are to be useful, and that we should have great faith if we are to be greatly useful. . . . We, above all men, need the mountain-moving faith, by which, in the old time, men of God "subdued kingdoms, wrought righteousness, obtained promises, stopped the mouths of lions, quenched the violence of fire, escaped the edge of the sword, out of weakness were made strong, waxed valiant in fight, turned to flight the armies of the aliens."[3]

If we are to be obedient to our Lord Jesus Christ in our neighborhoods and spheres of influence, God's people need to be led out into new ventures of faith, whether in evangelism, church planting, or other enterprises. Faith's secret is large views of God our Savior —and He is so great that our views can never be large enough. As shepherds and teachers, we need to cultivate daily personal Bible study and helpful reading of Christian literature that fans and nurtures faith. In that way we serve God's people by stirring and feeding their faith through example, sometimes almost unconsciously, since we cannot measure the degree to which our exhibition of faith encourages it in others.

Purity

Purity in its widest possible sense is required of those who shepherd and teach God's people. Our Lord Jesus Christ Himself is pure (1 John 3:3), and so those who belong to Him should also be pure. Such purity is an essential part of our relationship to God through our Lord Jesus Christ. Purity can be achieved only as it is our de-

liberate aim. Job knew that. He did not pretend not to be tempted, but he knew what to do with temptation when it came. "I made
a covenant with my eyes not to look lustfully at a girl" (31:1). Henry
Martyn, an early English missionary to India, prayed for the purity of a young woman whose beauty easily attracted him in unhelpful ways. He found that in praying for her holiness and purity, he
could not at the same time harbor impure thoughts.

Purity demands that we deal honestly with ourselves, so that
even the spiritual need of someone of the opposite sex does not
become a pretext for helping that person on account of the pleasure we find at being in her company.

If we are married, our total and uncompromised allegiance is to
be to our wives (1 Timothy 3:2, 12; Titus 1:6). A man's wife must
be the sole fountain from which he drinks for the fulfillment and
satisfaction of physical and sexual desires—both in thought and
physical act. We are to love our wives not only as we did in our
youth, but with a growing love.

Our behavior with those of the opposite sex is to be above re-
proach and worthy of respect (1 Timothy 3:2, 11). Spiritual leadership constantly brings shepherds and teachers into contact with
women in a variety of situations. There is natural pleasure and helpful stimulus through the interaction of the sexes in everyday life—
this is part of God's gift to us. But in a fallen world—and with our
fallen natures—there is plenty of scope for temptation and moral
failure. We shall deal later with this subject in greater detail, for it
is an area we dare not neglect. At this stage we simply underline
that as with so many other virtues, purity of life begins with
purity of heart. As we think, so we are.

Speech, life, love, faith, and purity: These are the priorities. The
reason for their importance is that as "overseers" or "elders" we
are "entrusted with God's work" (Titus 1:7). The flock we care for
is not ours, but Christ's (John 21:15–17). The blood that was shed
for them was Christ's blood—God's own blood (Acts 20:28). We
should set high standards for ourselves so that in imitating us

Christ's flock may find themselves imitating Him (1 Thessalonians 1:6).

There are many other characteristics that become those who lead and teach Christ's flock—such as earnestness and patience—but they are all comprehended in the five priorities we have considered.

AREAS OF GROWTH

These spiritual priorities of life and character all constitute areas for growth. Love and faith are constantly referred to in the New Testament as virtues in which we are to abound. Our speech and lifestyle should increasingly honor God as the Spirit's fruit grows. Our purity should increase as we learn from our mistakes and face up to the call to purity the gospel gives (1 Thessalonians 4:3).

God often achieves our spiritual growth in these areas through the difficulties He permits us to pass through in the course of our ministry. Paul's faith in God's power to deliver grew, for example, as he proved it in places like Philippi (Acts 16:25–26). His understanding of God's power to comfort developed as the sufferings of Christ flowed over into his life (2 Corinthians 1:5).

Paul would not have been the useful apostle, shepherd, and teacher he was had he not suffered so many disappointments and hardships. Experiences we would run away from are sometimes further periods of training from God to make us better servants of His Son. George Whitefield wrote in his diary while in Gibraltar in February 1738, "Conversed with one of the devout soldiers, who was under strong spiritual trials; and God was pleased to give him comfort. I find it necessary more and more every day, that ministers should be tempted in all things, that they may be able experimentally to succour those that are tempted."

Someone has aptly said that character is what we are in the dark. Our secret and private life provides the clue to God's approval upon our more public life and service. If we had to sum up in one word what a shepherd and teacher's life should be like, it would be the word *godly*—even though it is much out of vogue. Its essence is doing what pleases God without any eye to the approval of others. Our secret life is the clue to our public usefulness. David was described by God as a man after His own heart who would do everything He wanted him to do (Acts 13:22). "Make me that kind of man": This must be the heartfelt desire and prayer of everyone genuinely called to be a shepherd and teacher. "Above all else," the writer of Proverbs urges, "guard your heart, for it is the wellspring of life" (4:23).

CHAPTER 3

GOALS AND PRIORITIES

It is sadly possible to have false or mistaken goals, goals that are worldly rather than spiritual. The apostle John had no option but to condemn the example of a church leader—Diotrephes—who loved to be first (3 John 9). Our goal is not empire building. Although all called to serve our Lord Jesus Christ would accept that, it is easy nevertheless to err in this respect through lack of personal watchfulness. Lording it over others has no place in the work of shepherds and teachers (2 Corinthians 1:24; 1 Peter 5:3). The key title for those in Christ's service is servant. Shepherds and teachers are for churches, not churches for shepherds and teachers. Churches do not exist for our benefit or for our livelihood. We exist rather for their good.

Our goal is not to be well known and respected. Our goal is not to have a large church or congregation, which draws forth the admiration—and perhaps jealousy—of others. Our goal is not to draw people around us so that they are loyal to us, rather than to our Lord Jesus Christ. Our goal is not to make ourselves indispensable. Such are goals of ownership, whereas ours are goals of stewardship. Those whom we pastor and teach are entrusted to us—they are not ours but Jesus Christ's (1 Peter 5:3).

We cannot remind ourselves too often that the local church is not ours but His. That understanding conditions and dictates our goals and priorities. Although it may be only a small thing, it is wise to avoid the habit of referring to a church as "Mr. So-and-so's church" or of speaking of "my church." Rather we may discipline ourselves to say "the church to which Mr. So-and-so belongs" or "the church to which I belong." The effort of doing this alerts us to unhelpful attitudes we may be adopting toward the church.

To establish goals brings benefits and dangers. The principal benefit is that we know at what we should be aiming, and thus we avoid dissipating our energies on secondary matters. The main danger is that we may become so goal-oriented that we set unrealistic targets, which then become a rod for our own backs and discourage rather than spur us on. But this danger is no reason for not establishing proper goals. It is simply a snare to avoid. Our purpose is to determine the goals God wants us to have, rather than those of our own imagining. A substantial amount of current writing on this subject owes more to business practice than to biblical precept. It is imperative that we take our direction from the Scriptures.

FEED THE FLOCK

The Scriptures identify a number of pastoral and teaching goals, and our purpose is to draw attention to them. The starting point is in no doubt, since it must be the instruction our Lord Jesus Christ gave Peter when He restored him to fellowship with Himself after the Resurrection (John 21:15–17).

Our goal is to feed our Savior's flock. Peter's love for his Lord was to be displayed above all in his care of his Lord's lambs and sheep. The threefold instruction—"Feed my lambs" (verse 15), "Take care of my sheep" (verse 16), and "Feed my sheep" (verse 17)

—highlights three principal areas of pastoral care. The young—both in age and in faith—are to be carefully fed (verse 15); all Christians require general pastoral care (verse 16); and established Christians need to progress toward maturity (verse 17). Peter did not forget this goal, for besides providing lush spiritual pasture for Christ's flock in his two New Testament letters, he exhorts the elders of the churches in Asia Minor to "be shepherds of God's flock that is under your care" (1 Peter 5:2).

A shepherd's priority is to lead his flock into green pastures; and that is his principal task in handling the Scriptures. He is to enlarge the flock's understanding of the faith so that they may render a better obedience to Christ (Romans 1:5). As they are properly fed, they will be strong in the Lord and in the grace that is in Christ Jesus (Ephesians 6:10; 2 Timothy 2:1).

Every time we teach, it is appropriate to ask, "Am I providing good pasture for God's flock? Will this nourish their souls by causing them to feed upon our Lord Jesus Christ Himself and to respond to Him in obedience?" A mark of good feeding is that it causes faith to grow. That makes sense in that our faith had its beginnings as we heard God's Word and responded to it. The ministry of God's Word should always do God's people good. As Paul anticipated a further opportunity of ministering to the Philippians, he expected its result to be their "progress and joy in the faith" so that their joy in Christ would overflow (Philippians 1:25–26).

Although as we expound the Scriptures our task will sometimes be to rebuke and correct, it will always have as its end that God's people, responding with the obedience of faith, will know an overflowing and inexpressible joy in Christ. Our task as friends of the heavenly Bridegroom is to bring before the members of His church, His bride, the wonder and benefits of her union with the Bridegroom and the absolute perfection of His character, so that they obey Him with ever-increasing joy.

Joy—resulting from proper feeding—has so many beneficial consequences. When Christians are joyful in their Lord, they praise and thank God by their lips and lives. When Christians are joyful in Christ, they want to serve Him, and they do so with the gladness that befits His service. When Christians are joyful in Christ, they face their sufferings with peace and persevering faith. When Christians are joyful in Christ, they are in a position to help others. If Christians do not rejoice, it is not because they are Christians, but because they are not Christian enough. Joy is the rational state of the Christian in view of his spiritual position in Christ. Our goal to feed Christ's flock has this greater goal beyond it of the Christian's joy in Christ being complete (John 15:11).

PROCLAIM THE WHOLE WILL OF GOD

Proper feeding demands a balanced diet. Our goal, to quote Paul's words to the Ephesian elders, is "to proclaim . . . the whole will of God" (Acts 20:27). Having achieved this goal among the Ephesians, Paul could claim that no man's blood could be laid upon him (Acts 20:26; cf. Ezekiel 33:1–6). He had sought to share every aspect of gospel truth as he knew and understood it.

To proclaim the whole will of God we must faithfully expound the complete Scriptures. We must make plain God's will in regard to salvation, beginning with God's foreknowledge through to glorification (Romans 8:29–30). We must teach the whole will of God concerning sanctification, that it is not something vague and fanciful, but practical and relevant in that it means avoiding sexual immorality in all its forms and learning to control our bodies in a way that is holy and honorable (1 Thessalonians 4:3–4). Where the Scriptures are plain, we are to be plain, whether about Christian doctrine or behavior. We are not to hesitate to preach anything that may be helpful to God's people.

That Paul should go to such pains to emphasize his practice implies that we may be tempted sometimes not to declare the whole of God's will. We may hesitate because of the anticipated reaction of fallen human nature to an unpalatable divine truth. But such hesitation is wrong, since where there is a true work of God's Spirit in people's lives, they will be taught by Him to accept truth God wants them to receive, whether for their regeneration or sanctification. An important example is repentance (Acts 20:21)—a priority principle to be taught to both unbelievers and believers.

It is not easy to be balanced in our presentation of God's truth. William Burns, an early Scottish missionary to China, wrote in his diary,

> How hard it is to unite in just proportions the humbling doctrine of man's inability to come to Christ without regeneration, and the free gospel offer which is the moral means employed by God in conversion! Oh! Spirit of Jesus, my Saviour, lead me, a poor, ignorant, and self-conceited sinner, to the experience of this great mystery of grace, that I may know how I ought to declare thy glorious gospel to perishing fellow-sinners! Amen.

That is a prayer we do well to make our own.

To declare the complete will of God to His people we must deliberately teach them from the whole of the Scriptures. If we keep the notes of our addresses and sermons, it is salutary to review how balanced our teaching and preaching have been. Have we maintained a balance between Old and New Testaments? Have we given the kind of balance we find in Ephesians between doctrinal teaching and moral instruction? Since the whole of the Scriptures—both Old and New Testaments—is "useful for teaching, rebuking, correcting and training in righteousness" (2 Timothy 3:16), we are faithful to God's people only as we put the complete Scriptures to use in these ways, both in public teaching and in the more informal teaching of pastoral visitation in homes (Acts 20:20). They will then genuinely rejoice that "everything that was written in the past was written to teach us, so that through endurance and the encouragement of the Scriptures we might have hope" (Romans 15:4).

When we make it our goal to proclaim the whole of God's will, using the whole of the Scriptures, we avoid emphases that make us unhelpfully distinctive because of particular axes we are known to grind. G. Campbell Morgan told the story of the Baptist preacher who had a fixation with baptism and referred to it constantly. One morning he announced his text—"Adam, where are you?" (Genesis 3:9). He continued, "There are three lines we shall follow. First, where Adam was. Second, how he was to be saved from where he was. Third and last, a few words about baptism." The best reputation we can have is of faithfulness to Scripture, rather than even to a doctrinal position, and to be obedient ourselves to Scripture—and therefore to God—wherever that obedience may lead.

PRESENT EVERYONE PERFECT IN CHRIST

Feeding God's people and proclaiming the whole counsel of God are not ends in themselves. They serve a greater end—the goal of presenting everyone perfect in Christ. Paul shared this great objective when he described the essence of his ministry in his Colossian letter: "We proclaim him [Christ], admonishing and teaching everyone with all wisdom, so that we may present everyone perfect in Christ. To this end," he continued, "I labor, struggling with all his energy, which so powerfully works in me" (1:28–29).

The phrase "in Christ" underlines a great wonder of salvation: We are personally united to Jesus Christ. Christ is in us, and we are in Him. God's ultimate purpose, as the consequence of our reconciliation to Him and our union with Christ, is to present us before Himself in holiness, so that we may be with Him forever. But this work of sanctification is already in progress, and God employs His Son's undershepherds to forward it. Hence Paul's ambition for the Corinthians, to present them as a pure virgin to Christ, their heavenly Bridegroom (2 Corinthians 11:2), was entirely right.

We must motivate Christians to grow. Nothing does this better than their seeing in the Scriptures His glorious purposes for them in Christ. An important motivation we may easily overlook, perhaps because we take it for granted, is the constant and regular exposition of the gospel itself. Paul's plain purpose in Romans 12 onward is to motivate his readers to strive after mature Christian character and conduct. Significantly, chapters 1 to 8 expound in great detail the gospel by which we are saved—with chapters 9 to 11 interrupting his argument for him to express concern for his own unbelieving people, the Jews. Chapter 12 takes up where chapter 8 ends and significantly bases all its exhortations upon the little phrase "in view of God's mercy" (verse 1).

When our eyes are upon God's mercy we can't help but feel tremendous gratitude, the gratitude that leads to obedience and growth. Rather than forever rebuking believers about their failures, we must joyfully set before them the objectives of Christlikeness and spiritual maturity, as much a privilege as a duty. The enthusiasm with which we present them, plus the reality of our own pursuit of them—a most important factor—will encourage them to do the same.

Our goal is the holiness and the unreserved obedience to Christ of every believer. We are to hold before them and ourselves our Lord's instruction: "Be perfect . . . as your heavenly Father is perfect" (Matthew 5:48). While absolute perfection in this life is impossible, that fact provides no grounds for not aiming at it. God's Spirit, who indwells all believers, can enable us, and those whom we teach, to achieve virtues and standards of conduct that otherwise would be impossible. We are able to love our enemies, loving them as God loved us when we were His enemies. We can forgive others, as God has forgiven us. We, and those for whom we have responsibility, can become more and more like Jesus Christ. We may demonstrate in daily life the reality of our new birth by living as our Savior did.

We may helpfully think of God the Holy Spirit as both a sculptor and a potter. As God's people come regularly under the influence of His Word and pastoral care, they—like us—are in the hands of God the Holy Spirit. He has always before Him the person of our Lord Jesus, and it is His purpose, through the Word taught and preached, to chip away like a sculptor at our characters so that we increasingly conform to the image of Jesus Christ. He molds us like a potter as He helps us to apply the principles of His Word to our circumstances, and as a result we become more useful utensils in God's household.

The word *everyone* should not be overlooked in Colossians 1:28—"admonishing and teaching everyone." Shepherds and teachers are to be concerned for every Christian, without exception. Men and women—young and old—whom God brings into our care will be at different stages of spiritual experience. Starting where they are, we are to bring them to where God wants them in obedience and holiness of life.

The word *present* is also worth pondering in Colossians 1:28— "that we may present everyone perfect in Christ"—in that it reminds us that we are to have in view always that glorious moment of presentation when our Lord returns and His servants meet Him to give an account of their service. Think of the joy of presenting on that day all those for whom we have had responsibility. Paul explained to the Thessalonians the excitement this prospect gave him, especially when he found the going tough: "For what is our hope, our joy, or the crown in which we will glory in the presence of our Lord Jesus when he comes? Is it not you? Indeed, you are our glory and joy" (1 Thessalonians 2:19–20). Wise shepherds and teachers look for their reward then, and not now.

The means by which this goal is achieved is spelled out in the words that precede it: "We proclaim him [Christ], admonishing and teaching everyone with all wisdom . . ." (Colossians 1:28). First and foremost, it involves proclaiming Christ. This sounds so commonplace that we may fail to take proper notice of it. We must ensure that in all our shepherding and teaching we present the person of Christ. Right teaching always leads to Him and shows the relationship of all other truths to His saving work and His supremacy in God's purposes. As we give spiritual counsel, we must direct people to that aspect of Christ's character and work that most relevantly applies to their circumstances. In encouraging right behavior, we must point to the example of Christ, which is to be followed. The enemy of souls has won a significant battle when any shepherd or teacher performs any task without reference to the person, example, and teaching of his Lord.

Alongside the proclaiming of Christ, there must be admonition and teaching. Paul placed admonition first because he was a realist. Aware of his own need of constant correction, he appreciated that of others, too. Admonishing and warning are the special responsibility of undershepherds (1 Thessalonians 5:12). To give warnings is an expression of Christian realism—of dealing with things as they really are. Since all Christians are in the spiritual battle (Ephesians 6:10–18), they must be alerted to moral and spiritual dangers. All need to be warned against perils such as pride, self-confidence, Satan and his devices, false teaching, unhelpful emphases, and idleness (Acts 20:30–31; 1 Thessalonians 5:14). There are dangers along the road, and the task of the shepherd and teacher is to put up the "road signs" and to keep them freshly painted and up-to-date in the information they provide. Paul reminded the Ephesian elders that for three years he never stopped warning each of them night and day with tears (Acts 20:31). The addition of the words "with tears" provides an important clue as to how admonition and correction are to be exercised—they require compassion, the spirit of a father caring for his children (1 Corinthians 4:14–15).

Both spiritual exhortation and teaching call for considerable wisdom (Colossians 1:28). The wisdom is not so much that which comes from training and the gaining of expertise, but the wisdom that comes from the fear of the Lord, respect for His Word, and sensitivity to His Spirit—the wisdom that is from above (James 3:17–18).

The goal of presenting men and women perfect in Christ requires hard work. To this end Paul worked hard, struggling with all Christ's energy, which so powerfully worked in him (Colossians 1:29). The word used for struggling means literally to engage in a contest, and usually in the context of fighting with weapons. The only weapons adequate for this struggle with Satan and his influences are prayer and the Word of God. Satan places every possible hindrance he can in the way of Christians' progress to spiritual maturity. This awareness should increase the intensity of our conviction to frustrate him by employing the proper weapons and by availing ourselves of the power of the Lord Jesus, which is always available when our concern is to care for His flock.

Aware that he had to work hard, Paul knew too that the secret of success was Christ's energy in him. There is something of a mystery about the relationship of our working hard and the truth that as we do so, Christ's energy works in us to achieve His great purpose. We do not have to understand this spiritual principle fully in order to benefit from it. Our Lord Jesus gives the same Spirit who anointed Him to those who continue His work, and this guarantees that the work will be successfully accomplished.

PREPARE GOD'S PEOPLE FOR WORKS OF SERVICE

Alongside this great purpose of presenting everyone perfect in Christ, and as an essential part of it, our further goal is to "prepare God's people for works of service" (Ephesians 4:12). Although the body of Christ requires the gift of shepherds and teachers, it equally needs the other gifts Christ gives to His body. What is more, new shepherds and teachers are continually given to the church throughout her history, and they are to be recognized and encouraged in the development of their gifts alongside the gifts of others. Shepherds and teachers' particular responsibility is to prepare God's people for their individual works of service.

Every Christian has a function in the body of Christ (1 Corinthians 12) and unique service to perform for the good of other members of God's family. The shepherds and teachers' task is to fit every believer to fulfill his or her God-ordained place in Christ's body. They are to help Christians first to discern their gifts, and then to use them.

Once spiritual gifts are discerned, we help motivate people to exercise them by going out of our way to suggest means by which they can be developed and put to use. To pass on a book concerning the service people can give may be all the stimulus they require. We may suggest that people go on relevant training courses, or we may link them with those of similar gifts who are more experienced in their use.

Sometimes the gifts that the shepherd and teacher possesses have been so magnified in the church that the development of other gifts has been neglected. It has been foolishly assumed that the shepherd and teacher should somehow or other possess all the other necessary gifts for ministry, too. The shepherd and teacher is the key person to put this situation right where it exists. We must make it plain by our attitude and our teaching that our gifts are only gifts among other gifts. As we take pains to expound carefully and fully the teaching of passages like Romans 12, 1 Corinthians 12, and 1 Peter 4:10–11, we may demonstrate the interdependence of members of the body and that the purpose of all spiritual gifts is not selfish enjoyment but the profit of other members of God's family. The gifts are given so that we may share in bringing one another on in spiritual maturity—in other words, the presenting of one another perfect in Christ. (Ephesians 4:13 is an expansion of Colossians 1:28.)

As we teach the necessity for works of service, we must also provide opportunities for them. In the church fellowship to which we belonged in Edinburgh we found it helpful to provide a booklet entitled "Opportunities for Service," which was produced after an exposition of Romans 12 and then given to each new member. It lists various aspects of church life and the different gifts of service that members may be able to offer. People are invited to check those they either feel gifted for or in which they would be prepared to give help. It is not an infallible means of discovering gifts, and offers of service are not necessarily synonymous with the gifts required for that service. But they often are, and it is only by opportunity and testing that gifts come to light. It is by doing a task that a person discovers spiritual giftedness for it.

As part of our pastoral care, we should seek to identify the gifts of each member of the flock and to encourage them. This should not be a haphazard exercise but a deliberate one. Only good can come from bringing every member on the church membership roll before God in prayer in daily rotation, and asking for His help in identifying each member's gift, and for wisdom to encourage its use if its employment is not already obvious.

When we meet together as undershepherds to consider the well-being of the flock, the development and recognition of spiritual gifts within the church fellowship should be a regular item on the agenda. We will do well to be asking ourselves at something like six-month intervals, "Are there gifts God is giving to members of our church fellowship that we need to recognize and encourage?" It takes discipline to ensure that an important subject like this is not forced to the bottom of the agenda by the pressure of other business or even by being considered unimportant. If we are to teach God's people to be prepared for works of service, then we must make sure that those works of service are recognized, begun, and completed.

EQUIP GOD'S PEOPLE TO BE
FISHERS OF MEN AND WOMEN

The body of Christ is not only to care for its spiritual maturity, but it is also to grow. Our responsibility is not solely for the flock already gathered in, but for those other sheep that are to be called. The body of Christ is healthy as, through the works of service her members are equipped to fulfill, she reaches out into the world and obeys her Master's final commission to preach the Good News to every creature. A true pastor's concern is for the other sheep that have not yet heard the Great Shepherd's call (John 10:16).

Our goal is to equip God's people to be fishers of men and women. This was a priority purpose of our Lord Jesus Christ for His disciples. As potential apostles their special call was to evangelism. But that call is given to all members of the body of Christ, although some will be more gifted in it than others. In order to make His disciples fishers of men, our Lord Jesus took them under His instruction for three years, and they learned "fishing-for-men" by listening to His teaching and by watching Him do it. Those for whom we have responsibility need to be able to learn in the same way.

We must first teach evangelism, and we must then also teach it by doing it. Regular courses of instruction on evangelism have a place within the framework of the church's annual program of teaching. However, we best teach and encourage evangelism by the manner in which we ourselves regularly preach the gospel on every possible occasion. Nothing fires evangelism more than our people glorying in the gospel message as they hear it proclaimed. As we engage in apologetics, we provide our Christian hearers with guidance to help them answer the questions people ask concerning the hope in Christ they display.

Evangelism is seldom if ever easy work. So often the people invited to give talks on evangelism are specially gifted, and they may lead the less gifted to despair and to intense feelings of guilt and inferiority. Shepherds and teachers are by no means always gifted with the gift of the evangelist, and we may greatly help people by stating from time to time the difficulties we ourselves have in sharing the gospel and the things that have helped and encouraged us.

Rather than forever rebuking Christians for their failure to evangelize, we need to equip them for it. We may recommend a new evangelistic book that has been published, or a biography describing someone's conversion, which they could profitably read themselves and then pass on to someone for whose conversion they are praying. We may encourage them by the testimony of those who have been converted through the influence of ordinary people who have showed by their lives the power of Christ.

All our goals are interrelated. As God's people discover the whole will of God, they discover their responsibility for evangelism. As they are brought on in spiritual maturity, their light becomes brighter and their saltiness greater, and they thus increase their readiness for witness. Changing the picture from one of fishing to farming, our Lord bids us now, as He did His disciples, to open our eyes and "look at the fields" since "they are ripe for harvest" (John 4:35). At Parkside we have encouraged our people by reminding them frequently that it is our shared prayerful desire to see unbelieving people become committed followers of Jesus Christ.

KEEP WATCH OVER YOURSELF
AND THE FLOCK UNTIL THE TASK IS COMPLETE

Our final goal is to keep watch over ourselves and all the flock over which the Holy Spirit has made us overseers (Acts 20:28), not only for a while or a period of our lives, but until we complete the task the Lord Jesus has given us (Acts 20:24). At the time of our Lord's betrayal by Judas, the Shepherd was attacked and the members of the flock—the eleven disciples—were scattered. The enemy of souls always aims his strongest blows at the undershepherd. If he can do him harm, or damage his example, he brings hurt to the whole flock. Our top priority must be to keep watch over ourselves. When pastors turn aside from the way, they cause many to stumble by their example (Malachi 2:8).

Taking heed to ourselves, we are then in a position to keep a proper watch over the flock. A true pastor aims at providing not only pasture for the flock but also its security and deliverance (John 10:9). He remembers that it is no accident that he is an undershepherd. Every true undershepherd is where he is by the appointment of the Great Shepherd. He must watch carefully for the well-being of every soul entrusted to him. William Burns, as a young man, preached one Sunday in Blairgowrie in Perthshire, Scotland. What stuck in his mind all his life was that a godly woman exhorted him with spiritual earnestness afterward to watch for individual souls, saying, "You may lose a jewel from your crown; though you do not lose your crown, you may lose a jewel from it." To be faithful pastors we must be faithful to the end.

OUR NATURAL FEELINGS OF INSUFFICIENCY

As we ponder these goals we cannot help but be overwhelmed by their challenge. We are compelled to ask ourselves, "Who is equal to such a task?" (2 Corinthians 2:16). The answer is that no one is if he tries to do it uncalled of God and by reliance on human resources. But if a man is called by God, and does it with His resources, then he is equal to the task. Those whom God calls, He equips—that is the testimony of the Bible, of history, and of experience.

Our personal goal must be to do our best to present ourselves to God as workmen who do not need to be ashamed of their work and who correctly handle the Word of Truth—Paul's direction to Timothy (2 Timothy 2:15). We will consider this further when we look at the place we must give to study. Each of these identifiable New Testament goals requires an understanding of the Scriptures and their careful application. We must not only use the Word of God, but we must ourselves be under its constant instruction and discipline. Then we may expect God's gracious hand to be upon us—the hand that gives power and good success.

CHAPTER 4

PRAYER

If ever a subject requires honest and thorough treatment it is prayer in the life of the undershepherd and teacher. None would dispute its importance and priority. But its priority is not easy to achieve.

PRAYER AND OUR PERSONAL
RELATIONSHIP TO GOD

More important than being a shepherd or teacher is being a son of God. Prayer is the principal expression of our relationship to God through our Lord Jesus Christ. No privilege is greater than being able to call God "Father," and knowing that it is true. A priceless benefit of our new birth and adoption is that the actual Spirit of God's Son, Jesus Christ, lives within us, enabling us to cry, "Abba, Father." More important than employing prayer in the course of our pastoral ministry is our using prayer as the primary privilege of our personal relationship to God. A prayerless Christian is a contradiction in that if our life is under the control and influence of Christ's Spirit, we pray to the Father with delightful confidence. The first priority for a shepherd and teacher is to live as a Christian ought to live, and that means using prayer to the full.

It is healthy to have a fear of professionalism in our Christian service, of falling into the snare of praying publicly because we are expected to do so but not actually being men of prayer in private. Effective prayer in pastoral work arises from the habit of private prayer for prayer's own sake—or, better, for the sake of fellowship with God.

Since our relationship to God is the key to everything, it is the principal area of attack upon our Christian life. Honesty and realism are required of us here. The New Testament urges us to be "clear minded and self-controlled" so that we can pray (1 Peter 4:7). If we are confused or hazy in our thinking about prayer, and how to ensure its correct place in our life, we are bound to fail in achieving its proper priority. If we do not inject a fair amount of discipline into our life, we will be unable to control the contrary elements that continually militate against prayer.

Self-control begins with the time we get up in the morning so as to give time to prayer. For the majority of us the only real opportunity to be quiet and undisturbed is early in the morning. Pastoral duties often mean that we go to bed quite late. Part of the discipline of getting up early is to exercise equal discipline in the time we go to bed. That is not an easy thing, in that few of us can go straight to bed and to sleep if we have come in late from an elders' or deacons' meeting or a demanding pastoral situation. But where we are in a position to get to bed at a reasonable hour we must aim to do so with a good start in the morning in view. Our Lord Jesus clearly found that in His case the one way He got time to be quiet with His Father in prayer was to get up even before it was daylight. To achieve a time of quiet before the beginning of the working day is what we expect of those engaged in other callings, and by achieving it ourselves we show that it can be done and we are able to identify with others' difficulties.

Self-control is necessary to overcome practical difficulties in prayer, such as loss of concentration and getting into a rut in the manner in which we pray.

DP I prefer to pray on my knees when I am on my own, but I find that there is a limit to the time I can do so without its becoming uncomfortable and my concentration lapsing. I spend part of my prayer time like this, and then I spend the remainder going out of the house and praying as I walk. I find it helpful to pray aloud if other people are not around, and the earlier it is in the morning, the easier it is. We all need to determine what the best pattern is for us personally. Once we have found what suits us best, we should stick with it. One means of avoiding a rut in the method we use to pray is to alter our approach once a week. Each week, on my day off I, dispense with my prayer diary and pray without it.

Since prayer is one of the areas where we most want our people to win the spiritual battle, we ourselves must win it if we are to encourage and help them with any conviction. As we are in prayer, so we may expect our people to be. We all long to be part of a praying people. That is achieved not by continually scolding people for not praying, but by setting an example ourselves, as much in private as in public. What we say about prayer in public will have the ring of truth about it—and will be backed up by the Holy Spirit —as it is true in private.

Biographies show prayer to have been at the heart of the ministries of those whom God has been graciously pleased to use. John Welch ministered in the southwest of Scotland, in Kirkcudbright and at Ayr. A great revival took place under his preaching, and Samuel Rutherford bore testimony to its fruits when he settled in Anwoth in 1627. People who knew Welch spoke of his giving eight hours a day to prayer when other pastoral duties allowed. On the coldest winter nights his wife found him lying on the ground, wrestling with God in prayer for his people. Overwhelmed with grief on one occasion, he explained to her that he had a burden on him as an undershepherd that she did not bear in the same way—the responsibility for three thousand souls—and he did not know where many of them stood in their relationship with God. And so it was that he prayed. The real challenge this presents is not to match Welch in his timing but in his fervency.

AN UNDISPUTED PRIORITY
FOR SHEPHERDS AND TEACHERS

Prayer is our principal and main work. It has priority over the ministry of the Word in that it must come first. It is by prayer that the sword of the Spirit, the Word of God, is effectively unsheathed. Prayer perfectly complements the ministry of the Word. The apostles established the pattern for themselves and for us in Acts 6 when they determined that others should be appointed to do the duties that hindered their performing their most important tasks: "prayer and the ministry of the Word" (verse 4). That decision had immediate consequences of blessing for the church, as Luke significantly records: "So the word of God spread. The number of disciples in Jerusalem increased rapidly, and a large number of priests became obedient to the faith" (verse 7). How different things would have been if the apostles had allowed themselves to be swamped by tasks that others could have done and that deflected them from prayer and the ministry of the Word.

It is one thing to say that prayer is an undisputed priority and another thing to practice it. There are always the pressures of the urgent and the immediate. A principal temptation in the ministry is to be carried along by its sheer busyness to the neglect of prayer. Henry Martyn, an early missionary to India, frequently complained of the time it took him to prepare his sermons, a task that did not come easily to him. He lamented his "shortness of prayer through incessant sermon-making." After listening to Charles Simeon preach one evening, he wrote, "Mr. Simeon, in his excellent sermon tonight, observed that it was more easy for a minister to preach and study five hours than to pray for his people one half-hour."[1] Most would agree. The next piece of sermon preparation always seems more urgent than the time we should give to prayer.

Prayer is crucial because of the spiritual battle in which we are engaged. The importance of a shepherd and teacher's work automatically makes him the target of the enemy of souls. Like all Christians, we know a constant struggle between the flesh and the Spirit. The strength of Jesus Christ, obtained through prayer, is the necessary and sufficient resource for victory. As spiritual leaders, some of the temptations we experience will be unique to our tasks, and it is through prayer alone that we find insight to recognize them and power to avoid them. An unrelenting foe demands unrelenting spiritual watchfulness through prayer. Satan delights to make casualties of those who have encouraged others to fight the good fight of faith.

Satan places an amazing variety of temptations in our way, and it is foolish to imagine that we know them all already. He will try to overwhelm us by the sheer magnitude of our task of shepherding and teaching, especially when people are a disappointment to us. He will try to sow the seeds of discouragement as we realize how hard the hearts of men and women can be toward God and His truth. He will do his best to make us focus on our weakness and limitations. But prayer can thwart all Satan's attacks. Through prayer disappointments turn into opportunities to prove God. Through prayer the hardness of men and women's hearts melts. Through prayer the limitations of our human nature are countered.

The primary way to overcome Satan is on our knees. "Pray continually" is the order for every day for spiritual leaders in particular (1 Thessalonians 5:17). To fight the good fight of faith (1 Timothy 6:12), the weapon of prayer is indispensable (Ephesians 6:18).

Our Lord Jesus is our example here, as elsewhere. He, the Chief Shepherd, demonstrated the priority of prayer in pastoral work. He prayed when He needed to make decisions, such as the choice of the Twelve (Luke 6:12–16). He prayed when He and those around Him were subject to temptation (Matthew 14:23; John 17). He prayed before asking the disciples a key question about their understanding of His identity (Luke 9:18–22). He prayed when people had false views of Him (John 6:15). He prayed for those closest to Him in the light of the dangers He knew them to be in (Luke 22:32).

Every time we find it difficult to maintain prayer, we will be helped by remembering that this is simply an indication of its key importance in the spiritual battle. It is sheer foolishness to pray only when we feel like it. When we are lethargic, there is a place for stirring ourselves up to pray on the grounds that our Lord Jesus tells us that we ought always to pray and not give up (Luke 18:1). Prayer is the principal means of our deliverance from whatever ills beset us. The experience of Christmas Evans, a Welsh Baptist preacher, is helpful, in that as a pastor he found himself in a cold and arid state because of the influence of unhelpful teaching. He knew he needed to get out of this lethargic spiritual state, and he describes how it happened.

> I was weary, weary of a cold heart towards Christ and His sacrifice and the work of His Spirit, a cold heart in the pulpit, in secret prayer and in the study. For fifteen years previously I had felt my heart burning within me, as if going to Emmaus with Jesus. On a day ever to be remembered by me as I was going from Dolgelly to Machynlleth and climbing up toward Cader Idris I considered it incumbent upon to me pray, however hard I felt in my heart and how-

ever worldly the frame of my spirit was. Having begun in the name of Jesus I soon felt as it were the fetters loosening and the old hardness of heart softening, and, as I thought, mountains of frost and snow dissolving and melting within me. This engendered confidence in my soul in the promise of the Holy Ghost. I felt my whole mind relieved from some great bondage, tears flowed copiously, and I was constrained to cry out for the gracious visits of God, by restoring to my soul the joys of His salvation, and that He would visit the churches in Anglesey that were under my care. I embraced in my supplications all the churches of the saints, and nearly all the ministers in the principality by their names. This struggle lasted for three hours; it rose again and again like one wave after another, on a high flowing tide driven by strong wind, until my nature became faint by weeping and crying. Thus I resigned myself to Christ body and soul, gifts and labours, all my life, every day and every hour that remained for me; and all my cares I committed to Christ. The road was mountainous and lonely and I was wholly alone and suffered no interruption in my wrestling with God.

From this time I was made to expect the goodness of God to the churches and myself.[2]

Reluctance to pray obviously has something to do with our evil hearts, but its chief cause is our enemy, Satan, who knows that prayer is our supply line, our means of drinking deeply at the wells of salvation. He wants us to forget that the throne of God has become a throne of grace for us. Nothing must be allowed to rob us of this understanding and of the glorious truth that this throne is always open. This is particularly relevant when we are tempted to turn tail or to flinch from continuing in the battle as we ought. Our enemy may seem as impressive and big as Goliath must have appeared to David and the onlookers of that significant battle. But David's simple weapon with God's blessing on it was more than a match for Goliath. So, too, the simple weapon of prayer can demolish Satan's strongholds (2 Corinthians 10:4).

INTERCESSORY PRAYER AS
PART OF OUR PASTORAL CARE

The principal part of our pastoral care is unseen by those who benefit from it, since it is exercised in secret. Called to be shepherds as well as teachers, we must be intercessors for the members of Christ's flock entrusted to us. Prayer is one way in which we keep watch over the spiritual well-being of the lambs and sheep of the flock. If no one else prays for them, we must. It is significant that the ministry of intercession is the one ministry that our Lord continues in heaven now on our behalf. We are never nearer to His heart than when we bear up in our prayers the concerns and well-being of His flock.

"All the saints" (Ephesians 6:18) are to be prayed for, since all Christians in this world are in the battle, without exception. Some require daily prayer because of crises, and all have a call upon our regular prayers because of the needs all constantly have. We must not pray for people only when they are ill! Spurgeon made this point in a somewhat amusing way when talking to pastors: "When a man is upstairs in bed, and cannot do any hurt, you pray for him. When he is downstairs, and can do no end of mischief, you do not pray for him. Is this wise and prudent?"

Our primary concern must be the believers who are our pastoral responsibility. Some churches follow the helpful practice of producing a list of church members, divided up among the days of a month. But sometimes a church membership may be too large to make this a manageable proposition.

DP I found it helpful to take our church membership list and to pray for the people on one page each day. This meant praying for ten individuals or families. This number was as much as I could cope with each day, and a

smaller number might have been better, in order to give
more time to thinking about them and praying for them
intelligently. In addition, I carry a sheet in my loose-leaf
prayer diary for urgent needs to be remembered daily until they are graciously met by God. This sheet can be constantly updated. Within my own personal prayer diary I
also pray on a monthly basis for new converts, aware that
they ought to be regularly in my prayers. William Burns,
an early missionary to China, wrote in his diary one of his
prayers for such: "O Lord, keep these dear young disciples from the devil, the world, and the flesh; perfect Thy
love in their hearts, Thine image in their souls, and grant
to me in Thine infinite grace to experience more pure and
tender love for the lambs of the flock. This I ask in the name
of my Lord Jesus. Amen." His prayer is worth emulating.

AB I must confess that while I have tried to emulate
Derek's structured discipline in this matter, I have been
less than successful. This is due in part to the nature of
the spiritual battle and in some measure to a difference in
personality. I achieve the same objective of praying consistently and intelligently for "our sheep," but I do so in a
more random fashion. One of my colleagues shames me
with his lists. In contrast I tend to make the matters of
the moment and the people in the spotlight the focus of
my prayers.

As elders we pray routinely for the membership and
we have a pastoral care list that is updated daily. I find
that apart from my private devotional exercises I can pray
for the members of our pastoral team and staff and their
families while I am jogging. I work my way around the
building in my mind's eye, praying for the custodial staff

and the administrative people as well as my colleagues in ministry on the pastoral team. At the same time I have been trying over the years to learn what it means to cultivate the presence of Christ in the routine of life. I have been helped by these comments on prayer from the late William Still of Aberdeen.

> Prayer for the Christian is a matter of believing that God is, and that He does respond to those who believe in Him. That's the start. Now the real Christian is indwelt by the Holy Spirit, and the Holy Spirit is God, and is, naturally, in vital touch with the Father and the Son. On the basis that we know something about this God from the Holy Scriptures, we begin to speak to Him internally, and should do so as naturally, in a sense, as we speak to ourselves—our "better" selves, born of God in Christ Jesus. That's prayer. But we have to believe that He is there and listening. . . . If you are real about this, and believe in what you are doing, prayer, instead of being a matter of times and seasons and special or routine occasions, becomes a life, or it becomes such a vital part of life that it re-focuses one's whole outlook.

While spontaneous and extempore prayer is the norm, there is a value in writing down requests we feel we should make to God for people. Those who take prayer seriously also take seriously their preparation and thought for prayer. We find Paul, for instance, actually writing down in some of his letters the prayers that he offered for his fellow believers—good examples are Ephesians 1:15–19, Ephesians 3:14–21, and Colossians 1:9–12. One way to keep our prayers fresh is to use Paul's prayers in rotation for the believers for whom we have responsibility. As we first pray the prayers for ourselves, we will be in a better position to pray them for others.

Another aid to freshness in prayer—since everything habitual can lead to unhelpful ruts—is to make a habit of asking today for others the identical things we have sought from God for ourselves in view of what we have read from the Scriptures.

DP For many years now I have written in a notebook— preferably in a brief sentence or phrase—what has been most meaningful in my daily Scripture reading. For instance, my entry yesterday was from 1 Peter 4:2, and I wrote down, "Live . . . for the will of God." That became the principal theme of my praying for myself and then for others. Today it was "the Spirit of glory and of God rests on you" (1 Peter 4:14), and I found my thoughts turning to the manner in which each person of the Trinity is referred to in relation to glory (1 Corinthians 2:8; Ephesians 1:17), and that glory is our ultimate destination. Stirred to pray that I may realize afresh the wonder of my salvation in Christ, I prayed the same for those in my prayer diary today. This makes prayer fresh and different each day—and, more important still, relevant and in accord with God's will.

AB I have also found this to be a good pattern, and I enter the verse or phrase in my journal. I also use Spurgeon's *Morning and Evening,* and sometimes his phrase becomes mine for the day. John Baillie's *Diary of Private Prayer* has also proved helpful. My copy has a blank page for each morning and evening, providing space for the names of those for whom I am praying.

This morning a phrase from his prayer struck me. "Let

me keep no corner of my heart closed to Your influence."
I was challenged to take this seriously and in turn to pray
the same for my colleagues and family.

One unique benefit of praying regularly and systematically for
those for whom we have spiritual responsibility is that it prompts
concern and action. It is frequently used by the Holy Spirit to create a sensitivity to people's needs. Nothing surpasses this kind of
regular praying in making us acutely aware of blessings and benefits for which we should be asking God for others. In addition, we
should always pray for members of the flock as their names come
to mind throughout the day, sometimes for no apparent reason.
No prompting to pray is to be ignored, and often we discover later
that there was an acute need in the lives of those for whom we
prayed.

DP There have been occasions when I have felt it right to
let people know that I have been praying for them, and
sometimes what it is that I have believed I should ask
God on their behalf. The apostle Paul frequently expressed in his letters his prayerfulness for his readers, and
also something of his longings for them (e.g., Romans
1:9–11; Philemon 4–6). Occasionally—probably about
half a dozen times a year—I have dropped a brief note to
individuals, saying something like, "As I was praying for
you today I felt a particular concern for you, and found
myself asking for the Lord's special help for you . . ." I
have also done the same by phone or when I have "happened" to meet someone for whom I prayed earlier that
day. Knowing myself what an encouragement it is to dis-

cover that people have been praying for me, it is an equal encouragement for people to know that their undershepherd prays for them.

AB The tremendous impact of this practice (which I also try to keep) came home to me some years ago. In 1986 I had the privilege of sharing the speaking with Alex Motyer at a Bible Conference in Northern Ireland. We had never met before and we were together for a week. When we parted he told me that he would pray consistently for me and for my family. Some three years passed without any contact, and then one Good Friday I phoned him out of the blue to thank him for the help I had received from his commentary on Isaiah. When he heard me on the phone he said, "My dear boy, Beryl [his wife] and I have just paused for tea, and we were praying for you and for Cameron, Michelle, and Emily." The fact that he was able to name my children told me that his promise in 1986 had become a pattern in the ensuing years. Knowing how helped I was by his faithfulness, I have sought to follow his example.

Prayer and Preparation
for Teaching and Preaching

The apostles linked prayer with the ministry of the Word (Acts 6:4). As we spread each day before God, we will naturally share with Him the tasks that are before us, including our preparation for the teaching of His Word. There is value also in deliberately pausing to pray every time we are about to open our books for study, so that we remind ourselves of our dependence upon the Holy Spirit for enlightenment in preparation as well as for power in delivery.

DP Often as I have begun a day I have so felt the pressure of getting ready for the next meeting that I have wanted to get on with my preparation as quickly as possible, only to find myself struggling and not really getting anywhere. Frequently it has been because I have not looked to God for His help as I have begun. It is as impossible to understand the Scriptures without the Spirit's help as it is to read a sundial without the sun.

While I have not done it as often as I would have wished because of busyness—and so it may be something of a counsel of perfection—I have found great benefit in setting aside a morning or half a morning once or twice a year to pray through my preaching plan for a new session, perhaps even for a whole year. My purpose has been to keep the balance between Old and New Testaments, between doctrine and ethics, and between the exposition of doctrinal passages and character studies. I have to admit that God has been gracious in guiding me as I have gone along so often, but forward planning in an attitude of prayer is eminently worthwhile.

When the time comes to give a talk or sermon, there is much to be said for praying home its lessons for our own life before we apply it to the lives of others. I find that if I have read my notes through four times I am ready to use them. I do my fourth reading on my knees, praying through my own obedience to the truth I am going to share. Prior to preaching, I usually pray a prayer that came together through God speaking to me through three separate verses of Scripture, and it goes like this: "Help me, Lord, to speak as in Your sight, and to be prepared to fall into the ground and die so that I may bear much fruit. May my concern not be what people are thinking about me, but Your praise and Your people's good. Thank You that You have not given me a spirit of fear but rather of power, love, and self-discipline."

I try to remember to pray especially for the people who will be on the receiving end of the preaching, remembering their preciousness to God and His desire to feed them. We may become so caught up with our own sense of responsibility that we forget the very people for whom God's Word is intended, and for whom we have been preparing the whole week.

AB Once again, the fact that I follow an almost identical pattern illustrates the formative nature of my years as Derek's assistant. I am constantly asking God to grant me genuine humility of heart and demeanor, clarity of thought, brevity of expression, and an authority that comes by the power of His Word. After my father died one of his friends told me that my dad's prayer for me each Sunday was that my preaching would be marked by clarity, conviction, and compassion. I can understand why it is said that Spurgeon walked to his pulpit saying to himself, "I believe in the Holy Spirit."

PRAYER WHEN VISITING AND COUNSELING

Prayer is the best starting point in determining where and when to make pastoral visits. Sometimes the choice will be made because of crises and needs brought to our attention. Both at the beginning of the day and immediately before making the visit we should pray, trying, where we can, to anticipate what we feel the situation may be that we have to face or share, and asking God to direct us to appropriate Scriptures. We may find that other Scriptures come to mind when we are with the person concerned, but we will find it helpful to consider prayerfully beforehand where we should go in the Scriptures if no other direction is given.

Even as we are about to make a visit, it is appropriate to pray. During the course of a visit, if it takes an unexpected turn or a difficult question arises, an arrow prayer is appropriate and right, as Nehemiah discovered (Nehemiah 2:4). Prayer should be part of every pastoral visit. Once we make it our habit people will always expect us to pray with them, and they will be disappointed if we do not. Praying together should be seen as a principal purpose of a pastoral visit. Visits may be the ideal opportunity, too, to share with the person or people concerned the way in which we have felt we should pray for them in private. Where it is not an embarrassment, it is helpful to get people to pray audibly so that it is not just we ourselves who pray. This will be an encouragement to them and will make it easier to pray in this way the next time. "Let both of us pray" or "Let us all pray" are suggestions that may draw forth unexpected streams of prayer. Where the Scriptures have been read first, prayer finds its natural starting point in what God says in His Word.

What we have said about prayer and pastoral visiting applies equally to prayer and counseling. An important part of Christian counseling is showing a person what the Scriptures have to say about a problem or an issue, and indicating the benefits and guidance for which it is appropriate to ask God. The time spent in counseling should conclude therefore in prayer, relating the Scriptures to the situation, and asking God specifically for that which it is clear He wants to do or give. Where the person counseled is in a fit state to do so, it may help him very much if he can pray aloud, too, for the help he needs.

PRAYER AS THE NORM WHENEVER
ANYTHING OF MOMENT IS DISCUSSED

Whether in the context of pastoral visitation, conversations in people's homes in the course of social visits, or matters raised when Christians come together, we would recommend prayer together as the norm. We have found it helpful never to discuss any subject of moment or consequence with another Christian without then praying about it together. That may mean praying wherever we are —in our study, in the hallway, or by the church pew.

So often on a Sunday, for instance, a critical situation may come to light in the lives of those for whom spiritual leaders have responsibility. One or more of them may raise the matter with us, and perhaps we may only be able to talk for a few moments. We would there and then say at the conclusion, "Let's commit the matter to God." We do not need to sit down, but simply stand together while either we or someone else prays. A member of the church fellowship may raise an issue or, more difficult, a criticism, which cannot be properly discussed there and then. As a future date is fixed to talk it through, we would seize that present opportunity to say, "We'll pray now, and ask for God's help for when we discuss it more fully."

This practice has many advantages. It means that the care we share for people is cast upon the Lord, rather than merely carried by us—no small thing. It sweetens attitudes if the subject or issue happens to be a touchy one. It encourages prayerfulness by example rather than by instruction. It means that we do not forget to pray for the matter concerned. So often we can make a mental note to pray for something, but the pressure of other things pushes it out. But praying at the time means that the issue has not been left unprayed for, and praying together writes it all the more on the mind for future prayer. It further underlines, too, the value of united prayer. If a subject is worth discussing, it is worthy of prayer—that is the best rule.

Praying with people over the telephone is an extension of this practice. Those about to go for an important interview or those under stress because of responsibility for caring for the seriously or terminally ill may be greatly encouraged by a brief phone call to give an appropriate verse of Scripture and to pray. Some phone calls may be initiated by others to discuss a difficult issue. If so, we follow the principle of suggesting at the conclusion, "Let's pray together about the matter before we ring off." As Paul knelt down spontaneously with the Ephesian elders and prayed (Acts 20:36), so we should do the same as a natural application of the instruction to "pray continually" (1 Thessalonians 5:17).

PUBLIC PRAYER

Shepherds and teachers are expected to lead in public prayer more than most people and not least in the conduct of the corporate worship of God by His people. In some parts of the body of Christ a liturgy or prayer book is used, and extemporary prayer is not the norm. Most who use set prayers find it best not to be limited to them in that to do so imposes an unhelpful restraint when relating prayer to the changing needs of God's people. Set prayers and free prayer are ideally combined. So many of our convictions about forms of prayer arise from our background rather than from our understanding of Scripture.

What counts is reality, since God looks upon our heart whether we are praying set or extemporary prayers. When we pray publicly, care is required in our language in a way that does not apply when we pray privately. We are not suggesting that we should be clever in our use of words, or that the actual words themselves are the important issue. Rather we are suggesting that when we regularly lead others in prayer, there is a danger of using the same words, and of our prayers becoming so stereotyped and predictable that people almost know what we are going to say in the next sentence. That may be an exaggeration, but we all know exactly how certain people will pray when called upon to do so publicly.

The best public prayers are those that come from the heart

and are prompted by the Spirit. Bearing in mind that necessary and first principle, the best prayers are those that arise from our current reading and application of the Scriptures to our lives, for then they will be both fresh and different every time we pray. It is in public prayer especially that we must be cautious of anything approaching professionalism—of simply using words that are expected rather than words that flow from our hearts.

Extemporary prayer in the context of services for the worship of God needs to be prepared for, not in the sense that prayers should be written out word for word, for then they would cease to be extemporary! Rather we should carefully think and pray beforehand concerning the praise and worship we should offer God, and the matters for intercession to bring before Him. The next step is to consider which Scriptures guide us in what we should be saying to God and asking from Him.

DP I keep 104 envelopes—two for each Sunday of the year—in which I place skeleton outlines of prayers that I prepare Sunday by Sunday. I will often prepare an outline and find myself praying quite differently at the time. I am not sorry about that but glad, in that I recognize that I may be following the prompting of the Spirit. At the same time I may be following the same prompting of the Spirit in using the skeleton prayer I asked Him to help me prepare beforehand. The more important we believe prayer to be, the more time we are ready to give to preparing ourselves for it.

AB Once again, I am not as meticulous in my preparation. However, my concern is always the same—that my pulpit prayers would be marked by integrity, clarity, and fervency. There is probably no more vulnerable place for the pastor than standing before the congregation in prayer. It will quickly become apparent whether or not he is growing in his personal awareness of God's grace and goodness. I am always on the lookout for prayer books. I often resort to language from the *Book of Common Prayer*, and I have benefited greatly from *Parish Prayers* edited by Frank Colquhoun, as well as the Puritan prayers that are collected in *The Valley of Vision*.

OUR OWN NEED OF THE PRAYERS OF OTHERS

As this is an area seldom spoken of, it ought to be mentioned at this point. Shepherds and teachers need the prayers of God's people and should not hesitate to ask for them. "Pray for us," the writer of the letter to the Hebrews urges his readers (13:18). Paul constantly sought the prayers of his fellow believers (Romans 15:30; 2 Corinthians 1:10–11; Ephesians 6:19; Colossians 4:3), because he knew his dependence upon them and the effectiveness God gave to them (Philippians 1:19).

We should never allow those to whom we minister to imagine that we are somehow super-Christians who do not have the same temptations as they do and identical dependence upon God. When in the course of our exposition of Scripture we are dealing with passages where prayer was sought by Paul and others, we may then solicit prayer for ourselves and other undershepherds. In prayer letters we write, we can thank people from time to time for their prayers. When people assure us, perhaps in the course of pastoral visitation, "I pray for you regularly," we should tell them how much we appreciate their prayers. No Christian knows how much he owes to God for the prayers of others, and not least shepherds and teachers.

CHAPTER 5

DEVOTIONAL LIFE

OUR SECRET AND PERSONAL LIFE

Behind our public life there needs to be a hidden life where our roots are firmly fixed in God Himself (Psalm 1:3). As we turn our attention to our devotional life, we have in view that most private part of our daily life when we go into our room, close the door, and spend time with our Father in secret (Matthew 6:6). We will rightly teach others the importance of this daily practice. It is all the more vital for us, because we may lack those who care for our souls as we do for others. We firmly believe that the latter ought not to be the case, and we will return to that subject later when we consider pastoral care. But where it is so, then we need to be all the more watchful for the growth and development of our own spiritual life.

Before ever we are shepherds and teachers, we are first and foremost sons of God, and our spiritual life demands to be nurtured. One of the hazards of pastoral ministry is to be so caught up with the legitimate spiritual needs of others that we neglect our own. Such a situation becomes counterproductive, since we effectively help others only as we ourselves are spiritually healthy. To give heed to our devotional life is to recognize that our relationship to God is more important than our service. God wants us and our fellowship with Him more than He wants even our pastoral and teaching ministry, important as it is.

LOVE FOR GOD MUST BE
THE PRIORITY OF OUR LIFE

"Devotional" may not be the best word, since it tends to make some of us think of devotional literature, which may not have much body or substance to it. But it is an appropriate word in that it lays stress upon our devotion to God and to His Son Jesus Christ. The priority of our lives must be to love God—the summary of the commandments underlines this (Luke 10:26–28), and Paul significantly ends his letter to the Ephesians with the words, "Grace to all who love our Lord Jesus Christ with an undying love" (6:24). God the Son is the supreme object of the Father's love, and we are never more in harmony with God than when we delight in His Son and love Him.

In recommissioning Peter as an undershepherd, our Lord made it plain that Peter's service was to find its driving force in his love for his Master—only then would it be acceptable (John 21:15–17). The more we love Christ the more we must guard that love, since it will be an object of attack by the enemy of souls. It is possible to enjoy being a shepherd and teacher for the wrong reasons, perhaps because of the seeming importance or prominence that it gives. As we take care of our love for Jesus Christ, we avoid such snares.

In concentrating upon our devotional life we have three areas of our more secret and personal life in view. First, there is what we may describe as our walk with God. No Old Testament character stands out more as a man whose personal relationship with God was right than Enoch, who "walked with God" (Genesis 5:24). He no more saw God with his physical eyes than we do, and the writer to the Hebrews reminds us that Enoch's life was one of faith like ours (Hebrews 11:5–6). Walking with someone implies being in step with that person and sharing his friendship and fellowship. A preeminent purpose of our devotional life is to keep ourselves in step with God, to check, as every new day opens and closes, that we are in harmony with Him. In our devotional life we share our life with God as a man does with his closest friend (cf. Revelation 3:20).

Second, we have in view the sustaining of our spiritual life. Like those whom we endeavor to help, we do not live by bread alone. Our never-dying souls, having been redeemed and made alive spiritually, cry out for spiritual nurture by prayer and Bible reading. Our inner being needs to be renewed day by day (2 Corinthians 4:16). Our union with our Lord Jesus Christ is our most valuable possession, and as we meet with Him by means of prayer and meditation upon His Word, He renews our spiritual life. A branch of the vine is healthy only as it is in vital touch with the life of the vine (John 15:5).

Third, we have in view the development of our own Christian character. A pastoral objective is to see others grow in their likeness to their Lord and Master, and we must not neglect that priority ourselves. Christian character develops aright as we add to "faith goodness; and to goodness, knowledge; and to knowledge, self-control; and to self-control, perseverance; and to perseverance, godliness; and to godliness, brotherly kindness; and to brotherly kindness, love" (2 Peter 1:5–7). All these virtues are exemplified in our Lord Jesus, even as the fruit of the Spirit is. A key aspect of our devotional life is our meditation upon the person of our Lord Jesus Christ and deliberate self-examination to ensure that we are making it our aim to be like Him. So often when we tell God that is what we honestly want, He answers us in surprising ways. Trials may come—and especially trials arising from our God-given ministry and service. They are frequently the means God employs to perfect our characters and to answer our prayers for Christlikeness. Only as we possess these qualities "in increasing measure" will we be kept "from being ineffective and unproductive" in our knowledge of our Lord Jesus Christ (2 Peter 1:8).

We are naturally concerned to be successful shepherds and teachers; but our overriding concern must be to live a godly life rather than to achieve what others may consider success. As we make personal holiness our aim—God's stated priority for our personal life—we may leave it to God to add to us whatever else we need (Matthew 6:33; 1 Peter 1:15–16). Paul's example helps here. While throughout his letters he exhibits a concern for spiritual success in terms of fulfilling his ministry (Romans 15:20; 1 Corinthians 9:22, 27), in sharing his ambitions he emphasized that above everything else he wanted to know Christ better, and to take hold of that for which the Lord Jesus took hold of him. He was constantly aware that he had not yet arrived and that he had much to learn and more of Christ to enjoy (Philippians 3:10–14). To share honestly such ambitions and convictions is spiritual maturity (Philippians 3:15).

AVOIDING PROFESSIONALISM

Taking care of our secret life with God is the clue to avoiding the snare of professionalism, especially if we have been set apart to give the whole of our time to the work of an undershepherd. By professionalism we have in mind the snare of reading the Scriptures principally with a view to their application to others, rather than first and foremost to applying them to our own lives; or praying for others publicly in a way we do not pray for ourselves in private; or doing things that are expected of a shepherd and teacher simply because they are expected, rather than out of joy because we know they please God.

A danger inherent in being paid for a task is that we may end up doing it only as a job. We are not suggesting that those called to give their whole time to shepherding and teaching should not be properly and fully supported—the New Testament is clear that they should be (1 Corinthians 9:1–14; 1 Timothy 5:17–18). But this may be one of the reasons Paul sometimes chose to engage in tent making, so that he could offer his services freely. He was not only keen that people should see that he did not shepherd and teach for material advantage, but he also wished to keep himself from what we have described as professionalism. He underlined his philosophy when he wrote to the Corinthians, "Unlike so many, we do not peddle the word of God for profit. On the contrary, in Christ we speak before God with sincerity, like men sent from God" (2 Corinthians 2:17). A peddler is always intent upon dispensing his goods for the sake of gain; not so the Christian undershepherd and teacher. As we safeguard our personal relationship with God through our daily fellowship with Him, we ensure our sincerity, so that when we speak to others our words ring true and our hearers discern that we are men sent from God.

GOD'S REQUIREMENT IS
QUALITY RATHER THAN QUANTITY

Some lessons we learn slowly, and one that we have found particularly difficult is that God wants quality of life from us rather than quantity of service, and that the latter is no substitute for the former. More important than all our preparation for ministry and our careful administration of church life is that we should live our lives for the will of God and reflect His Son's grace and character in all our dealings with others.

The most powerful influence we can have upon people is example. The strength of our example—of which we ourselves are seldom, if ever, aware—comes from the reality and sincerity of our inner and secret life with God. Moral failures, which can so tragically ruin a man's testimony and terminate his ministry, invariably stem from neglected daily fellowship with God. Walking daily in the light increases sensitivity to the first approaches of temptation and sin and strengthens our capacity to resist it by the power of the Spirit.

The continual presence of the Spirit with us is both a tremendous encouragement and a serious challenge. The encouragement is that He is always present to assist us; we have but to cry for His help and it is there. The challenge is that we can never deceive Him, much as we may deceive others and even ourselves. He knows the truth about our devotional life, whether it is our excuses or our deep heart-thirst after God. Paul's final exhortations to the Ephesian elders began with the timely words, "Keep watch over yourselves" (Acts 20:28).

FOUR ASPECTS OF OUR DEVOTIONAL LIFE

1. Worship

It may seem artificial to divide our devotional life into various parts, since one aspect continually flows over into another, but it is helpful to do so to establish what ought to be included. The right place to begin is worship. It is no accident that the word itself, both in its Old and New Testament usage, can be translated, according to context, either worship or service. Acceptable service is offered only by those who genuinely worship; and service itself is part of our worship of God as we have His praise as our objective.

Worship is what we were originally created for, and then recreated for in Christ. It is tragic if we feel obliged to lead God's people in public praise and worship but are devoid of heartfelt praise and worship when we come before Him in secret—and yet that can be the case.

DP I have sometimes felt this to be an area of particular poverty in my life, and I have found several practices helpful and have used one or another of them at a time. First, in the loose-leaf prayer diary I keep, I have written down a different aspect of God's character for meditation on each day of the month. Where Scriptures have prompted me to think of an aspect of God's character, I have written out the verse of Scripture, too. I have then begun each day by meditating upon this facet of God's character, and it has stimulated worship that has been different from the day before and that has properly exercised my mind in fresh appreciation of God. Second, I find a hymnbook or a Christian songbook helpful, especially in the sections relating to the worship of God for all that He is and all that He has done for us in Christ. I use one with which I am not familiar, so that it exposes me to the possibility of new expressions of praise and worship. Third, I value psalms that I can make my own in my praise of God as I pray them through aloud. They then always prompt me to express praise in my own words, in ways I would not have done without the psalm's help. It is valuable to compile our own list of psalms that we find particularly suitable when worship does not come as easily as we would wish to our souls. Since the worship of God is so fundamental to our appreciation and love for God, all effort involved in growing in our ability to worship Him is worthwhile and will be graciously taken up by the Holy Spirit to our profit.

AB In the flyleaf of my diary of private prayer I have written this verse:

> *Weak is the effort of my heart*
> *And cold my warmest thought*
> *But when I see Thee as Thou art*
> *I'll praise Thee as I ought.*

This is a constant reminder to me that genuine worship is an affair of the heart. My heart needs to be "tuned" to sing His praise, and that does not happen apart from a deepening experiential knowledge of God. Again the hymn writer helps us: "'Tis what I know of Thee my Lord and God, that fills my lips with praise, my life with song." Growing up in Scotland I learned many of the metrical psalms by heart, and seldom a day passes without my benefiting from them. I am also helped by playing the music in my car first thing in the morning—not least of all on a Sunday when I make my way to church. Horatius Bonar speaks for more than himself in these words:

> *Fill Thou my life, O Lord my God*
> *In every part with praise*
> *That my whole being may proclaim*
> *Thy being and Thy ways.*
>
> *So shall no part of day or night*
> *From sacredness be free;*
> *But all my life, in every step*
> *Be fellowship with Thee.*

2. Prayer and Meditation

We considered prayer in our last chapter, but it clearly has a unique place in our devotional life. We worship God by means of prayer; and it is by prayer that we share our life and our innermost desires with Him. The picture of a child coming to a father is the one we should always have before us, and we must not allow anything to rob us of prayer's simplicity (Matthew 7:7–11). As undershepherds we gather to ourselves all kinds of cares with regard to Christ's flock, and it is in prayer that we rightly off-load our anxieties onto the Chief Shepherd (1 Peter 5:7). Whatever bothers us is a subject worthy of prayer. Whatever causes us anxiety is to be cast upon Him.

We all long to keep fresh in prayer, so that it does not become a mere matter of words or meaningless routine. Anything we do habitually possesses this inherent danger, and so we should not be ashamed of it, but rather watchful to avoid it.

DP The only answer I know is to pray deliberately against it when I become aware of it happening, and at the same time to ensure that my prayer is essentially a response to God's Word as I read it daily. If we make a point of consciously responding to God by means of His Word, our prayers are kept fresh. While I pray for God's help as I begin to read the Scriptures, I read them before my main time of prayer, rather than the other way around. I do this because the Scriptures provide a new agenda for prayer each day.

To respond adequately to God as He speaks to us in His Word demands meditation on our part, since it focuses our thoughts upon God and what He says to us. But I do not find meditation easy. Here my prayer diary has its uses again. When I find one or more verses of Scripture especially meaningful and relevant, I capture them for the future by writing them down on one of the pages of my prayer diary. When I come to them the next month, I meditate upon them again, often with renewed profit, allowing them to prompt prayer, whether of worship, praise, thanksgiving, petition, or obedient submission to God.

A prayer diary is an extremely personal matter, and my pattern may not be the best for others. But some kind of method is indispensable if we mean business. I divide my prayer diary into three parts. First, there is a page that lists urgent needs, which I regularly update and rewrite.

Then I have a page for each day of the week, for people and matters that I feel I ought to pray for on a weekly basis. In view of the importance of the guidance our Lord gives in the pattern prayer, I have inserted into this section the skeleton agenda the Lord's Prayer provides, with one petition for each day of the week except one. Thus I pray on six consecutive days for: 1. The honor of God's name in the world; 2. The extension of the Church and the coming of God's kingdom through the preaching of the gospel everywhere; 3. The obedience of God's people to His will—beginning with myself—and for God's overruling in human affairs; 4. My daily practical needs and those of others; 5. My relationships and the practice of forgiveness, and then the relationships of all God's people; 6. My temptations and the spiritual battle in which all believers are involved. I frequently put aside this weekly skeleton so as not to get into a rut. The benefit of using it on a regular although occasional basis is that it extends my vision and helps me to avoid the peril of thinking only of the urgent matters in my own situation.

The third section of my prayer diary is the longest, in that I have a page for each day of the month, and over the period of a month I pray for all for whom I feel I have some responsibility. Whatever method we use, there is the danger of mere routine. In an effort to avoid this, I dispense with my prayer diary each week on my day off, and pray and meditate without it. I then include in my prayers the next day the people my prayer diary would have reminded me to pray for the previous day.

3. Bible Reading

Each aspect of our devotional life involves the Scriptures in some way. Love for Christ—our greatest priority—expresses itself in our obedience to His words (John 14:15, 21, 23). Walking with God means keeping in step with Him by daily obedience. Psalm 1 explains what it means to walk with God, and it links meditation with obedience to God's Law. The spiritual food that His Word provides nourishes our spiritual life. It is through His Word that we gain glimpses of Christ's glory so that our characters are transformed "into his likeness with ever-increasing glory" (2 Corinthians 3:18).

The professionalism we have warned ourselves of must be avoided especially when we read the Scriptures. We can so easily handle them with others in view, rather than for our own benefit. There will always be the next preaching and teaching opportunity for us to think of and for which to prepare. We must aim to read the Scriptures for ourselves first, rather than for others. What we discover for ourselves, we can then share with Christ's flock with integrity.

DP Although it takes a lifetime—and probably more—to cover the whole of the Bible in regular exposition, it is important that we, as shepherds and teachers in particular, should expose ourselves to the whole of the Bible. Even to write that is something of a personal rebuke, because on only two or three occasions have I ensured that I have read the whole of the Bible through in a year, using the excellent scheme devised by Robert Murray M'Cheyne. I am not suggesting that there is particular merit in accomplishing it in the space of a year, but any method is valuable that means I regularly and frequently read through the whole of the Scriptures. I would recommend doing this sometimes with a Bible translation with which we are unfamiliar, and marking with a highlighter those words, verses, or passages that stand out in a fresh way. Later we may review and explore these new treasures in depth.

But as well as reading whole chapters each day, it is imperative that we should read a briefer passage, in order to meditate upon it in the manner we have suggested, with a view to prayer and obedience. Bible reading aids abound, and they all have their individual advantages. Since I have profited over the years from the Scripture Union Notes, I use them for my daily devotional reading, as much for their systematic covering of Scripture and method as for the notes themselves.

As shepherds and teachers we will be familiar with most of Scripture, and so there is the danger of our reading a passage with such familiarity that we do not really take it in or look for anything new. It is imperative that we pray against such a peril whenever we are aware of it, and that we cry to God for His Spirit's help to read it with new insight. The most helpful practice I know to maintain freshness is never to read my daily passage without writing down a word, a phrase, a sentence, or a whole verse that is especially meaningful, or through which I feel God is speaking to me. This stops me reading the Scriptures unexpectantly, and it also provides me with something new upon which to meditate prior to my praying.

This morning I read 2 Peter 1:1–9 and my thoughts latched on to verse 3: "everything we need for life and godliness," and so they are the words I have written down for today. They prompted me to thank God for His provision for my material and physical needs, as well as for my spiritual. They stirred me to pray about the priority of godliness in my life, having pondered once more the nature of true godliness.

Sometimes in my systematic reading of Scripture I will be in a particularly difficult passage or a historical narrative where nothing stands out and speaks to me. When that happens, having read the passage concerned, I turn to the book of Psalms or Proverbs and read until God's Word speaks to my heart and condition. If something arrests my attention so that I feel I need to meditate upon it again or regularly, I will not only write it down in my list of daily verses, but I will add it to a page in my monthly prayer diary.

4. The Reading of Christian Books

Christian classics and books that stimulate devotion to our Lord Jesus Christ and personal holiness have an invaluable place in our devotional life. Their potential in our lives is greater than that for other books. One of our principal difficulties as shepherds and teachers is that rather than being ministered to, we tend to be ministering always to others. An effective way of putting this right is to let others minister to us through their writings.

DP I cannot measure the profit I have gained from spending five or ten minutes each day reading a book that feeds my love for Christ and makes me glory in my salvation. I usually do this before I read the Scriptures and pray. I do not read at this stage in the day books that relate to my work or to controversial subjects, but those that nourish my soul and focus my attention on God's greatness and glory. The biography of Cyril Forster Garbett, a former Archbishop of York, reveals how he regularly read through the *Preces Privatae* of Lancelot Andrews, *The Imitation of Christ* by Thomas à Kempis, and *The Scale of Perfection* by Walter Hilton.

It is good to balance the reading of an old book, well proven over the years, with a more contemporary book. Nothing has been more helpful to me than John Owen's *The Glory of Christ.* But having read it, I would balance it with something like J. I. Packer's *Knowing God.* I have read through two volumes of *The Works of Richard Sibbes,* a sixteenth-century Puritan, and I would balance reading these with the writings of someone like A. W. Tozer.

We will all find some books more helpful than others, but besides those already mentioned it is worth considering some others if they are not familiar to you: Richard Baxter's *The Saints' Everlasting Rest;* Andrew Bonar's *Heavenly Springs;* John Bunyan's *The Pilgrim's Progress* and *The Holy War;* Robert Murray M'Cheyne's *Memoirs and Remains;* William Law's *A Serious Call to a Devout and Holy Life;* Jeremy Taylor's *Holy Living and Dying;* Samuel Rutherford's *Letters;* Henry Scougal's *The Life of God in the Soul of Man;* and A. W. Tozer's *Knowledge of the Holy.* The majority of these are old books that are tried and tested. More contemporary books should be sought as well, but we should not shirk the effort required in tackling some of these Christian classics, in that they have been wells of unique refreshment to many of our predecessors.

The ideal pattern for such reading is not to read much at a time—perhaps just a section or a page or two, so as to read and meditate. Having done this, I then read the Scriptures, and try to include in my prayers what I have learned first through the Scriptures and then through my reading of my current book. The criterion for the choice of a book for this period each day is that it must feed my soul and lead me to Christ Himself. If I start a book and find it does not do this, and that it is spiritually arid, then I will change it.

Only good can come from taking stock of our devotional life, for upon it depends our walk with God. Shepherds and teachers are the enemy's prime target, and his most powerful and sustained attacks will be upon our walk with God. If possible, he will encourage us to keep up all our outward and public activities to the neglect of the inward nurture of our souls and the cultivation of the secret place. He knows that then we will soon forfeit our inward peace, since we will let slip our ease in casting our anxieties upon the Lord. He knows, even if we forget, that if we neglect our fellowship with God, we will lose our assurance of God's presence, the certainty that we are in the right place, and the power to succeed in the tasks to which God has called us. He knows that out of touch with God we lose our sensitivity to His guidance and become vulnerable to temptation and moral failure.

Happily, the converse is true: As we keep watch over our walk with God, we enjoy the peace He promises, the consciousness of His presence when we most need it, the assurance that we are where He wants us to be, the guidance of His Spirit, and the power to withstand all Satan's fiery darts and to accomplish successfully our God-given tasks and privileges.

CHAPTER 6

STUDY

STUDY AND EFFECTIVE MINISTRY

Besides study being an obvious priority for the shepherd and teacher, it is also a tremendous privilege. Although not a few hardships may be ours because of our pastoral responsibilities, we have a tremendous bonus in the call God gives us to study. What may and can be but an occasional activity for some Christians, we may engage in every day for several hours, and some understandably envy us. When study becomes demanding, we should remember our privileged position.

There is no conflict between the place of study in successful ministry and dependence upon God the Holy Spirit. Some have considered hours of study to be in conflict with faith in the Spirit's help in ministry. But those who have known the Spirit's blessing most in ministry have been most aware of their need to study the Scriptures in secret with His help. Charles Spurgeon was one such, and he commented on this when addressing a group of pastors:

Some of our people think that we have little or nothing to do but to stand in the pulpit, and pour out a flood of words two or three times a week; but they ought to know that, if we did not spend much time in diligent study, they would get poverty-stricken sermons. I have heard of a brother who trusts in the Lord and does not study; but I have also heard that his people do not trust in him; in fact, I am informed that they wish him to go elsewhere with his inspired discourses, for they say that, when he did study, his talk was poor enough, but now that he gives them that which comes first to his lips, it is altogether unbearable. If any man will preach as he should preach, his work will take more out of him than any other labour under heaven.[1]

It would be foolish not to recognize that there are dangers in study. It can become an end in itself. We can study with the wrong motivation. John Owen, the Puritan theologian, admitted with a sense of shame in later life that one of the reasons he studied so hard as a young man was an ambition he had to rise to power and distinction in the Church. David Brainerd, an early missionary to the North American Indians, found that study could feed his pride. When on one occasion opportunities for study were much more difficult to find than before, he concluded, "The reason, I judge, why I am not allowed to study a great part of my time is, because I am endeavouring to lay in such a stock of knowledge as shall nourish self-sufficiency." Certain as David Brainerd was that it was his duty to study and qualify himself in the best manner he could for his duties, he was conscious that study all too easily made him self-confident. The energies of our enemy, Satan, are always directed at making a bad thing of a good thing, and that applies to study as to everything else. To be aware of the dangers is a first step in combating them.

The Church is in urgent need of shepherds and teachers who will study. The pressures and pace of contemporary life make that an increasingly difficult goal to achieve. Christ's flock on earth depends upon its undershepherds to lead it into the fresh pastures of God's Word. Undershepherds maintain an effective ministry as they extend their own understanding of God's Word. If we are constantly pouring out without pouring in, we will soon cease to pour out anything that is of value to others.

INSTRUCTING OTHERS AND
OUR PERSONAL OBEDIENCE TO GOD

Ezra's ministry was successful, and the manner in which it is summed up is instructive: "The gracious hand of his God was on him. For Ezra had devoted himself to the study and observance of the Law of the LORD, and to teaching its decrees and laws in Israel" (Ezra 7:9–10). Ezra's devotion to study is clearly commended in this statement. We know from the Old Testament book that bears his name that many practical and urgent matters demanded his attention, but he nevertheless gave the proper priority to study. More than that, he observed the right order of things: study, followed by personal obedience, leading to effective teaching of others. Before he instructed others in proper obedience to God's Word, he obeyed it himself.

The key to success in study is that we always study with a view to our own obedience first. A trap Satan regularly tries to set is for us so to concentrate upon others' obedience to God that we neglect our own obedience. Whatever we study in the Scriptures—even though we inevitably have our preaching to others in view—we must first relate to ourselves, and practice. Then we may teach others what we ourselves are striving to obey. This ties in with the emphasis we have given upon the importance of our example. Study becomes merely academic and arid if we do not put into practice what we learn. Teaching from the lips of those who fail to live in the good of what they teach soon lacks the ring of reality. Ezra's permanent and lasting influence flowed from what happened in secret as he studied God's Law. As we carefully link our study of God's

Word with practical obedience, we save ourselves from the subtle snare of professionalism in the ministry. We are ordinary Christians before we are shepherds and teachers.

DETERMINING THE BEST PLACE TO STUDY

The place where we physically study is important. We may not have much choice, but, when we do, it is worth giving careful thought to it. We are all creatures of habit and are helped by atmosphere. If we associate a particular room, or even a table or desk, with study, we will find study much easier when we come to it. If it is possible to set apart a complete room—no matter how small— just for study, that is a great boon.

DP Having experimented over the years, and having lived in a house provided by the church, I came to prefer an upstairs room in that it tends to be quieter, and I was not so inclined to be disturbed by callers at the front door or by what might be going on elsewhere within the house. The first study I had was not only downstairs but also the room nearest the front door. The doorbell never went off without my being disturbed and overhearing the conversations at the door or within the hall. People could also tell that I was at home by looking through the window, and that encouraged more interruptions still during my study time!

Some may find it advantageous to have their place of study at the church rather than at home because of the smaller likelihood of interruptions. That is worth considering, especially if a room is not available at home. It is vital, however, to have all our books in one place rather than in two, as there are few things more frustrating than finding that the book we want is in the other place!

The one caution I have about using the church as the place of study is vulnerability when it comes to unexpected callers. I have particularly in mind the unexpected arrival of someone of the opposite sex. I have made it a practice never to have a conversation with a woman in empty church premises or at my home when my wife is not also at home. The only way to avoid perils that some have fallen into through the sexual temptations that pastoral work may create is to put up the proper barriers.

AB Some of us are more influenced by our environment than others. It is almost embarrassing to admit to this, but I find that I am particularly sensitive to issues of color, light, and sound. It is imperative that the study "nest" we create is conducive to our best work. In Scotland my study was in my home on the ground floor, and I relied upon my wife to field the interruptions. I was able to work there until the children came along. At that point I moved to my vestry in the church building, but I had to carry my books with me each day. There was no telephone there to interrupt me, but its absence also isolated me in an unhelpful way.

For the past twenty years my study has been in the church building. As our pastoral team has grown and as the busyness of the office has increased, I have created what I refer to as "the cave." This is simply another room away from everything else that affords me the kind of privacy that helps me to say focused. Some of my colleagues seem able to study well in short bursts. They can walk away and return to the material later. If they are like Harrier Jump Jets, then I am more of a lumbering Jumbo. It

takes me a long time to get airborne, but once aloft I can
stay there (and need to stay there) for long stretches.

NO SUBSTITUTE FOR DISCIPLINE

Most of us will be tempted to neglect study, and some more
than others. Study requires not only devotion but also discipline
to make it effective. As we begin any day, there will invariably be
other matters that could preoccupy us, and apparently quite legiti-
mately. Seemingly urgent practical matters regularly threaten the
more important that may not be labeled urgent. Urgent does not always mean important. It is helpful to ask, "What are the main hin-
drances to my studying?" and, on identifying them, to be honest and
realistic in applying remedies.

DP Correspondence is a hindrance as far as I am concerned. I enjoy receiving letters and e-mails, although I
am not so keen on answering them because of the time
involved. I have a fear of my correspondence tray so piling
up or my unanswered e-mails so accumulating that they
become a burden and something of a nightmare. Because
the main post comes at the beginning of the day, there is
a temptation to deal with it there and then. But it frequently takes more time than anticipated. The discipline
I have determined for myself, therefore, is never to answer letters or respond to e-mails in the morning. Correspondence does not involve the same degree of
concentration as study, and so I relegate correspondence
to a part of the day when I am not at my freshest and

when it does not matter if I am disturbed. For me that is either immediately before or after our evening meal.

AB For me the mail does not arrive until the afternoon. If at all possible I like to deal with it there and then. If I can't and it begins to pile up, I find it best to tackle it in the early morning before my assistant arrives. With it out of the way I then find it easier to study.

If we have been set apart by God's people to give all our time to shepherding and teaching, it is imperative, where possible, to devote our mornings to study. There may be exceptions, but it remains the general rule. Men whom God has conspicuously used have found this to be the case, and we are wise to learn from their experience. J. H. Jowett accepted an invitation to minister in New York at Fifth Avenue Presbyterian Church; later he was to be minister at Westminster Chapel in London. Sharing his plans with a friend, he wrote,

> I am learning to resist almost every hour of the day the tremendous forces that would push me here and there. I do not know what time ministers here spend in their studies. They are evidently engaged in a hundred outside works that must leave them very little time to prepare their message. I am going to stand steadily against this pressure, even at the cost of being misunderstood. When I get into my own home I shall allow nothing to interfere with my morning in the study. If the pulpit is to be occupied by men with a message worth hearing we must have the time to prepare it. I feel the preaching of the Word of God is incomparably my first work in New York.[2]

Dr. W. E. Sangster held the same conviction:

> The man who jealously guards his morning hours for deep study,
> and study which centres in God's Book; who lets it be known to his
> people that, while he is available at any hour of day or night for the
> dying (and other needs which brook no delay) he expects to be left
> undisturbed in his pulpit preparation until lunch-time; who uses
> these fenced hours, first for praying, then for brooding on the Bible
> and for the flinty kind of thinking which will enable him to go
> twice a Sunday to his pulpit and really feed his people from the
> word of God—that man will not lack his reward.
>
> I do not say that the multitudes will crowd to hear him—
> though they might. I do say that an expectation will grow among
> his people for the word he has to give, and that not only will the ex-
> pectation grow but, if they never become a multitude, the numbers
> will grow as well.[3]

If correspondence can be a hindrance to study, the phone is perhaps a greater problem. People unaccustomed to study have little idea
of how a single telephone call can hinder our whole flow of thought
and study. Obviously we want to be immediately available to any
member of the flock in a moment of crisis. But crises apart, we should
encourage people to avoid phoning us during the morning.

DP I have found it helpful to ask people to ring me either
before nine in the morning or after twelve noon, so that I
may aim at three hours of uninterrupted study.

AB Since we have a telephone receptionist who screens
the calls and passes them on to my assistant, I rely upon

her wisdom in passing along the emergencies and in saving the routine calls to be handled later. I can be my own worst enemy by making phone calls when they come to mind and thus interrupting myself!

A prompt start each morning is imperative, especially as we are responsible for the organizing of our own time. The promptness with which we would expect others to present themselves at their place of work is the promptness we should expect of ourselves. We should not despise small practicalities that encourage discipline.

DP For example, I do not work in my study with my slippers on. Slippers imply leisure and casualness, and so to help my attitude of mind I wear shoes. Others may not require such practical helps, but I find them beneficial.

AB For the same reason each of us on the pastoral team arrives for work in collar and tie. This is increasingly unusual, but we do it to make the point for ourselves if for no one else: This is serious business. We relax the rule on Fridays just to prove that we are not incapable of studying without a tie!

Our determination to study should never be influenced by our feelings. Governed by feelings or distractions, we will either become lazy or hopelessly diverted from our priority. If we limit our study to when we feel fresh and enthusiastic about it, we will accomplish little. But if we determine to study, no matter how we feel, we will soon discover ourselves excited at familiar and new truth and refreshed by it, beyond all expectation.

Part of self-discipline in study is to determine an order of priorities.

DP So often I find myself bewildered—and, to be honest, almost paralyzed—by the number of study tasks before me. What I find most helpful is to take a sheet of paper, write down the tasks in a priority order, and assign an appropriate time for each. This procedure delivers me from the paralysis of indecision, the waste of nervous energy in wondering how ever I am going to cope, and the mistake of jumping from one task to another without proper planning.

Many of us find there is a limit to our concentration upon one subject. If we work for too long at a single assignment we may become stale at it. It is frequently helpful to turn to another assignment, so that although somewhat tired or stale at working with the first, we come to the second with freshness. I frequently divide my mornings into two, so as to deal with two aspects of study. I often accomplish much more working this way in a morning than in simply maintaining the pressure on one assignment. Then the following day I complete the two tasks, once more in their two halves.

AB Even as I write I find myself battling with this issue. Writing deadlines are fighting for the time I need to give to sermon preparation. Inevitably and rightly Sunday wins and other study projects must take their turn. As I mentioned earlier, I am not as good as Derek at dividing my mornings. Each of us must learn what is best for him. For me to attempt Derek's regimen is akin to David's dressing up in Saul's armor.

AN AREA OF TENSION: FINDING TIME FOR GENERAL READING AND STUDY

There is considerable tension for most shepherds and teachers in giving appropriate time to preparation for ministry and the time they feel they ought to give to general reading and study. It is the tension of always having in view the next address or sermon to be given so that there is little or no time left for study and reading apart from what is necessary to prepare for the immediate preaching responsibility. We confess that sometimes we have fallen into the snare of feeling sorry for ourselves in this. But we hope that we have learned better now, since self-pity is always out of place.

This "hand-to-mouth" experience has one invaluable benefit—it means that our approach has the potential of consistent freshness since we are always having to break new ground, something that is an incalculable benefit both to our hearers and ourselves. Although we may not be able to study other areas of Scripture and read books unrelated to the subject in hand, if we are systematic in our preaching, our study and reading will be increasingly comprehensive over a period of years—and almost unconsciously so. There is no better way of grasping Christian doctrine than extended study of the whole of Scripture.

PLANNING OUR WEEK

We all have the same number of hours in a week, and it is those who plan carefully who get the most out of them. As Hannah More put it, "It is just as in packing a trunk; a good packer will get twice as much in as a bungler."

DP I reckoned I required four hours' study each working day to keep on top of my preparation for the weekly demands of ministry in the pastorate. In order not to be overwhelmed by this requirement, I needed to plan my week's work carefully. Pastors' responsibilities vary, and each must work out what is best for him and be prepared to adjust his program as circumstances change. In the hope that it may be helpful, I will outline my typical week of teaching responsibilities in a pastorate and how I tried to organize my preparation for them.

In a normal week I had responsibility for two Sunday services, and the Sunday morning included a children's address as an integral part. On a Monday night I usually had to give a brief address at the church prayer meeting. Every Thursday there was a church Bible study, and for two-thirds of the year I taught at it. In addition, there were the inevitable extras of young people's meetings, University Christian Unions, the church women's meeting, and invitations to preach elsewhere.

I found initially that it was all too easy to say yes to extra meetings months or even years ahead, but hard to cope with them when the time came to prepare for them. So often they put extreme pressure upon me in a week when I had a funeral or an unexpected pastoral demand. Preparation for the extra event could then make inroads into time that ought to have been spent in study for the forthcoming Sunday or Bible study. To avoid this I restricted myself to one extra speaking commitment each week—whether within the church fellowship or outside it—and I ruthlessly refused other invitations, no matter how attractive or pressing, recognizing that the principle was right, and that God graciously determined the order in which invitations came to me.

On a Monday morning I first prepared for the church prayer meeting. This involved a brief—ten-minute maximum—development of a thought or verse to stimulate and encourage prayer. I decided that because of the legitimate demands of other preparation, and because the prayer meeting is not primarily a meeting for Bible ministry, I should not devote more than half an hour to preparation. I sought to speak more extemporaneously at the prayer meeting than at any other time, trying to spend the half hour's preparation in ensuring that I really understood the text or passage and its immediate application to our gathering together for prayer.

Having prepared for the prayer meeting, I then determined where in the Scriptures I should preach at the two services the following Sunday. That was usually no problem when I was preaching systematically through a Bible book or a series dealing with a subject or Bible character, in that one passage always led on to another. This is one of the benefits of systematic exposition: It saves a lot of nervous energy in worrying where we should be going next.

As part of that preparation, I wrote down on a large sheet of paper every thought that came to my mind relating to the subject or the passage, first for the morning message and then for the evening. At this stage I did not try to discern or impose any order, although if possible ways of dealing with the subject or passage came to mind, then I scribbled them down as well. I then laid aside these two preparation tasks—rather like leaving pots to simmer. I ought to mention at this stage that Tuesday was my day off. The advantage of beginning this preparation on a Monday was that I came to it fresh again later in the week, having already done the preliminary work on Monday. I frequently found that my unconscious mind had been working away at it during the intervening period, so that I could see ways of presenting the material. On Monday morning I tried to do the same for the Thursday Bible study.

On Wednesday morning my first task was to take the rough notes I had written on Monday for the Thursday Bible study and complete my preparation. If I could not complete it in the morning, I continued through the early part of the afternoon—pastoral duties permitting—until it was done. I tried to avoid preparing on the Thursday itself the material I was to give that evening. If I left it as late as Thursday, I did not have much peace of mind on Wednesday night, because I knew it only required a pastoral emergency the next day and my preparation would be put in jeopardy and I would be under pressure. I believe God helps us remarkably when we are under pressure, but I find that I cannot call upon Him for help in the same way when the pressure is of my own making.

On Thursday morning I aimed to finish my preparation for Sunday morning, and Friday morning likewise was devoted to Sunday evening. Saturday mornings were important in my planning in that I spent the first hour or so going over my two Sunday sermons—and sometimes, but very exceptionally, completing one of them if pastoral pressures had been great that week. I then spent what time was left looking ahead into the next week to begin preparation for any extra meeting. If it held no extra preaching commitment, then I seized the opportunity to start the preparation I have described as Monday's priority.

That is the hand-to-mouth pattern I followed for thirty years. It clearly left little time for reading other than that relating to the passages and subjects we were studying in church. Looking at it another way, however, it meant that over those thirty years my study and reading related to the whole of the Scriptures. Different circumstances demand different programs—but some disciplined program is imperative if we are to make the best use of our limited time.

AB There is little doubt that many who read the outline of Derek's week will feel that they have never really planned their time at all and that they are the most disorganized pastors in the universe. Or is it just me who feels this way? In the relative orderliness of life in Scotland I approximated that pattern. Here in America, it is hard to come close to it. Certain social patterns work against it. Something as simple as a breakfast meeting can immediately alter the complexion of the day. One must either decide to rule out such meetings or to have them very early in the morning, or deal with the impact that they inevitably have upon the balance of the day. I routinely begin the week meeting for breakfast with one of my pastoral team so that we can reflect on the Lord's Day just passed and begin to plan for the immediate future.

I have learned that it takes the same amount of effort and time to prepare for the Sunday sermons whether I find that time in the mornings or the afternoons. In my own case when I am traveling midweek, I have to become increasingly creative in the way in which I organize my days. There is no doubt in my mind that Derek's outline is a good target, but failure to fit that particular framework need not mean failure to do the necessary preparation of mind and heart.

BOOKS

A pastor's books are as essential as the furniture of his home. Dr. David Bogue of Gosport was a trainer of students for the mission field at the end of the eighteenth and the beginning of the nineteenth century in what was known as Bogue's Academy. Listed among the practical matters of ministerial ethics that Bogue dealt with is the question, "What proportion as to expense ought a minister's library to bear to his furniture?"[4] Whatever answer we may give, the question underlines the importance of books.

Books play a vital part in study. They are necessary equipment for ministry. Time for reading is so valuable that it is imperative to use it well, and not to waste it upon material that is ephemeral. We should read books that will exercise our minds and stretch our mental powers. It is better to get stuck into a book of solid worth that will take a month to read than two or three insubstantial paperbacks. Rather than being daunted by the growing pile of new books we have acquired, we should recognize that if we devote just half an hour a day to reading we will accomplish a tremendous amount in a year.

Our starting point must be books that help us to get to grips with the text, such as Hebrew and Greek lexicons, Bible dictionaries, and theological word-books. Second, we need to give priority to obtaining single-volume commentaries on all the Bible books, starting with those we are currently studying with our people. Third, we need to build up a basic library of books dealing with the doctrines of the faith, beginning with a book of systematic theology. If we know one book of systematic theology well, we are able to check the interpretation we give of any verse or passage in relation to the teaching of the whole Bible.

There is considerable value in producing what is in effect our own systematic theology. If we draw up a doctrinal framework, guided by our chosen book of systematic theology, we may add to it throughout the years as we explore the Bible more fully. The effort involved in writing down the main points of every important Christian doctrine will do more than anything else to imprint them upon our memory. As shepherds and teachers we are to defend the faith and to safeguard the understanding of those under our care; we can do this only as we ourselves are well instructed in the faith.

Our fourth priority is our need to know the Christian classics, the books that have proved themselves and made an impact upon Christians over a long period of time. Fifth, we need books that deal with the practicalities of the Christian faith—Christian ethics and conduct, missions and evangelism. Sixth, we need to read Christian biographies, for besides stimulating faith, they illustrate from human experience so many of the truths we teach. Finally, we need to read secular books that stretch our minds and keep us in touch with contemporary life and thought.

The ministry of God's Word requires a well-furnished mind, and we should neglect no field of knowledge. There is a place, for instance, for reading the editorial of our daily newspaper, and asking ourselves what the Christian response or attitude is to the subject under discussion.

THE RETENTION OF THE FRUITS OF STUDY

Every effective teacher of the Word develops his own ways of retaining information and benefiting from what he studies. We invariably discover far more in preparing a sermon or an address than we actually use in delivering it. It is imperative that we retain and conserve anything that may be helpful in future ministry. We have profited by discussing this with others, and as we share our different methods it is not to suggest that others should copy them. Rather the hope is that our approaches may spark ideas for different and better approaches, but with the end result that the fruits of study are put to the best use.

DP I began with a biblical index, and then extended it into a subject index—and I use the second even more than the first. In my scheme I have a separate card for each chapter of the Bible. It is not necessary to write out all the cards beforehand but simply to produce them as there is information to record for any chapter. Take, for example, Philippians 1:6. If I find an interesting comment on that text, or some illustration of the way in which God continues His good work in Christians, I list it on my Philippians 1 card as follows: "Philippians 1:6. See A. N. Other: *A Helpful Book,* p. 100." Let us imagine that my illustration of God's continuing work in believers relates to God's faithfulness; I then also list it under that heading: "FAITHFULNESS, GOD'S: An illustration of God's faithfulness in His good work in us. See A. N. Other: *A Helpful Book,* p. 100." Here the subject index comes into its own, because Philippians 1:6 also describes what happens at new birth, and so I also list the Scripture reference and my comment and illustration in my subject index under NEW BIRTH. The value of this is that while my concordance would not lead me to Philippians 1:6 on the subject of new birth, my index does.

While reading a commentary we will often find our minds latching on to some new understanding of truth that does not have immediate relevance to our subject in hand. If we do not record it we are almost certain to lose it—either by forgetfulness or by not remembering where we read it. An indexing system solves this difficulty and proves increasingly valuable. I have found it a mistake to try to put the information onto my cards as I read, since that slows down study and concentration. I find it better to jot the notes down on scraps of paper, and then transfer them to my index later.

AB I have adopted this same pattern from the beginning, and I am currently working with my assistant to transfer the material to computer programs so that when I travel I can take large amounts of background material on a CD or in an MP3 format. The most important aspect of this is not the form our system takes but that we have some system. Although laborious in the beginning, it will save us a lot of time in the long run.

"Much study wearies the body" is the practical comment of the writer of Ecclesiastes (12:12), and since there is really no end to study we need to beware of getting its importance out of perspective. Our study is not an end in itself: Its purpose is the proper feeding of Christ's flock. One of the advantages of our calling is that we are both shepherds and teachers, so that our time is not to be given completely to study. Too much study is bad for us; it needs to be linked with other activities.

BIBLICAL DIRECTIVES

Paul's instructions to Timothy provide clear-cut directives: "Until I come, devote yourself to the public reading of Scripture, to preaching and to teaching. Do not neglect your gift, which was given you through a prophetic message when the body of elders laid their hands on you. Be diligent in these matters; give yourself wholly to them, so that everyone may see your progress" (1 Timothy 4:13–15); "Do your best to present yourself to God as one approved, a workman who does not need to be ashamed who correctly handles the word of truth" (2 Timothy 2:15).

Study is part of our devotion to God's Word and the ministry He has committed to us. It requires our personal best. We are to be diligent in study. God does not expect from us what He expects from others. He knows what we are capable of, and that alone is what He wants. Our motivation is to be God's approval. "The minister of the gospel," A. W. Pink wrote,

> is to be no slacker and shirker, but rather "a workman that needeth not to be ashamed" (2 Tim. 2:15 [KJV]). Whether he rises early or . . . finds it more expedient to burn the midnight oil, he is in honour and duty bound to spend at least as many hours in his study as does the farmer in his field, the clerk in his office, or the labourer in the factory. He has no warrant to expect God to use him unless he be industrious and denies himself.[5]

"Approved" is a word from the world of industry where something is expected to come fully up to standard. As God's workmen in the Word, our concern must be that we shall not be ashamed when He tests our work. Our task is to release and apply God's most precious Word so that we and all His people grow in holiness and godliness. Our difficult responsibility is to present God's truth in its perfect balance. George Whitefield recorded in his diary one night after having preached in Bristol, "The congregation consisted of thousands, and God enabled me to lay before them His threatenings and promises, so that none might either despair or presume. Oh that I may be taught of God rightly to divide the Word of truth!"

As shepherds and teachers we will do well to read Psalm 119 several times a year—a section a day—so that our reverence for the Scriptures is not only maintained but also deepened. Dealing with

God's Word each day must never make it appear commonplace—it is the living Word of God. All study of the Scriptures is fruitless without divine illumination. "There must be Spirit in me as there is Spirit in the Scriptures, before I can see anything," remarked the sixteenth-century Puritan Richard Sibbes. Although those whom we teach may not realize the amount of time we need to give to study, our Master does, and, as Thomas Goodwin put it, "The reaper is equally paid even for the time in which he sharpens his sickle."

CHAPTER 7

PREACHING

All genuine shepherds and teachers are such by the appointment of the Great Shepherd of the sheep, our Lord Jesus Christ. Because He is our pattern and example, preaching claims priority in our work. He began His public ministry by standing up to read the Scriptures in the synagogue at Nazareth at the place in Isaiah where it is written, "The Spirit of the Lord is on me, because he has anointed me to preach good news to the poor. He has sent me to proclaim freedom for the prisoners and recovery of sight for the blind, to release the oppressed, to proclaim the year of the Lord's favor" (Luke 4:18–19). The gospel records demonstrate that preaching the Good News was His priority for three years.

"Faith comes from hearing the message, and the message is heard through the word of Christ" (Romans 10:17). As we proclaim Christ in all the Scriptures, men and women come to faith in Him. As we go on to proclaim the whole will of God revealed in the Scriptures, men and women go on to maturity of faith in Jesus Christ.

THE CONTEMPORARY CLIMATE OF
OPINION REGARDING PREACHING

Preaching has lost its central place in many parts of the church—to its great loss—and there has been something of a reaction to the prominence traditionally given to it. Part of this reaction reflects the age in which we live, in that it is not thought appropriate to tell anyone else what to do. Psychiatrists tend to be nondirective in their approach rather than directive. That may well be entirely appropriate to them, but it is not the case for the undershepherd and teacher who is called upon to speak "as one speaking the very words of God" (1 Peter 4:11). If we handle God's Word aright, we will regularly direct ourselves and others into God's ways, without apology. Preaching is deliberately directive, and it ceases to be biblical if it is nondirective.

Preaching, like other good gifts of God, has been abused. Some have used the pulpit as a coward's castle from which they have made pronouncements without having to take public criticism in return. They have used it to forward their own ideas rather than gospel truth. But our concern is with the preaching of God's Word, not the propagation of human ideas or opinions.

In subtle ways the primary nature of preaching can be eroded even by those who believe in its fundamental importance. Other activities may be put in its place. Considerable contemporary emphasis is placed upon dialogue and discussion, and the value of small groups, so that instead of men and women listening to teaching and preaching, group Bible study and the sharing of ideas may replace it. Small groups are of profit, and it does not have to be a matter of either/or, but it can work out that way in practice. Much blessing has come through a new understanding of worship, but a danger is that far more time may be given to singing than to listening to God through His Word. Several decades ago Dr. Martyn Lloyd-Jones recognized the beginnings of a contemporary trend: "You have a song leader as a new kind of official in the church, and he conducts the singing and is supposed to produce the atmosphere. But he often takes so much time in producing the atmosphere that there is no time for preaching in the atmosphere!"[1]

We need to bring these issues out into the open in as positive a way as possible. First, we should affirm the place there is both for listening to teaching and preaching by those whom God has called to it, and for group Bible study. But the second must not preclude the former. Second, we must show how one of the important purposes of singing is to enable the Word of Christ to dwell in us richly (Colossians 3:16), and that worship is not limited to singing but it includes careful listening to God and joyful submission to His Word. Rather than worship and singing preceding the preaching of God's Word, there is equal place for its following the preaching as part of our response to it.

The Distinction Between Teaching and Preaching

A helpful and significant distinction is made in the New Testament, and especially in the Acts of the Apostles, between teaching and preaching, although both activities are comprehended in our commonly accepted understanding of preaching. Acts 5:42 tells how the apostles did not cease teaching and proclaiming Jesus as the Christ. Then in Acts 15:35, for example, Paul and Barnabas are described as remaining in Antioch "where they and many others taught and preached the word of the Lord." Where a deliberate distinction is made between the two it underlines the twofold approach we are to have in view. In teaching we aim to give people an understanding of God's truth. Beginning often with the first principles of a doctrine, we will make sure that people grasp it as best they can in all its aspects. Then in preaching we make an appeal to people's wills, as well as to their emotions, to respond to the Word that they have now understood through teaching.

To neglect this distinction between teaching and preaching

creates difficulties. Considerable harm may be done to people if they are called upon to act without first possessing a proper foundation in their understanding for that action. Many have made an emotional response to preaching, and have not understood afterward what they have done. That is irresponsible of the preacher and damaging to the hearers. Preaching at its best maintains a balance between teaching and preaching. First, there will be careful exposition of God's truth, so that hearers clearly understand what God says, and then there will be an appeal to men and women's wills to respond with reasonable obedience. When the two words are used together, preaching relates to the application of the Word that has been taught, since, once understood, it must be applied to our lives.

The more we know the people we teach, the more sensitive we will be to the necessary mixture of teaching and preaching required in every message. It is interesting to notice in Acts that when the apostles went into a Jewish situation where the Scriptures were already known, the emphasis was upon preaching. When, however, they went into a Gentile situation, where little or nothing was known of God's revealed truth, the stress was upon teaching and then preaching. A skillful preacher discerns how much teaching is required before it is right to expect an intelligent and spiritual response to the Word.

THE GENERAL BACKGROUND TO OUR PREACHING

Before considering the practicalities of preaching, we must remember that our best preparation is maintaining everyday priorities for effective ministry. First, we must cultivate our knowledge of the Scriptures, and our obedience to God through them, so that we ourselves grow in our knowledge of Him. If we are to expound the whole will of God, we must know His will in detail, and that can be achieved only by a grasp of the whole of Scripture. Admittedly, it is a lifetime assignment, but that provides no excuse for laziness. We should beware of preaching only from passages of Scripture with which we are already familiar. It is easy to neglect the Old Testament, since we tend to be more familiar with the New. But we need the instruction, encouragement, and comfort of all the Scriptures, and if shepherds and teachers do not lead God's people into the pastures of the Old as well as the New, the sheep are unlikely to lead themselves into them. To bring our people into fresh pastures we must continually break new ground.

Second, wide reading of every kind is invaluable. Top of the list must be theological reading. If we find benefit, as most preachers do, from the Puritans and others of past centuries, we should balance the reading of these well-tried books with contemporary theological books and commentaries. Often the books that have proved their worth over many generations are the more profitable, but we must expose ourselves to what God is teaching His people today by His Word.

DP I find it helpful to read as widely as possible in other fields, although time so often precludes this. Biographies are invaluable because of the insight they give into the way in which people think and behave. Here again balance is vital, and I aim to read first a Christian biography and then a secular.

AB I also find great profit in reading biographies. We should all read the two-volume biographies on Martyn Lloyd-Jones, John Stott, and George Whitefield. I enjoy the biographies of politicians, musicians, and golfers. Novels that pass the Philippians 4:8 test are also profitable in stretching our imagination and developing our powers of description. I find it helpful to read the book reviews in *The New York Times,* and even the obituaries. As time allows, it is also important to read material from competing perspectives. This helps us sharpen our wits and keeps us on our theological toes.

Third, experience of life enhances effective preaching. That experience comes about in two principal ways—first, our own, and second, that of those whom we serve in the gospel. God allows us to pass through experiences that we may find hard at the time and that make us wonder what His purpose is. What we discover so often is that God enriches us through them, and they enhance our grasp of spiritual truth as He makes it relevant to our situation.

DP One reason I would discourage a young man from training for the ministry straight from school or university is that he probably does not have that experience of life that will be so important in relating his ministry of God's Word to men and women's real life situations. There is much to be said for working for a while in ordinary employment, no matter how humdrum, so as to share what is the experience of the majority of people. The Reverend John McNeill, whose ministry was outstandingly fruitful, spent the early years of his life as a station booking-office clerk, first at Greenock and then in Edinburgh. He frequently referred to it later, saying, "There was a lot of human nature in front of a booking-office window to provide useful study for one who was ultimately to be a minister."[2]

AB From time to time, as in my own case, there will be an exception to this rule. When I sensed God's call to pastoral ministry I left my course of study in economics and worked for a year prior to beginning at the London Bible College. That year proved in the providence of God to be a "crash course" in reality. From the rough and tumble of a butcher's shop in Yorkshire (with weekly trips to the abattoir) and the mundane tasks of a "cleaner/handyman" in an all-girls teacher training college, to selling clothing to the golfing community at the British Open, I learned a great deal in a short time. Long before that, I can see now, God was using the companionship of my grandfather as we traveled together regularly around the city of Glasgow on public transport. Even after all these years I find myself using illustrations from scenes etched into my memory from that period in my life. To the extent that the absence of a prolonged secular work environment represents a lack or a weakness, God may choose to use it as another necessary means to create an increased sense of dependence upon Him.

The linking of shepherding with teaching demands teaching earthed to reality, so that we deal with genuine and not merely hypothetical situations in our preaching. A great benefit of being the pastor of those whom we teach is that we are able to apply the Word carefully to the known needs of the people under our care. We do not mean by this that when we discern a need, we immediately frame a sermon to meet it. That is likely to prove unhelpful and embarrassing to the hearers. But as we get to know people well, visiting them in their crises and serving them in various circumstances, our application of God's Word will be unconsciously and helpfully colored by our assimilation of their experiences and cries for direction.

Fourth, we should discipline ourselves not to lose seed thoughts for sermons and talks.

DP As I listen to the Scriptures being read, or taught and preached, or in my daily reading of the Bible and other books, I find ideas for sermons—perhaps a sermon outline—coming to mind. If I do not write it down, I lose it. I have learned to stop whatever I am doing in order to write it down, together with thoughts for its development. I then file it away, either under its Bible reference or the subject to which it relates. I have no idea how many hundreds of seed thoughts I have collected, but the point is that they are there when I want them, and so many have come to life when worked on further.

Fifth, as we mentioned when dealing with the question of study, it is important to be building up a scheme to recall material we have read over the months and years. It is impossible to calculate the value of this accumulated material and the hours it saves us from thumbing through books looking for that elusive reference we vaguely remember having read somewhere.

AB Unlike Derek, who has hundreds of seed thoughts that are "there when he wants them," I find myself asking, "Where are they when I need them!" While finding myself equally stirred and stimulated by listening to others preach, I may serve as more of a warning than an example. Although I have made his pattern my own when it comes to a retrieval system, I have in this particular instance not been as disciplined as I should. It is unwise to assume that we will be able to rely upon our memories. This is a good place to reinforce the vital necessity of a workable filing system.

PREPARATION FOR PREACHING

Preparing a sermon or a talk is a very personal process, and the reason we share our own approach is that we have been helped over the years as we have asked others how they set about the task. Whatever our method, prayer and personal obedience to the Word of God must come first. The very spirit in which we prepare should express our dependence upon God and our personal willingness to be obedient to what He reveals to us to pass on to His people.

DP There are two ways in which I prepare. The first is when a Scripture suddenly becomes alive to me, and I think I see its relevance and a possible way to expound it. I then take the largest sheet of paper available and write down all that comes to mind, in whatever order. I jot down other Scriptures that are similar or explanatory, together with illustrations and thoughts regarding application. No matter how higgledy-piggledy the thoughts come, I put them down on my sheet of paper. Having run myself dry, I read around the particular verse or subject, using commentaries and my index. By the time I have completed this, I usually discern some pattern or order and a possible skeleton outline. Having drawn up the skeleton outline, I determine the way to introduce the subject and I also decide, in brief outline, how to apply it. I then tidy up the skeleton outline. That done, I begin to write, adding the necessary flesh to my skeleton. My own practice is to write or type out the sermon in full.

The second situation is where I systematically expound a book or part of a book. That has been my custom, although I take regular breaks from it so as to give balance and variety. My approach then is to study the passage first in as much depth as I can, ensuring that, as far as possible, I understand every word in context, and I read other passages in the Bible that relate to the subject. While doing that preparatory work, I will be quick to write down any thoughts that occur to me about the best means of dealing with the passage in preaching. The preparatory work done, I will try either to find a key phrase or sentence as a window through which to look at the whole, or to see if the passage breaks up into natural parts as a key to its presentation.

A danger when we first begin to preach is to try to say everything we have discovered about a subject or a passage! We then make what we say indigestible. Hours spent in preparation do not mean that we have to share all our thought processes with our hearers. Ruthless pruning ensures we are as clear and simple in our approach as possible. The mark of a good teacher is that what is difficult and complicated becomes simple to understand. We need to be selective in our use of what we have learned from a passage and to beware lest a mass of information obscures the actual message God wants us to convey. The benefit of systematic exposition of Scripture is that we touch upon subjects that otherwise might not be dealt with, but that God uses to bless people in a remarkable manner as they sit under the regular exposition of His Word.

Exposition is what we have in view, not imposition. It is more important to let the Scriptures guide us as to our subjects than for us to have a subject in mind and then try to find a Scripture upon which to latch what we want to say. One of the exciting features of a series of sermons on a subject, a character, or a Bible book is that God, in His gracious sovereignty, so regularly times the applicability of that exposition to the present needs of a congregation. Every shepherd and teacher will be able to recall instances of God using the systematic exposition of Scripture in remarkable ways.

DP During a series on Abraham, I came to Abraham's attitude on the death of Sarah. Unknown to me, a widow was visiting us for that one Sunday, and she was having difficulty relating her faith to her grief. Her whole attitude was transformed through the Word God spoke to her. Expounding 1 Corinthians on another occasion, I was not looking forward to dealing with chapter 7, and felt it best to take the whole chapter in one sermon. I did not know that a couple were present whose marriage was breaking up—it had reached the critical moment of decision—and that Sunday morning God brought them together in reconciliation and love. If I had deliberately chosen to speak on that subject, they might have thought that I knew about them and was preaching at them. But as a sermon in a planned series, it was obvious that while I did not know about them, God did.

Charles Simeon's sermons have always impressed me, and most of all the care he took in his application. When we prepare we have several hours to ponder the application of God's truth to our lives. Our hearers have a few moments. After expounding truth, it is vital we apply it so that the hearers go away with an awareness of what the verse or passage has to say to them in their immediate situation and how they may be doers of God's Word.

The variety of the Scriptures themselves should be reflected in our methods of presentation. Systematic expository preaching is not limited to preaching through the books of the Bible. We may equally well deal with Bible characters or Scripture's basic truths and themes. Preaching systematically through the books of the Bible is a most effective means of ensuring that the whole will of God is presented over a period of time, but it is not the only way. To follow the same method relentlessly can become monotonous and boring.

Our Lord Jesus used a variety of forms of teaching. He gave straightforward ethical teaching, as in the Sermon on the Mount. He illustrated His teaching by everyday occurrences that captured His hearers' attention. But He also used stories or parables, and He sometimes took recent events—like the collapse of a tower or the slaughter of innocent people—to teach a lesson. Expository preaching should not mean lack of variety—rather it should bring infinite variety!

One danger of expository preaching—especially when we begin—is the tendency to be too long in one book or subject. Expository does not need to be synonymous with exhaustive and exhausting!

When I have done an extended series on a New Testament letter like Romans, I have divided the exposition into periods of approximately ten weeks, and then paused for a few weeks to do something entirely different. Both speaker and hearers then come back to the main subject with freshness. A refreshing contrast from Romans, for example, would be the life of Abraham or Joseph, so that narrative provides relief from the closely connected thought and concentration required for Romans.

AB I remain fascinated by the variety of approaches that preachers take in preparing their sermons. In our preparation as well as in our delivery we must "to our own selves be true." When I am asked to summarize my method of preparation, I mention the following points, which I learned from the late Leith Samuel. They essentially follow the pattern that Derek has just outlined.

1. Think yourself empty.

   As strange as it may sound, we must be careful to ensure that we do not avoid sound thinking. The temptation to respond emotionally to a passage (this is how this makes me feel) is not unique to our listeners. If we are to have "thinking" congregations it is incumbent upon us to be "thinking" pastors! We do not want to be uncertain by the time our study ends, but it is surely right and proper to begin with the perspective "I must know what this says, and I must learn what this means."

2. Read yourself full.

3. Write yourself clear.

   Aside from the essential empowering of the Holy Spirit, if there is one single aspect of sermon preparation that I would want to emphasize, it is this. Freedom of delivery in the pulpit depends upon careful organization in the study. We may believe that we have a grasp of the text, only to stand up and discover that somewhere between our thinking and our speaking things have gone badly awry. The missing link can usually be traced to the absence of putting our thoughts down clearly.

4. Pray yourself hot.

There is no chance of fire in the pews if there is an iceberg in the pulpit! Without prayer and communion with God during the preparation stages, the pulpit will be cold. In 1752 John Shaw reminded the incumbent pastor beginning his charge in Cambridge, Massachusetts: "All will be in vain, to no saving purpose, until God is pleased to give the increase. And in order to do this, God looks for their prayers to come up to His ears. A praying minister is the way to have a successful ministry."[3]

5. Be yourself, but don't preach yourself.

A good teacher, like John the Baptist, clears the way, declares the way, and then gets out of the way.

EVANGELISTIC PREACHING

To teach and preach the gospel to those who are unbelievers with a view to their conversion is an awesome privilege.

DP My own conviction is that where there are two services on a Sunday, one should be evangelistic in character, recognizing, however, that a service does not have to be directly evangelistic to be the means of a person's conversion. My experience is that people have frequently been converted at services where the preaching has been addressed to Christians. When an unconverted person hears the preaching of God's Word to believers, he will often be constrained to ask himself, "Why doesn't this truth apply to me?" or "Why can't I rejoice in these truths as these Christians do?" But the advantage of having unconverted people in mind in one of two services is that it keeps the priority of gospel preaching before God's people, and it encourages Christians to bring their non-Christian friends.

AB In my study I keep the following quote from *A Quest for Godliness* by J. I. Packer: "If one preaches the Bible biblically, one cannot help preaching the gospel all the time, and every sermon will be, as Bolton said, at least by implication, evangelistic." In certain circles the predominant notion is that "we gather for edification and we scatter to evangelize." Although this encourages the congregation to engage in personal evangelism, it also results in an absence of evangelistic preaching. Some contemporary books on preaching do not even have a chapter on evangelistic preaching. I am helped by reading the evangelistic sermons of Lloyd-Jones, and I try consistently to ensure that our congregation has regular opportunities to invite friends to hear the Good News being preached. The morning services have more unbelievers in them than the evening ones. However, our baptism services in the evening provide suitable occasions for evangelistic preaching.

Gospel preaching in the context of regular Sunday ministry is not an easy practice. Maintaining freshness is a continual challenge. We may have to fight against the dampening effect of seeing only familiar faces or few unconverted people present. But to give in, and to abandon gospel preaching, only serves to accentuate the problem. Part of the answer is to deal with passages of Scripture that make plain the gospel but that also serve to instruct Christians. For example, if we systematically expound one of the four Gospels we instruct Christians. But at the same time we preach the gospel as the apostles first proclaimed it. If we expound the Acts of the Apostles, we instruct believers, but we also preach the gospel itself through the account Acts gives of the apostolic preaching and of lives changed through the gospel. In a similar way the book of Job can be expounded by means of the questions Job asked, and they are extremely relevant questions for the unbeliever.

Gospel preaching is hard work. We must begin by taking nothing for granted. Sadly, we may use jargon or "in language" that is intelligible to Christians but not to others. We must use the Bible's own vocabulary to explain the gospel, taking trouble to explain basic words like repentance, faith, and justification. We must make every effort to understand our hearers, rather than expecting them first to understand us. We need to ask ourselves, *What would I be thinking and feeling if I heard the gospel for the first time?* or *What does the word* repentance *mean in everyday language, and how is the Christian use of it different?* Our love and concern for our hearer is seen in our effort to put ourselves in his place.

We must work at removing misconceptions. The enemy of men's souls encourages wrong ideas about God, the person of Christ, and salvation. While ultimately the Holy Spirit alone can shine into men and women's hearts to reveal God's glory in the face of Jesus Christ, He calls upon us to work with Him. Part of that partnership is removing common misconceptions about God, the gospel, and the nature of the Christian life.

We must make sure we go back far enough in our preaching of the gospel. When the apostles proclaimed the gospel to the Jews they could assume their hearers knew God's Law. The preaching of the Law was a God-given schoolmaster to bring their hearers to repentance and faith in Jesus Christ as their Savior. But the apostles knew that they could not take this background for granted when they preached to Gentiles. The Acts of the Apostles illustrates how they then went back to God the Creator (Acts 17:24ff). This makes sense: God's Law convicts of sin only as I appreciate whose Law it is I have broken. We need to be in Genesis 1 and 3 as well as in John 1 and 3.

We must declare the gospel in all its fullness, ensuring that no constituent part is neglected. This cannot be done on every occasion the gospel is preached, but most if not of all of its elements will be present, although the spotlight may be upon only one. It is helpful to remind ourselves from time to time of the six main elements in the apostolic declaration of the gospel, once they were sure that they had gone back far enough to enable their hearers to realize that their message was from the one true God, the Creator and Supreme Law-Giver.

> *First, the appointed time,* concerning which the Old Testament prophets had spoken, and to which God's chosen people had looked forward, has come. Through Christ, God has visited and redeemed His people (Acts 2:16–21).
>
> *Second, this act of God intervening in human history* is to be seen in the life of Jesus Christ, the Messiah, sent by God, rejected, put to death by men, and raised up by God on the third day (Acts 2:32, 36).
>
> *Third, by His death and resurrection, Jesus Christ has conquered sin* and has opened the kingdom of heaven to all believers. Salvation is to be found in no one else (Acts 4:12).
>
> *Fourth, the proofs of God's present power in the world* are to be found in the fact of the resurrection of Christ and the evidence of the Holy Spirit's working in the church (Acts 4:33; Romans 1:4; Ephesians 1:19–20).
>
> *Fifth, this is but the beginnings of God's kingdom.* Our Lord Jesus Christ will return again as Judge, and God's kingdom

will be finally established (Acts 3:20–21; 17:30–31; 2 Thessalonians 1:7–10).

Sixth, all men and women, therefore, should repent and be baptized in the name of Jesus Christ the Messiah and Lord for
the forgiveness of their sins, and they will receive the gift
of the Holy Spirit (Acts 2:38).

Now gospel preaching is not a matter of simply taking this outline and preaching it as it is! But it is the backcloth to all we say.
In essence the entire gospel is here, and our task is to use the whole
of the Scriptures to show forth its wonders and glories.

Our single-minded purpose in declaring the gospel is to give a
clear and accurate presentation of the person and work of our Lord
Jesus Christ. The Father purposes and delights in His Son's supremacy in everything—and not least in the gospel and its preaching. Gospel preaching fails if it does not set forth the glories of
our once crucified and now risen and glorified Savior. Everything
we proclaim about the gospel must be viewed in its relationship
to Him.

In proclaiming Christ we must not overlook the explaining of
the numerous benefits of salvation such as reconciliation with God
(2 Corinthians 5:18–21), justification (1 Corinthians 1:30; 6:11),
deliverance from condemnation (John 3:18; Romans 8:1; 1 Corinthians 11:32), belonging to the people of God (Acts 2:41, 47;
1 Corinthians 1:2; 6:1–2; 16:1, 15; 1 Peter 2:4–10), membership
of God's kingdom (1 Corinthians 6:10; Colossians 1:13), the gift
of the Holy Spirit (Acts 2:38; 1 Corinthians 2:12; 6:19), eternal life
(John 3:16; 11:25–26), and the resurrection of the body (1 Corinthians 6:14; 15:12–57). These benefits are worthy of detailed exposition and find countless illustrations in the Bible, providing
endless scope for variety of presentation.

We must explain the response God requires to the gospel.
Whether it was on the Day of Pentecost when the crowds cried out,
"What shall we do?" (Acts 2:37) or answering the Philippian jailer

who asked, "What must I do to be saved?" (Acts 16:30), the apostles were careful to give a clear response. In answer to the crowds' question, they replied, "Repent and be baptized, every one of you, in the name of Jesus Christ for the forgiveness of your sins. And you will receive the gift of the Holy Spirit. The promise is for you and your children and for all who are far off—for all whom the Lord our God will call" (Acts 2:38–39). To the jailer they said, "Believe in the Lord Jesus, and you will be saved—you and your household" (Acts 16:31).

Repentance and faith need frequent explanation. At the same time we must encourage men and women to count the cost. It is possible to neglect this, but it was never overlooked in our Lord's gospel preaching. None was allowed to become His disciple without first knowing what was involved and how costly it might prove. We have no need to be afraid of the consequences of honestly explaining the cost. Those who genuinely seek Christ will find their desire to follow Him intensified.

We need to know what to expect as a result of gospel preaching: We look for conversions! There is a relationship between what we expect and what we receive. In preaching, as in every other aspect of the Christian life, "without faith it is impossible to please God" (Hebrews 11:6). Preaching is an activity of faith. We are to be men of faith every time we preach, expecting God the Holy Spirit to accompany His own Word with power and conviction (1 Corinthians 2:4–5).

More often than not people will be converted through the preaching of the Word without any personal contact with the preacher. On other occasions people may seek us out, perhaps after a service or more privately. When they do, we must look for conviction of sin, arising from an awareness of God's holiness, and the deflation of pride. If God's Spirit is at work in them, they will accept the authority of what God says in His Word, and the necessity of obeying what He says, no matter how costly. No joy surpasses that of witnessing new birth!

PREACHING TO CHILDREN

We have principally in mind the children's talk that may be given in a Sunday service. Children are part of the congregation, and it is appropriate that they should be present and that parents should be encouraged to bring their children, so that they worship together as families. As undershepherds and teachers we have responsibility for every age group; we are to provide milk for the lambs and pasture for the sheep. Even as the Scriptures address themselves to each age group, so must we. Our Lord taught that the kingdom of God is open to children as well as to adults (Mark 10:14). The conversion of children and their growth in grace and in the knowledge of our Lord Jesus Christ are pastoral objectives. Our children ought to feel part of the church family and to know they have a value to God and His people. Giving time to them in the context of a church service furthers this.

A regular children's talk provides a relationship with the children of the church fellowship that we would not otherwise have. This is especially the case when we involve children in the talks in some way. Parents should be encouraged to see the children's talk as a family talking point over Sunday lunch, so that the instruction of the service overflows naturally into the family conversation, with the parents seizing the opportunity of discussing the Christian life.

Children's talks are no different in purpose from the rest of the ministry of the Word: We aim to instruct children in the revelation the Scriptures give of God in the person of His Son, and the gospel He came to make possible and to proclaim. The talk should explain Scripture truth so that it is an integral part of the service. Preaching to children must have the same basic content, although in simpler form, as all Christian teaching. Where possible, it is helpful to gain the children's participation, as this increases their interest and writes the teaching more indelibly upon their minds. Visual aids—whether flannelgraph, the overhead projector, PowerPoint, or simple drawings or objects—are invaluable, although never as an end in themselves. Visual aids do not need to be outstanding for their artistic value; it is more important that they should be bold and clear. If we can illustrate what we say by something seen, it will be better remembered.

Conveying spiritual truth simply, without being childish, takes considerable effort. Children's talks that center around a non-biblical story—perhaps for a story's sake—are to be avoided. Taking what at first appears to be a difficult subject and determining that we will make it intelligible to children is one of the most fruitful approaches. (We usually end up making it much more intelligible to the adults as well!)

A rewarding series is a children's catechism, which provides scope to present the whole of basic Christian doctrine, together with an opportunity for the children to participate by learning the questions and answers by heart. John Bunyan's *Pilgrim's Progress*—in both its parts—and *The Holy War* are full of scriptural truth and lend themselves to visual presentation.

DP Series help to sustain interest, and also mean that we do not dither in deciding what to do next. I have done a number of alphabetical series such as "Guess who I am?" in which I have described a biblical character and gotten the children to raise their hands as soon as they identify the person. One of the most rewarding was an alphabetical series entitled "What the Lord Jesus means to me" beginning with A for Advocate. I have encouraged the children to make their own scrapbook or record of a series, and then rewarded them at the end. This has again given me a relationship with the children, and the instruction on a Sunday has overflowed into the home.

To talk effectively to children requires diligence, sincerity, liveliness, and naturalness. We must be diligent in looking out for helpful ways of expressing God's truth, being prepared to wrestle with hard subjects until we see a way of presenting them simply and intelligibly to children. We must never talk down to them or be condescending. Children have a unique ability to discern sincerity, and they soon know if we are really concerned about them. Children tend to be lively, and liveliness in our presentation identifies us with them. We are not proposing a false liveliness for liveliness' sake, but we are suggesting that we should be as forceful and as enthusiastic as we can naturally be. As in all teaching and preaching, we must be ourselves.

When children are taught effectively in congregational worship, everyone gains something, and the teaching addressed primarily to the children becomes part of the instruction of the adults. When we learn to teach children effectively we probably increase our powers of communication to adults. For that reason a children's talk needs to be prepared and written out as carefully as any other.

AB When I began my ministry here in Cleveland I had come from the context just described. While it did not work to introduce this concept in the morning, I found that there was an opportunity in the evening. For the first few years I took time in the evening service to speak to the children, employing some of the material just mentioned. The response was terrific, and the resulting sense of fellowship and growth in attendance was due in no small part to this particular emphasis. This in turn gave way to a program for youngsters in the same time frame as our evening service. We call it Kids of the Kingdom, and it is essentially a form of children's church. Not only does this provide a context in which the children are learning, but it also provides an environment in which we are able to train teenagers and college students in the realm of children's ministry.

NOTES OR FULL MANUSCRIPT?

Whether we speak from a full manuscript or notes is a matter of personal preference. Whichever we use, we must ensure that we are not bound by either.

DP For the first seven years of my ministry I wrote out in full everything I intended to say, and I still do the same if I have time. It helps to avoid wordiness, and it enables me to be as critical as possible of my language and my approach before preaching. My usual practice is to have a full manuscript, having gone through it beforehand with a highlighter pen, drawing attention to the key word or thought in each paragraph or section as an aid to my eye and memory. Those who listen are probably unaware that I have full notes in front of me. Although more often than not I could manage without full notes—the highlighted sections are enough to keep my memory going—to have the complete notes before me is reassuring, especially if careful exposition of a difficult passage is necessary, where words need to be carefully chosen.

AB Following Spurgeon's advice I wrote out my sermons in full for the first five years of my ministry, and in the ensuing twenty-two years I have maintained that pattern. I do so not in order that I can read from it in the pulpit, but as a discipline of preparation.

BEING OURSELVES

We must be ourselves in our manner and style of preaching. So often when we begin to preach, we model ourselves, usually unconsciously, on our favorite preacher or the person who has been the greatest example and help to us. If we have the happy experience of a succession of young assistants over the years, it is important to encourage them to be themselves. Individual preachers made a conscious impression upon us in our formative years as preachers, and we thank God for them. But good as the influence of some may be, it is important to recognize that God has given us our own distinctive personality, which He can use in the communication of His truth.

Being ourselves, however, is not the same thing as not bothering about distracting mannerisms. Some mannerisms are part of our personality, and to rule them out would be to put ourselves in a straitjacket. But we need to be strict where any mannerism or habit distracts from our presentation of the truth. Constructive criticism from people we can trust is crucial. If we are married, our wives are the most likely persons to provide us with this. If we are not, then we should let it be known to someone whose judgment we trust that we are genuinely open to criticism and want it.

THE TRUTH WE MUST NEVER FORGET

In all our preaching we are dependent upon the Holy Spirit. Like frail sailing craft with their sails, we are helpless without the wind of the Spirit. No matter how well we have prepared and equipped ourselves, our words fall to the ground apart from the gracious unction that the Lord Jesus, the Head of the church, gives by the Spirit. Every time we genuinely minister in His name, His hand is upon us, and His Spirit is with our lips as we speak from His Word.

THE PERILS OF PREACHING

The most obvious peril of preaching is pride. The best corrective is to appreciate the danger, and to seek and accept constructive criticism from those whom we can trust to be honest with us. An opposite peril, and just as common, is despair and a sense of failure.

DP I doubt if there has been a Sunday I have preached when I have not had some such awareness. On occasions I have known deep despair because I have felt I have been so clumsy in my presentation of the truth. At such times we need to remind ourselves of God's call. I have come to recognize that God allows such things to happen so that I cultivate the humility that befits a teacher of His Word and to teach me my constant dependence upon Him. One of the most humbling experiences I know is to discover afterward that on the occasions when I felt I did badly God has been pleased to work in a special way in people's lives!

AB I am encouraged to know that Derek feels this way. I had hoped that this sense would pass with time. But it hasn't. As I stood to preach this past Sunday, I felt as though I was standing in a telephone box, and, although I could see the people outside and could hear my own voice (usually a bad sign), I had no assurance that they could hear me. Eric Alexander told a gathering of ministers that when he left the pulpit and returned to his vestry, he found himself saying out loud, "Lord, I am sorry." Lloyd-Jones was as outspoken on this matter as any I have read. "Any man who has had some glimpse of what it is to preach will inevitably feel that he has never preached. But he will go on trying, hoping that by the grace of God one day he may truly preach."[4]

The third peril is our inability to be frequently on the receiving end of preaching. Worse still, when we do listen to others preach, we can be most critical listeners. We must beware of such a snare, and cultivate being good listeners, looking for the Lord's Word, as we would wish others to expect when they listen to us. When we are not able to listen regularly to the preaching of others, there are the two readily available alternatives of listening to tapes or reading books that will nurture our spiritual growth. If we ever fall into the snare of only wanting to preach and not to be on the receiving end, professionalism has taken over, and we have ceased living a normal Christian life.

THE HIGHEST PRIVILEGE

There is no greater task in all the world than teaching and preaching the Word of God, for to us is committed the privilege of proclaiming the unsearchable riches of Christ and making plain the meaning of God's great plan of salvation that was kept hidden until the coming of His Son (Ephesians 3:8–9). No greater privilege exists!

CHAPTER 8

PASTORAL CARE

Those not engaged in pastoral work seldom understand or appreciate what it involves. "The average layman," William Sangster, a prominent twentieth-century Methodist preacher, wrote, "has only the vaguest idea of what is meant by the term 'pastoral work.' Indeed, people can be found outside the churches who honestly believe that a minister's whole duty is to conduct a couple of services on a Sunday and nothing more. Even among those who concede that he does little things on other days of the week, 'pastoral work' may suggest little more than a round of afternoon visits to the female members of the congregation, drinking tea, and indulging in hours of small talk." These words present something of a caricature, but such ideas do exist. In *Huckleberry Finn* a discussion takes place between Huck and Joanna about the role of ministers. She asks Huck what it is they do. He replies: "Oh, nothing much. Loll around, pass the plate—and one thing or another. But mainly they don't do nothing." "Well, then, what are they for?" "Why, they're for style. Don't you know nothing?"

What is done in public on a Sunday is like the tip of an iceberg. Behind all true preaching by shepherds and teachers there are hours of study and preparation linked with deep involvement in people's lives—an involvement in which there are no regular "working hours." Pastoral care is at one and the same time the most demanding and rewarding task there can be.

SHEPHERDING EQUALS PASTORAL CARE

Shepherding is synonymous with pastoral care: It is the practical, individual, and spiritual care of Christ's people as His lambs and sheep. It goes hand in hand with the complementary function of teaching. Some shepherds and teachers may feel they have a greater gift for one than for the other. We may hear it said, "He is a better teacher than a pastor," or the opposite, "He is more of a pastor than a teacher." Because the functions are inseparably and uniquely linked in God's ordering of the Church's life, we should determine to be as effective as we can in both spheres.

The functions of the shepherd are more likely to be neglected than those of the teacher. Responsibilities for teaching can be much more readily defined—for example, we know how many teaching responsibilities we have each week, and we can plan the hours we should devote to preparation. We may find a sense of achievement in completing our preparation and giving what we trust are God-given expositions of His Word. But the limits of pastoral work are much more difficult to define, and one week's demands will seldom be the same as the previous or the next.

Shepherding and teaching should not be separated. Preaching and pastoral work help each other. Visiting enhances our preaching in that it helps us to appreciate how our fellow believers think, their problems, and their temptations. When we preach to those we know well, and whose situations we understand, we apply God's truth more relevantly, almost unconsciously—and probably the less consciously the better. Our visits and counseling have greater relevance too, because the members of the flock associate us with the Word they have heard taught and preached, and in one-to-one conversations we are able to apply that same Word more personally and in greater depth.

THE BACKGROUND TO OUR PASTORAL CARE

Pastoral care has as its objective the fulfillment of the goals we established in chapter 3: the feeding of the flock, the proclaiming of the whole will of God, the presenting of every believer perfect in Christ, the preparing of God's people for works of service, and equipping them to be fishers of men. Unless we keep these objectives before us, we may fall into the snare of simply engaging in pastoral work and visitation because it is expected of us, and we may feel we have accomplished all that is necessary by completing a set number of visits each week.

What is important is not how many visits we have achieved, but how effective they have been in furthering these objectives. Quality is more important than quantity. In pursuit of these goals, our concern is to see our people progress in the faith so that their joy in the Lord Jesus Christ overflows (Philippians 1:25–26). The Lord Jesus Himself must be as central to our pastoral work as to our preaching. The mark of a spiritually healthy people is that they rejoice in Jesus Christ (Philippians 3:3; 4:4), and our task is to nurture and deepen that joy.

ALL NEED PASTORAL CARE— INCLUDING OURSELVES

As we have in our mind's eye the Christian fellowship to which we belong, all associated with it require pastoral care—there are no exceptions. One of the reasons we are described as sheep is our natural perversity. As undershepherds, we may be so concerned for the spiritual welfare of the flock that we neglect our need for others to be concerned for our soul's well-being. For this to happen is to fall into the snare of professionalism. "Who is the undershepherd's shepherd?" is a key question. The first answer is that the Lord Jesus Christ Himself is; but as our Shepherd, He will raise up those who will show pastoral concern for us.

In the larger denominations the denominational structure usually aims to provide pastoral care for undershepherds, whether through episcopacy or a local presbytery. Free churches sometimes have area superintendents whose task is to keep a watchful pastoral eye upon ministers. Carefully and spiritually exercised, only good can come from such relationships. But they have a tendency to be remote, and to come into operation mainly in times of crisis, when often harm has already been done. Within a church fellowship itself the undershepherd needs to be someone's pastoral responsibility. If we genuinely hold to the parity of elders—and the New Testament demands that—the solution is for every undershepherd to be the pastoral responsibility of one of his fellow elders.

DP In the two churches to which I have belonged as pastor, the church membership has been divided into pastoral groups, with each elder, apart from myself, caring for a group, normally determined by the geographical location of the members' homes. I—as the presiding elder— have felt my primary responsibility to be the pastoral care of the elders and their wives and families. At the same time I—together with my wife and family—have belonged to the elder's group in whose area we have lived. I have felt it important to encourage him to feel responsible for my family and myself, and never to think that I do not need his pastoral care or to imagine that I will resent his feeling he should exercise it toward me. It is only as we own our need of pastoral care that we are able to exercise it with humility and reality to others.

AB Although our structure is not the same, the same role is played by my fellow elders. For the past twenty years I have enjoyed their guidance, admonition, fellowship, and encouragement. On one occasion I was reading to a group of them about an elderly friend of mine, T. S. Mooney. I was quoting from one of the chapters in a short biography written after his death: "He was by nature a person who sought to praise the good and, therefore, he had no time to find fault. The warmth of the man came from his intimacy with Christ. No one could have had a more sympathetic supporter than I found in Mr. Mooney. Despite being a bachelor he had an acute awareness of the pressures which can come upon the minister's family. He had the spiritual welfare of the minister at heart." Later, one of my elders came to me and said, "I want to be your T. S. Mooney." And in the goodness of God he is that to me and more.

BASIC PRINCIPLES OF PASTORAL CARE

Men should deal with men and women with women. We begin with this principle not because it is the most important, but because to neglect it has been the cause of some men making shipwreck of their call to the ministry. The principle as stated needs some qualification and amplification. It is not to be applied in a ruthless, unfeeling, and unthinking way. We are equally the undershepherds of women as of men, and we are to be available to all members of the flock and any others whom God brings across our path. Anyone—male or female—may call, requesting help, or seek our counsel following a meeting or service. We should respond to such requests with an openness to God and a desire to be His servants.

If a woman seeks help, we should ensure that we meet her either on church premises when someone else is around, or in our home when our wife is at home. Most requests for help are unique situations, in which guidance is given and there is no need for further meetings. If, however, we are called upon to give counsel to a woman, and frequent meetings are required, it is both wise and expedient that we bring in another woman who can help. If the person we are trying to assist does not want this, then we may be sure that there is all the more reason for doing so. If we are not happy to hand her over to someone else, then we too need to examine our motives. When a difficult decision has to be made of this nature, we should share it, if married, with our wife. The best rule we know is if in doubt about the wisdom of counseling someone, do not, but pass it on to someone else. A danger of sustained one-to-one counseling is that the person counseled can become too dependent upon the counselor, especially if of the opposite sex—and for this reason, among others, long-term counseling should be with those of the same sex.

We never know from what temptations God may graciously save us as we put up proper barriers or build in safeguards. When interviewing womenfolk at the church, we have always asked either our secretary or the church caretaker—usually the former—to answer the door and to bring the person concerned to the vestry, so that it is immediately apparent that someone else is on the premises. Similarly, our wives always answer the door to such folk when the visit is to our home, for identical reasons. If appropriate, we will say at the conclusion, "Do you mind if I share with my wife this matter so that we may pray together about it?" This helps to establish a relationship with us both. We must all determine what is wise for ourselves, but safeguards need to be built into our pastoral practice, not only for our own well-being but also for the honor of Christ. First Corinthians 10:12 has application to undershepherds in their pastoral care of womenfolk.

We must take time and make an effort to know people's names and circumstances. Basic to all pastoral care is knowing the sheep well and loving them in Christ as individuals. Describing His relationship to His sheep, the Lord Jesus said, "I am the good shepherd; I know my sheep and my sheep know me" (John 10:14). Good undershepherds know their sheep, and their sheep recognize them to be their undershepherds. To know someone we need to know both his name and character. We need to know the names of those for whom we are responsible, whether it is fifty people or five hundred. Part of our respect for an individual is the trouble we go to know his or her name. Paul shows such respect in so many of his letters, and especially in the last chapter of Romans when he sends individual greetings to many believers who had a special place in his heart.

Some find it easier to remember names than others do. But there are things we can do that help fix people's names in our memory.

DP I found one practice particularly helpful when I first came to the church fellowship to which I belong, and which I served as pastor in Edinburgh. The hundreds of names I needed to learn overwhelmed me initially. Convinced that I must master them as best I could, I always carried around with me in my early weeks and months a piece of paper upon which I wrote the names of every church member I met. When I spoke to someone for the first time, I apologized for my piece of paper and pen, and said, "Please excuse me if I write your name down to help me remember it." When I arrived home I transferred these names to my prayer diary, distributing the names over the different days of the month. If a particular topic had been talked about with the person concerned, I jotted down a single word or phrase to remind me. Praying for people by name quickly made them real people to me, and also served to write their names and faces upon my mind and heart. As the weeks and months passed, I used my piece of paper less and less, and added names in a more private way. Sometimes I met someone whom I had met before but whose name I could not remember. I either owned up, or later diligently searched through my list to identify who it was I had met again! Once I had managed to know the existing members of the church fellowship, it was easy to know the new members as they were added one by one.

AB I do my best in this area, but I have to content myself with knowing the names of our "committed core group," and even that I find to be an increasing challenge. Of the thousands of people who attend on any given Sunday, I know only a small number by name. I am not happy about this, but it is the case. I recently met a couple who are new to Parkside. The wife's name being the same as my mother's, I remember. The husband told me a story about how he capsized his boat on Lake Erie. He did this so that I might remember his name. Sadly, I only know him as the "shipwrecked sailor" who is married to a lady called Louise!

Knowing a person's name is only a preliminary step to getting to know the individual. Some people we will get to know quickly, whereas others it will take much longer and even years. Some people are open and forthcoming; others are shy and reserved. But pastoral responsibilities soon bring us into contact with most people.

Knowing people's names and circumstances provides a basis for intelligent intercession for them. We referred to this earlier in considering our prayer life and its wide-ranging character. Prayer is the most effective means of pastoral care. We can pray for people when we cannot visit them. We can pray for people when they would not want us to pray with them. We have been set apart as shepherds and teachers so that we may give time to intercessory prayer. It is no accident that the one present activity of our Lord Jesus Christ, the Great Shepherd of the sheep, to which the New Testament refers is His continuing intercession for us (Hebrews 7:25). We are never closer to His heart than when we intercede in His Name for His sheep. Praying for people promotes spiritual sensitivity to their needs as nothing else does. As we pray for people, we will often sense the prompting of the Spirit to visit, phone, or write to them. Without prayer, that prompting may not be known.

We must aim at loving all the flock with the same love. Love for the Lord Jesus and for His people is the preeminent motive for pastoral work (John 21:15–17). Those whom we serve should be in no doubt of our love, and we should take trouble, where necessary, to assure them of it (cf. 1 John 2:7; 3:2, 21; 4:1, 7, 11; 3 John 2, 5, 11). Pastoral concern lies at the heart of pastoral success. A former bishop of London, William Wand, confessed nervousness about pastoral responsibilities when, as a young man, he took up his ministry at St. Mark's in Salisbury. He was greatly helped by an elderly gentleman in whom he confided who said, "You needn't worry about that, if you remember one thing; always let your people see that you are interested in them, and that will be enough."[1]

A temptation when we first undertake pastoral care is to be so concerned to get things right that we continually tell people what they ought to do and to be like, to the neglect of showing that we love them. Undershepherds benefit from the counsel of those who tell them when this is the case. Charles Warr, one-time minister of St. Giles, Edinburgh, related how his "ministry was helped beyond words" early on when he was minister of St. Paul's Greenock:

> One day Mr. Arthur Caird . . . looked in to see me. He was always perfectly groomed, and as everyone said of him, was just as nice as he looked. After some desultory conversation, he ran his hand over his silver hair, turned on me his kindly eyes that always had a twinkle in them, and delivered himself of some flattering and heartwarming words about my first year's ministry at St. Paul's. Then he paused and after a short sentence went on: "Yes, everything in the garden's lovely—or nearly everything." I waited, now a little anxious. Arthur Caird rose and came over to me and laid a fatherly hand on my shoulder. "My boy," said he, "the garden's still waiting for the blossoming of one flower without which the garden of no minister can be perfect." Another pause, "I know we're not everything we ought to be, and no doubt we need a lot of scolding; but we'd all be a great deal better than we are if only you would try sometimes, instead of lecturing us, to show us that you love us!"[2]

Charles Warr records, "These words were a turning-point in my ministry."

Our love for the flock should be like that of a father for his children (1 John 2:18, 28). Their concerns and needs should be constantly in our minds and upon our hearts. Separated from his flock, Samuel Rutherford, a seventeenth-century Scottish pastor, wrote, "My soul longeth exceedingly to hear whether there be any work of Christ in the parish. . . . I think of my people in my sleep. . . . I long exceedingly to know if the oft-spoken-of match betwixt you and Christ holdeth; and if you follow on to know the Lord. My day thoughts and my night thoughts are of you, while ye sleep, I am afraid of your souls that they be off the rock." That kind of love binds the undershepherd and his sheep together.

While it may be a difficult path to follow, we have the conviction that an undershepherd should avoid particular friendships within the flock so that he may honestly and genuinely be the true friend of all. Not all members of the flock will be naturally lovable; but then the same is true of undershepherds. It is the difficult who need loving most. Sometimes they are difficult simply because no one has really made the effort to love them. We must put them first on our list for the careful exercise of love. When people know that we love them, they will accept what we say, even when it has to be a rebuke. It disposes them to listen when otherwise they might be cautious, apprehensive, and suspicious. "Love me," said Augustine, "and then say anything to me and about me you like." Richard Baxter's flock used to say, "We take all things well from one who always and wholly loves us."

A practical expression of love for the flock is generosity with our time. If we love people, we give them time—and that includes our families, who must never be neglected because of our care of others. The stewardship of time in pastoral work is a constant battle. There are obvious limits to the time we have available, especially if it is in the morning when we properly give priority to study and preparation for ministry. But there are occasions each week when we can deliberately make ourselves available to people, and although they may not seem at first sight particularly significant, we believe they are.

DP I have in view those moments that follow services and meetings. Most undershepherds and teachers find themselves the last people off the premises. That is entirely what we should expect if we are available to people. I confess that on occasions I have been so tired that I have wanted to slip away quickly. But I also recognized that simply to be available to chat to people after a meeting made it easy to establish contact with them and to talk to people who might be too shy to make the first approach. When we find ourselves standing in a crowd after a meeting, we of all people should aim to talk with those who may be shy, lonely, and perhaps on the fringe of the church fellowship. To achieve this, we may have to steel ourselves against other folk monopolizing us.

AB I have blown hot and cold on this over the years. In Scotland 99 percent of the congregation exited through the main door. If I stood there, then I had an opportunity to greet as many of them as time would allow. Here at Parkside there is no such door. I find too that if I stand at the front of the auditorium at the end of the service it very often serves as an invitation to the same people to approach me. Although this is fine, it means that I fail to greet others who may be new or have a particular question.

My current pattern is to "disappear" following the first two morning services and then to linger after the third. In the evening I also am available often in *The Commons*—our church meeting area—where people tend to mingle after the service. The added challenge I find is related to what we noted earlier under preaching. Namely, I often feel so deflated after preaching that I have to try very hard to switch off from the burden of preaching and tune in to the concerns of my congregation. Only another pastor will understand the pain of receiving a sincere but trivial compliment that suggests that the person has been completely untouched by the message.

THE EXERCISE OF PASTORAL CARE

Shepherd is not the only title that expresses the duties of a pastor and teacher. He must also be a doctor of souls. When Isaiah describes the Messiah and His flock, he writes: "He tends his flock like a shepherd: He gathers the lambs in his arms and carries them close to his heart; he gently leads those that have young" (Isaiah 40:11). This telling description indicates the varying situations within the flock: Some are lambs, some have responsibilities for the young, and others are burdened, needing sympathetic care. The Lord Jesus leads them all to appropriate pasture. If He has a poor weak lamb, He does not push him on, but gathers him into His arms and supports him. He discerns the need of the individual and ministers to each accordingly.

Our concern in pastoral care must be to exercise God-given insight. As we have already suggested, nothing assists this more than systematic prayer for the flock. Our complementary concern must be to relate the Scriptures to the individual situations of the members of the flock. We need biblical knowledge, discernment to make a proper diagnosis, and then skill to prescribe the remedy Scripture provides.

Our daily study of the Scriptures has in view not only the public teaching and preaching of the Word of God, but equally its sharing and application in pastoral work. It is not inappropriate to think of ourselves as doctors in our personal contact with members of the flock. When a doctor is called in to visit a patient, his whole training makes him focus upon discerning the patient's physical need and the known answer to his condition. He prescribes the remedy, whether pleasant or unpleasant, since his objective is the patient's well-being. If the contact with one of his patients is routine, and not on account of a crisis or illness, his concern will be to encourage his patient in pursuits and habits that will contribute to his physical well-being. As we have contact with people in acute need, we should seek discernment, by the Spirit's help and our understanding of Scripture, to make an accurate diagnosis. Then we should recommend the action the Scriptures prescribe. Where our contact is in the course of routine pastoral care, we should talk about spiritual pursuits and habits that will encourage spiritual growth and health.

Although we must major on being good listeners, we must not hesitate to be directive, providing it is the Scriptures' direction we give. Our purpose is to show people how to live according to the Scriptures, including how not to go beyond what they say. "How good is a timely word," the book of Proverbs declares (15:23), and that is an axiom of pastoral practice.

Visiting an elder's wife who was laid low by a lingering and incurable illness, before leaving her bedside, Dr. Alexander Whyte quoted the Scottish paraphrase of Isaiah 40:31, "On eagles' wings they mount, they soar." "Then, at the door, he turned and added as an afterthought—dropping into the homely Scots, as he was wont to do in moments of intimacy—'Put that under your tongue and suck it like a sweetie.'"[3]

KEY WORDS IN PASTORAL CARE

There are at least four key words in the New Testament used of pastoral care, and they are of equal importance: encouragement, exhortation, admonition, and counsel. All Christians need encouragement, whether to persevere in godliness or personal evangelism or to develop their spiritual gifts and to discover their proper place in the body of Christ. Although all believers ought to encourage one another, it is the particular responsibility of undershepherds to do so. This is not surprising, since they are the chosen instruments of God the Holy Spirit, the God-given Encourager of His people. Filled with the Spirit, we encourage others. As we make a pastoral visit or sit down to help someone seeking counsel, our deliberate purpose should be to encourage that person. Paul singles out the timid and the weak as those who are in special need of encouragement (1 Thessalonians 5:14).

Alongside encouragement goes exhortation. They cannot always be separated, but exhortation has much more of a directional element within it than encouragement: It tells us what we should be doing. Two typical instructions like, "As we have opportunity, let us do good to all people, especially to those who belong to the family of believers" (Galatians 6:10) and "Rejoice in the Lord always" (Philippians 4:4) are exhortations, and they both tell us what we should be doing. The Scriptures consistently point us in the spiritual or moral direction we should go. In exhortation, using the Scriptures, we point one another in the right direction. When we counsel married couples, we will exhort them to love each other. Counseling children, we will exhort them to honor their parents. Although the exhortations are familiar, they should still be given.

Admonition—in terms of warning and correction—must, where necessary, accompany both encouragement and exhortation. In giving a warning or a rebuke, we should be quick to give praise where it is due (1 Corinthians 11:2), since that makes correction easier to accept. The New Testament regards admonition as the particular province of undershepherds (1 Thessalonians 5:12). We may have to warn against idols (1 John 5:21) or possible spiritual wolves (Acts 20:29). Admonition is much more difficult than encouragement or exhortation, since there may be greater uncertainty as to how it will be received. But that unknown factor must not hinder our exercising it. All need admonishing on occasions.

DP I mentioned earlier the importance of an undershepherd being under someone's pastoral care. Early on in my ministry in Edinburgh, I accepted a church anniversary preaching engagement that took me to the west of England. It happened to coincide with our annual missionary conference, which was always the last weekend in November. In making his pastoral visit to me at the end of that year my elder not only encouraged me, as he consistently did, but he also admonished me for my absence from the missionary conference. His reasoning went something like this: "Since missions are important, and we expect God to say something to us as a church about our corporate responsibilities, you ought to be present to hear what God has to say." I recognized him to be right, and I never accepted another engagement that coincided with that last weekend in November. His admonition was necessary and beneficial.

AB One of my elders called me the morning after our elders' meeting. "Last evening," he said, "you hurt Mr. X with your words." Not that what I had said was untrue, but the way in which I had said it was unkind. He continued, "I want you to call Mr. X and apologize, and then call me and let me know how you got on." Resisting the temptation to become defensive, I did as I was admonished to do, and all three of us were the better for it.

The context and atmosphere of all admonition must be love. We may often feel nervous in giving a rebuke, but our nervousness itself lets a person know that we do not admonish lightly or unfeelingly.

Counseling is exercised as much in casual conversations after meetings as on set occasions when people make an appointment to see us. When we visit the bereaved or the unwell, or people come to see us because of their problems or need of guidance, we engage in counseling—counseling that may involve at one and the same time encouragement, exhortation, and admonition.

The Holy Spirit does the most effective counseling as the Word that He has inspired is taught and preached. He after all is the Counselor. He is well able to apply the same straightforward exposition in different ways to every Christian listening to it. To one He may speak a word of encouragement, to another a rebuke, while to yet another He may give direction. This happens continually when the Scriptures are expounded in the Spirit's power. The best kind of counseling so often arises from, and follows upon, the preaching of the Scriptures. In regular exposition there will be times when it is appropriate, for example, to talk about God's gift of sex, and the honoring of marriage, whether in recounting the life of Joseph or David or dealing with basic New Testament commands like, "It is God's will that you should be sanctified: that you should avoid sexual immorality" (1 Thessalonians 4:3).

Looking back, we cannot remember many occasions when we have dealt with such subjects in preaching without someone seeking us out afterward for help, either to get right with God on the issue or to obtain advice. The counseling that then took place was a natural extension of the application of God's Word. Some contemporary emphasis upon counseling may arise from a neglect of the ministry of teaching and preaching. If our preaching is pastoral and practical in its application, we will be teaching people to take care not only of others but also of themselves.

Often the best counseling is spontaneous—the seemingly casual meeting of a member of the flock in the street, or the apparent haphazard conversation after a meeting when an important issue is raised. We need to learn to view the interruptions of our daily routine in that light, and not least telephone calls. John Newton was not bothered by the telephone, but he was by people coming to his home. He said, "When I hear a knock at my study door, I hear a message from God; it may be a message of instruction; perhaps a lesson of patience; but, since it is His message, it must be interesting." Behind many a casual telephone conversation or an unexpected call about something not important in itself, there may be spiritual need for which counsel is required. To share the verse we have chosen for the day can in itself be the encouragement a person needs, or it can provide the opening for him to disclose the real reason for his wanting to be in touch.

Part of our counseling ministry is to pass people on to others who may be able to help them better than we can. Among God's people there is an almost infinite resource of experience to be drawn upon. The comfort we and others have found can be shared.

DP I never felt more helpless than when early on in my ministry I had to visit the parents and family of a five-year-old girl who had been run over and killed on the last day of her first term at school. In the church fellowship another family had lost their young child some time earlier. It was natural to ask them to follow up my visit. Their comfort was invaluable; in fact, it contributed to the conversion of the whole family. The conversations that took place could have been described as "counseling," but they were simply one family sharing with another the way in which they had found comfort, support, and hope.

AB We have extended this principle at Parkside by establishing a number of groups that exist to provide help and hope in Christ. These care groups meet on Thursday evenings, usually for six-to-eight-week terms, and they provide biblical guidance and support in dealing with bereavement, marital failure, single parenting, drug-related problems, and even handling unemployment. In every instance the Scriptures are our rule and guide, but the participants have responded to the call: "Don't go it alone, you need Jesus and you need others."

Questions serve a useful function in pastoral work, and especially in counseling. To ask an appropriate question may open up a helpful conversation and avoid our beating about the bush. Paul asked pastoral questions. Writing to the Galatians, he enquired, "Who has bewitched you?" (Galatians 3:1), and "What has happened to all your joy?" (4:15). If someone comes to talk about uncertainties concerning the future, he may be helped to come to the point if we ask, "Where are your areas of doubt about the future?" It is appropriate to ask a Christian questions such as: "Do you find it hard to keep your relationship with God fresh?" or "Have you been able to maintain your spiritual joy in Christ?" If this is precisely the person's problem, it is then easy to talk about it. If the person is spiritually healthy, he will have much to share on the subject.

Our main task in counseling is to assist Christians to understand their own condition, and God's purpose in it, and then to recognize what their right behavior should be. Besides giving encouragement, we must not hesitate to exhort and admonish where necessary. We must not shrink from doing what may be dangerous in our work, or what will not be greeted with gratitude. Sometimes we may have the difficult task of reminding people of God's jealousy for their loyalty and love (1 Corinthians 10:22).

Our goal in counsel is not the pleasure of the people we strive to help, but pleasing God. Our concern must be to speak the truth in Christ—and with love—with our conscience confirming the fact by the Holy Spirit (Romans 9:1). People should always be encouraged to think through the counsel we give (1 Corinthians 10:15). Such encouragement shows that we are not authoritarian, although directive, and that our earnest desire is to present only God's truth—something God Himself will confirm to people's consciences (2 Corinthians 4:2).

RECOGNIZING OUR OWN LIMITATIONS

We are all out of our depth in pastoral work. Our confidence must never be in our expertise or training or experience, but in God's ability to use frail instruments filled with His Spirit. For this reason all pastoral work must be linked with prayer. Without the enabling grace of God, no encouragement, exhortation, admonition, or spiritual counsel will do any good; they must be backed by prayer (cf. Romans 15:5–6).

In counseling, we do not aim to compete with the doctor or psychologist or psychiatrist. We must recognize the point at which we have to say, "You need specialized help of another sort, not just spiritual help." We may do great damage if we fail to do this, because we may imply the person's problem is wholly spiritual, when it may be far from that. One way of testing whether or not a person's problem is spiritual is to apply the spiritual remedy. If that does not suffice, then we must consider the possibility of some other area, besides the spiritual, needing investigation. At that point we must not be slow to encourage the person to look elsewhere.

A practical way to show our recognition of our own limitations is to identify ourselves with others in any exhortation or counsel we give. It is always better to say "we" where we honestly can, rather than "you." Referring to the great objective of Christian experience, Paul wrote to the Philippians, "Brothers, I do not consider myself yet to have taken hold of it. But one thing I do: Forgetting what is behind and straining toward what is ahead, I press on toward the goal to win the prize for which God has called me heavenward in Christ Jesus. All of us who are mature should take such a view" (Philippians 3:13–15).

All for whom we care should be aware that we are in the same battle, and that we speak not as professional Christians but as members with them of God's family. Just as it is of immeasurable comfort to know that our Great High Priest was tested in every way as we are—although He, uniquely without sin—it is an encouragement to the flock to know that undershepherds are made of the same stuff as themselves.

OUR GREATEST CONFIDENCE

When we help God's people pastorally, we have one tremendous source of confidence: It is that when God begins a good work in people's lives He will continue it until the day of Jesus Christ. The hidden factor in every encouragement we give, or exhortation, or difficult piece of advice or correction, is that God the Holy Spirit indwells the believer to back it up, and to apply it with a force we do not possess. Our confidence that people will react and respond in the right way is not our confidence in human nature but our confidence regarding God's working in them. This explains why Paul spoke of being confident in the Lord concerning the behavior of Christians (2 Thessalonians 3:4; Philemon 21). Without that confidence we would despair; with that confidence we are brave and strong to fulfill any pastoral responsibility.

CHAPTER 9

PASTORAL CARE—
THE PRACTICALITIES

In turning to the practicalities of pastoral care, there will be tremendous variation in the circumstances and responsibilities placed upon undershepherds. In describing our own approaches, we are not implying that they are the best, but we hope that where undershepherds are in the early stages of their work our experience may provide some guideposts, and that others will find the stimulus of assessing other people's approaches helpful to their own.

VISITING PEOPLE IN THEIR HOMES

The expectations of a Scottish congregation and its American counterpart are one area where the cultural differences between Edinburgh and Cleveland are most obvious. In each context the objective is the same. We desire to exercise pastoral care and oversight in a manner that expresses a personal interest in and concern for people's well-being. In Scotland a telephone call might be taken as unwillingness to go the extra mile (visiting the home), whereas in America a visit to the home might be seen as an unnecessary exercise or even an intrusion. It is unwise to generalize, because there is a significant difference between the expectations of a small rural congregation in Louisiana and a congregation spread over fifty square miles in the suburbs of Chicago.

The fact that a well-known pastor and preacher seldom called on anyone gave rise to a story that may well be apocryphal. One of his elders was unwell, and the preacher, happening to be in the neighborhood, thought that he would drop in to see him. The elder, looking toward the door and seeing the preacher, exclaimed, "I'm not that sick, am I?" Although there are obviously situations where the pastor is not expected to engage in frequent visitation, much pastoral work needs to be done in families, and it should not surprise our people when we care for them in this way.

A pastoral visit is more than a social call. Nevertheless it is a social call in that we are interested in people as people, their families, their concerns and interests. In Scotland our calls are usually not formal occasions, where people feel they must have the house spick-and-span and show us into their best room, with the children duly cautioned to be on their best behavior. A surprise visit helps to avoid this kind of reception, and has much to be said for it. In America, on the other hand, unannounced visits may prove inconvenient to the people upon whom we call, and we will do far better to plan in advance for such a visit. In the States families are warmly appreciative of the pastor's expression of pastoral care in showing up at the children's swim meet or the Friday night football game. The more we know our people, the more we know the best approach.

DP If I visited an older couple without a family, who would have gone to a lot of trouble to prepare the home for a visit, I tried to call in when passing without letting them know beforehand. If it was a younger married couple with a family, I rang beforehand—sometimes up to a week ahead—and arranged a time when both husband and wife would be at home, and when the younger family members' routine would not be disrupted by my visit. We need to be sensitive to people's different circumstances. To ring up a week beforehand and plan a visit might cause supersensitive individuals to panic and to imagine some ominous reason for the visit. Far better to wait until we see such people at church, and to say casually, "I've been meaning to call and see you sometime. Would Wednesday or Thursday be convenient?"

AB With our congregation spread over such a large geographical area, home visits are almost without exception planned, and more often than not they take place to address a crisis. In more than twenty years I cannot think of any home visits that have not been on account of bereavement or a matter of church discipline or some other significant issue in the family.

A pastoral visit must never be simply a task to be done, in order that no one may say the home or individual has not been visited or to quiet conscience. Paul's concern to visit the Roman Christians "in the full measure of the blessing of Christ" (Romans 15:29) provides a good objective. We should always go ready to speak of spiritual things, and with the deliberate intention of doing so, providing God's Spirit puts no restraint upon us at the time. Our visit should do good; it should contribute something to the spiritual well-being of those we visit. As the sun shining upon our faces and bodies brings a sense of well-being, so our visits should bring an awareness of God's gracious shining upon His people.

All manner of subjects may be raised or discussed in a pastoral visit, and our aim should be to lift any discussion to the highest level, and whenever we can, to relate it to the person and work of our Lord Jesus Christ. This is not an artificial exercise. Urging humility and unity upon God's people, Paul did not hesitate to exhort them to have the mind of Christ in them (Philippians 2:1ff). Dealing with the complexities of the marriage relationship, he spoke of Christ's relationship to His bride, the church (Ephesians 5).

In the middle of a conversation, perhaps on a difficult subject, an arrow prayer to God asking Him to show us how to relate it to the person and work of Christ will not go unanswered, and will turn a visit that might be disastrous into one of considerable benefit.

Inevitably there will be occasions when people express criticism of other Christians. We have found it helpful to counter whatever is said by always saying something positive about the individual concerned, and then to deliberately include that person in a positive way in our concluding prayer together. This practice discourages people from voicing wrongful criticisms, and saves us from being quoted as agreeing with their criticism. More important still, it may be just the corrective someone needs to see the good in someone else rather than the bad.

DP Unless it is a first visit, I reckon half an hour to be the ideal length of time, except when an important matter arises in the conversation that demands to be talked through there and then. I would usually spend the first half of my visit talking about things in general, with the focus on people's family and work, so that in praying for them, I may pray intelligently. We must never forget that a purpose of our visit is to get to know people and their circumstances well, so that we can be faithful in private prayer for them. In the second half of the visit I aim to share something from the Scriptures and to pray about the matters that have occupied our conversation.

AB I have tried to adopt a similar pattern when meeting with individuals or couples for the same reason, but in my study rather than their home. It is all too easy to talk for longer while accomplishing less.

It is always better that people should feel our visit is too short than too long. Visits from Alexander Whyte—the much loved minister of Free St. George's, Edinburgh—were often brief but much appreciated. In a memorial booklet, Mrs. Robert Simpson wrote,

He could not accomplish all he would have liked, but many of us know what his visits meant to us. He did not stay long, he never said much, but what he did say—how concise, how true, how much to the point, how full of strengthening and comfort! One visit I shall never forget; he came in and stood at the couch and repeated:

> "He gives the conquest to the weak,
> Supports the fainting heart,
> And courage in the evil hour
> His heav'nly aids impart."

Then a word of prayer and he was gone. No doubt to several others that afternoon he brought strength and comfort by these words.

The words Alexander Whyte quoted are the fifth verse of Paraphrase 22 in the Scottish Psalter, from Isaiah 40:27–31.

If people are not at home when we call, it is valuable to leave a note or write a brief letter explaining our lack of success in finding them in. This means that the visit is not entirely wasted in that the person knows our intention was to see him, and it prepares the way for a further visit. Quoting the same paraphrase, having not found someone at home that day, Alexander Whyte wrote, "Had I seen you when I called, I would have given you the prophet's word when he was visiting the sick in Jerusalem—'He gives the conquest to the weak.'" Such a note can accomplish as much as the intended visit.

EVANGELISTIC VISITATION

Besides visits to members of the flock, there will be visits to those who are not yet Christians. As well as being undershepherds, we are to be spiritual physicians and midwives.

DP I have found these among the most stimulating and rewarding visits to make, and yet they can be pushed out by other pastoral duties. I found that the only safeguard against that happening was to reserve one evening a week for such visits. Most were prompted by people signing a visitor's card at church on a Sunday or making themselves known to me after a Sunday service, sometimes in the happy context of a desire to know more of the Christian faith. My general rule was to deal with the married couples myself, leaving it to single folk to visit those of their own sex.

I invariably preceded my first visit with either a telephone call or a letter. When people have a family, it is not always easy for them to say immediately on the phone which night will be convenient. In writing a brief note I put forward a date and a time, suggesting that if I did not hear from them I would take it to be convenient, and for them not to hesitate to give me a ring if they would prefer another time. So often the latter part of an evening is preferable where young children have to be put to bed and the house put in order after the day's busyness. For profitable spiritual conversation, unnecessary distractions are best avoided.

It is exciting to make a visit and to feel ourselves like a midwife who arrives just in time to witness the miracle of birth. I can look back to occasions when God's Spirit had already worked through the preaching of God's Word, and the individual or couple were waiting to respond to God's invitation in Christ to salvation. Other visits may indicate the beginnings of spiritual interest or genuine seeking after God. Where this is the case, nothing is more profitable than to suggest engaging in regular Bible study together. I found that I could not do this realistically with more than one or two couples in a week, and it is vital to bring in others who can share in this ministry.

I recall a number of couples with whom I went through 1 Peter over several months. My choice of 1 Peter was influenced by the manner in which it deals with every aspect of Christian doctrine in brief compass. My procedure with some of the couples was to arrange to meet after our church prayer meeting on a Monday evening. We limited ourselves to thirty minutes, which meant that the couple knew that our times together were disciplined, and it also meant that I was home by ten o'clock! We went through the letter verse by verse, with my explaining it as simply as I could. When we arrived at the end of the letter, they were often rejoicing in God's salvation and had started to see the benefits of Bible study. I wish that I had encouraged and trained more to share in this.

AB Such visitation is unusual for me now but not unknown. Without neglecting these opportunities I have had to learn to give them away not only to members of the pastoral team but to the congregation as a whole. It is a source of great encouragement to others as well when individuals on the occasion of their baptism tell how in the context of an evangelistic Bible study they came to faith in Christ.

HOSPITAL VISITATION

Hospital visits are one of an undershepherd's priorities. Seldom will we get closer to our flock, or will they look for our spiritual encouragement more, than when they are unwell, and when perhaps the future is uncertain so far as their health is concerned. The sooner a first visit can be made the better once we are aware of someone's hospitalization. Besides being reassuring to the patient, and an evidence of the immediacy of our caring, it means that we are never caught unaware by sudden deterioration or serious illness.

Hospitals are generous in granting us the privilege of visiting patients outside normal visiting times. Normal hours of visiting should be avoided, unless we need to meet the relatives and friends of the person who is unwell. It is not fair to usurp visiting time a patient may enjoy with his or her family and friends, and it is much better to be able to talk to people on their own rather than with others present. Privileged visitors, we should never enter a ward with-

178

out checking with the nurse in charge that it is convenient, and it is good to express our appreciation as we leave.

Particular discernment has to be exercised in hospital visits. If someone is seriously ill, and scarcely able to sustain a conversation, just two or three minutes is more than sufficient time for an appropriate verse of Scripture to be shared and the praying of a short prayer for God's help for the patient and His blessing upon those close to him or her. It is better to make frequent visits of two or three minutes than a lengthy visit that wearies and embarrasses. Where a patient is well able to have visitors, ten to fifteen minutes is probably the kind of time to have in view. Anything longer, outside of visiting times, may be overstaying our privilege and may weary the patient who will be too courteous to tell us.

It is useful to ask, "How would you like me to pray for you?" as it may make it easier for him to share his fears or anxieties, which otherwise he would not feel he could voice. Sharing in this intimate way will invariably bring relevant Scriptures to mind, and then praying together enables fears and anxieties to be brought honestly to God. When a verse of Scripture suitable for someone in the hospital comes home to us with particular force, it may be helpful to type it on a small piece of paper or card, and leave it with the person in the hospital.

Whether we are visiting people in their homes or in the hospital, we will sometimes feel that our visit has been ineffective and has accomplished little. Our resort must be prayer, not despair. Thomas Boston, whose practice was to visit each of his families in Ettrick, Selkirkshire, in the Scottish Borders, once a year, recounts how he was called in to visit a dying woman. He wrote in his journal, "Being with E. P. the night before she died, I had no satisfaction in converse with her; which affected me exceedingly. Thereupon I came in to my closet, and set myself to wrestle with God on her account; and then went to her again, and was much comforted in her; so that my spirit was more than ordinarily elevated. She said she fixed on that word, 'Thou hast played the harlot with many lovers; yet return again to Me, saith the Lord.'" Boston's example is helpful. A difficult or disappointing visit must not rule out a repeat visit, but rather encourage another after more prayer. There are few joys to exceed seeing a spiritual change for the better as God obviously honors perseverance.

The Place of Letters

The New Testament letters themselves illustrate the value of letters in pastoral work. Most of them are pastoral letters, and some were written to individuals like Philemon, Gaius, Timothy, and Titus. Sometimes a pastoral visit may not be possible, and there are situations where a letter is better than a visit or can prepare the way for it. F. W. Boreham, in his delightful autobiography, expresses the value of letters in pastoral work:

> It often falls to a minister's lot to approach people, and especially young people, on the most delicate and important subjects. Upon their decisions much of their future happiness and usefulness will depend. As a minister, I must therefore go about the business with the utmost care. Shall I seek an interview? But an interview is an embarrassing affair. I may not say exactly what I meant to say; and I force my friend into speaking immediately and without carefully weighing the issues. But see how much better I can do with the co-operation of the post office! I sit at my desk and write exactly what I want to say. I am under no necessity to complete a sentence until I can do so to my perfect satisfaction. I can pause to consider the exact word that I wish to employ. And if, when it is written, my letter does not please me, I can tear it up and write it all over again. I am not driven to impromptu utterance or careless phrase-ology. I am free of the inevitable effect upon my expression pro-duced by the presence of another person. I am not embarrassed by the embarrassment that he feels on being approached on so vital a theme. I am cool, collected, leisurely and free. And the advantages

that come to me in inditing the letter are shared by him in receiving it. He is alone, and, therefore, entirely himself. He is not disconcerted by the presence of an interviewer. He owes nothing to etiquette or ceremony. He has the advantage of having the case stated to him as forcefully and as well as I am to state it. He can read it with ease and in silence without the awkward feeling that, in one moment, he must make some sort of reply. If he is vexed at my intrusion into his private affairs he has time to recover from his displeasure and to reflect that I am moved only by a desire for his own welfare. If he is flattered at my attention, he has time to fling aside such superficial considerations and to face the issue on its merits. The matter sinks into his soul; becomes part of his normal life and thought; and, by the time we meet, he is prepared to talk it over without embarrassment, without personal feeling, and without undue reserve. In such matters, and they are among the most important with which a minister is called to deal, the post office is able to render a man invaluable assistance.[1]

DP Inevitably we will find ourselves helping those with marital problems, and it is here that letters may most helpfully prepare the way for a visit. If we ring beforehand we cannot help but talk to just one of the partners, and he or she may hesitate to speak on behalf of the other. The first reaction too may be one of resentment at our interest or intrusion. The advantage of a letter addressed to husband and wife together is that they both may read it, have time to overcome what may be their initial hesitation, and then find themselves prepared to receive us.

The Organization of Pastoral Care

While effective pastoral care requires organization, the best is frequently spontaneous and seemingly casual. However, behind the best spontaneity and the seizing of casual opportunities, there is usually organization.

DP I have in mind the habit referred to earlier of writing down each day a verse from Scripture which speaks to me, and upon which I may meditate. In whatever pastoral opportunities I have that day I aim to share that verse, where it is appropriate to do so. It may be in meeting someone in the street, or during the unexpected phone call, or sometimes as I write a letter. These are all important because God is sovereign in the organization of our day.

Each day is made up of a variety of contacts, and we can never be sure who may be most in need of encouragement, exhortation, or admonition. By recognizing that God may bring about our most casual meeting, telephone call, and letter, we begin to see that nothing should be thought of as an interruption but as an opportunity. The organization of pastoral care begins, as we have suggested earlier, in systematic prayer for those for whom we are responsible. It is helpful to pray at the beginning of each day for the unexpected opportunities we will have, since this alerts us to their possibility and gives us eyes to see them.

To organize pastoral care, we must establish priorities. We would put at the top of the list the new Christian. It is all too easy to rejoice in seeing people come to faith in Christ, but then to neglect their spiritual nurture. The time to encourage them to be instructed in the Christian faith is immediately upon their conversion. They are ready for it then as at no other time, and they need it most then too. As undershepherds, there are limits upon the amount of time we can give to new Christians as individuals, especially if we are privileged to have the care of several at a time. If the latter is the case, some kind of discipleship class is the best means of instructing them and of meeting them frequently. It has the added benefit of bringing the new Christian into contact with other young Christians. At the same time we should prayerfully link up the new Christian with an older Christian of the same sex who can keep a watchful eye upon him or her and ensure that one-to-one pastoral care is available. It is an advantage if that person can come along to the discipleship class with the new Christian, where possible.

Then there must come the unwell and the troubled. Within this group, priorities will also have to be determined. Some patients will have long-term stays in the hospital, particularly the elderly. Others will be emergencies, where life itself is in the balance. The latter clearly have prior claim.

Frequently we will be called upon to help those who are in distress. Our first task must be to discover whether or not the person is a Christian, by looking for a sense of sin and an awareness of God's love and of love for Him. If these are lacking, then we should deal with the person as someone who is unconverted. If the person is clearly a Christian, we must not fail to recognize that the distress may have physical or psychological roots. Someone may, for example, have a history of depressive illness. If we are clear that the problem is primarily spiritual, we should seek its cause either in unconfessed sin that perhaps has not been recognized, or in an attack of the enemy of souls, or in a period of temporary spiritual desertion for which God has good purposes.

Helping the troubled in mind requires much time and patience. If the problem is plainly not spiritual, we must be quick to say so,

and to encourage the person to seek medical help, which he may
well be resisting because of a wrongful sense of failure on account
of the distress. Our task then is to reassure the person and encourage the person to accept treatment as part of God's gracious
provision and care.

DP Christians with new experiences—such as those getting engaged or married, and those rejoicing in the gift of
children—must have a place in our priorities. Whenever a
couple get engaged, it is valuable to write to them
straightaway and, besides expressing congratulations, best
wishes, and prayers, to suggest that we will be delighted
to meet them after any service to pray for their future. I
always found this suggestion was taken up with enthusiasm, and it gave an opportunity to share their plans and
to pray together.

I planned to have one session with all whose marriages I was to conduct, in which I devoted most of the
time to talking about living together as a married couple,
trying to be as practical as possible, and using the Scriptures as our guide. I always wished I had had more time
to devote to this, but I felt it better to have a single session with each couple on their own rather than to bring
all the prospective married couples together for a series of
meetings.

As important as what we say in such meetings is the
establishing of a good relationship with each couple, as
that rapport can be of considerable significance in future
years in a time of crisis. I supplemented this session with
the gift of a Christian book on marriage, and the idea
evolved latterly of several married couples leading a series
of home meetings for those about to get married entitled

"Homemakers." Having discussed their format, I stood back, leaving it to the trusted couples, and this provision supplemented the instruction I tried to give.

To take time to visit new parents in order to pray with them in thanksgiving for the gift of children is always worthwhile, although I found that to do so was impossible sometimes because of the shortage of evening opportunities. My wife visited mothers whenever their babies were born, usually while they were in the hospital or immediately upon their return home. She was much more able to do this, and her arriving at the time of a baby's feeding did not cause embarrassment as my own might have done.

AB In the early days at Parkside I attempted to function in much the same way as Derek describes. Over time as both the congregation and the pastoral team have grown I have shared these privileges. For some reading this it might seem that this delegation is all to my advantage. On the contrary I find that aspects of pastoral care that were my responsibility when we were smaller I seldom if ever have occasion to enjoy. There is of course a peculiar danger in this, namely of becoming so divorced from the details that we lose any realistic sense of involvement in the lives of the congregation. Being alert to the danger goes a long way toward ensuring that it does not happen. The important issue for the congregation is that they are being cared for.

The urgent character of some pastoral needs must not push out the apparently nonurgent. If we devote our energies to crises, we may miss out on regular and systematic involvement that goes a long way toward anticipating problems, so that many may be prevented altogether. Even as preventative medicine is better than surgery, so regular pastoral contact is preferable to crisis encounters. One of the problems of pastoral care and visitation is that there is never an end to it, and we never feel we have done enough. However we approach it, we inevitably sense that we could have done more. The more we do, the more, too, is expected. Such considerations provide no grounds for discouragement, however; rather they point to the priority of striving to please God rather than people in our pastoral work, and to develop a personal program that is tailored to our own pastoral responsibilities, and to follow it, recognizing that God never requires more of us than is right, even though people may.

TWO PERSONAL PROGRAMS

We help ourselves by writing into the organization of our pastoral work the principles we feel we should work by, and determining at the same time that we will not be so rigid in applying them that they become a rod for our own back. We share that conviction with some feeling in that, on looking back, many of the pressures we have lived under in pastoral work have been self-inflicted —we have sometimes demanded more of ourselves than God intended. At the same time, every undershepherd prefers to demand too much of himself than too little. Whatever happens, we must not lose touch with the Chief Shepherd and forfeit His guidance and peace.

Every church fellowship situation is different—in its size, the age-spread of its membership, the area in which it is placed, and the number of people in the pastoral team. In sharing ways in which we have organized pastoral care, we do it not as a suggested guide to others —that would be presumptuous—but in the hope that it may stimulate ideas as to ways of doing it in a more effective manner.

DP My pattern was to carry around in my diary a note of those whom I ought to contact, visit, or arrange to see in the immediate future. There were always some visits that I did not look forward to as much as others—perhaps because of the opposition I anticipated, or because the purpose was to admonish on account of unhelpful behavior or criticism. I learned to do these visits first, and not to allow them to go to the bottom of the list and to be pushed out by legitimate but not so urgent visits. Invariably I found the visits then not so difficult as I anticipated.

I aimed to keep Monday afternoon free for my regular hospital visits. If people went into the hospital some other time in the week for an operation, I always went in the day before the operation in order to pray with them and to encourage them by means of a verse or passage of Scripture, often writing it out beforehand on a slip of paper or card to leave with them. This latter practice is an advantage if, as sometimes happens, the patient is unavailable because of preparatory procedures for the operation.

Each Monday evening—the night of our church prayer meeting—I devoted the three quarters of an hour beforehand to being available in the church office or vestry for people who had asked to see me, something that invariably happened the previous Sunday. I divided it into three fifteen-minute slots from 7:00 to 7:45 P.M. Fifteen minutes does not seem a long time, but I found that for the majority of matters it was about right, and it achieved a disciplined use of time. We tend to use whatever time is available. If more time was required, that quarter of an hour clearly established the fact, and I then arranged to meet the person concerned in the immediate future for a more open-ended conversation.

Each Monday night, applying the principle of caution mentioned earlier, one of the elders was on duty in rotation. It was his task to be around in the room leading to the vestry so as to welcome people and show them in. I felt that this was good both for me and for those who came, and it fulfilled the principle of never interviewing or counseling anyone of the opposite sex in an empty church building. To be available each week like this makes it easier for people to take the initiative in making contact, and particularly when, because of large numbers of people for whom we have responsibility, our main pastoral task is dealing with crises.

Paul Sangster, son of Dr. W. E. Sangster, quotes his father's words concerning a similar practice, and it is interesting to reflect that the kinds of situations that may present themselves to undershepherds have not really changed.

> Being the minister of a large central church, I can do little more, as far as visitation is concerned, than go to the very sick. Most of my pastoral work is done in my own vestry, my people (and others who seek my help) saving my moments by making the journey at the appointed time to me.
>
> Many, many hours of every week I spend this way.
>
> I pick up my old appointments book and filter the pages through my fingers. I, alone, can read my notes, but even a few pages remind me of the variety of needs on which my help has been sought.
>
> There are the homosexuals (mostly male) who come in all their pathetic need, to learn whether there is an answer to their problem in religion; there are the people who can't pray—to whom all their life (if they have kept up with it at all) it has been a duty and never a delight; there are the

people who have never had a personal experience of God and honestly don't know what it means, but who have been provoked by the preaching to enquire if the full, rich, evangelical experience is for all men; there are the masturbators of both sexes who overcome their self-loathing and tell their sad tale because it is well-known in the district that you can tell the minister anything, that he never appears shocked, and never tells; there are the cases of domestic incompatibility and marital infidelities; the illegitimate lad to whom, at the request of his mother, I had to tell the truth about his parentage; the poor nerve cases with their obsessions and persecution manias; the folk who find faith hard and with whom the intellectual problems are not just a screen for moral failure . . . the frustrated, the beaten and despairing.

I look back over the years and think of the multitudes my ordinary ministry must have touched. God alone knows how much good I did them. I tried! God knows that also. Many a night I dragged home almost too tired to undress.

But happy! Oh yes, happy! Fulfilling my ministry. Born to do this! Marvelling at the goodness of God in letting me do it all. Envying no man his job.[2]

I then kept one evening a week—usually the two or three Wednesdays in a month when I did not have elders' or deacons' meetings—to visit non-Christian folk with whom we had been brought into contact as a church, usually through their filling in a visitor's card on a Sunday. If I did not set aside this one evening to make such visits, the pastoral demands of the flock quickly pushed it out. I needed this contact with non-Christians, and the stimulus of personal evangelism; and many of these visits bore fruit over the years.

The remaining time available for pastoral visitation

each week, I devoted to systematic visitation of elderly folk and new families. I never visited women on their own in their homes unless they were old enough to be my grandmother. If pastoral care was needed, I invited them to our home, where my wife was around if not involved in the interview, or my wife and I would visit the single girls and women for coffee after the church prayer meeting.

AB It will already have become apparent to the reader that Derek's capacity and discipline in this, as in other areas, although he would not say so, are quite exceptional. Pondering his plan and its execution is almost like watching someone perform a feat of rare bravery and then noting the warning that appears at the bottom of the screen: "Do not attempt this on your own." The principles that underpin Derek's pattern should still be applied in our context even though it is different from his.

Our pastoral care should be exercised as we keep in touch with the Lord Jesus and know His peace and guidance.

Our pastoral care should not be chaotic or haphazard but planned. We should learn not to sidestep the difficulties, but to tackle them prayerfully and quickly. We should learn to "bundle" our tasks, taking advantage of time before and after meetings when we know others will be present. Our pastoral involvement must include "do[ing] the work of an evangelist" (2 Timothy 4:5). We must be circumspect in all our dealings, with particular care being shown not to visit any women in their home alone unless they are old enough to be our grandmother! Since Derek has been honest enough to admit that he has sometimes demanded more of himself than God intended, we may have to face the fact that we have offered less of ourselves than God desires.

THE DELEGATION OF RESPONSIBILITIES FOR PASTORAL CARE

The larger the church fellowship, the more the regular and systematic pastoral care and visitation needs to be shared, since the number of crises is multiplied—and it is when major problems arise that undershepherds are inevitably called in.

DP In my second church, which was a large city center fellowship, I found that once I had systematically visited all the house-bound members—about eighty to ninety in all—most of my pastoral work had to be devoted to helping people in their crises, and responding to those who wished to see me for advice and counsel. That compelled me to learn to share and delegate pastoral responsibilities.

The first sphere of pastoral delegation was within the pastoral team. For most of my time in pastoral charge—both in London and in Edinburgh—I had a young assistant and a deaconess/lady-worker. Since most crises tended to be brought to my attention first, I dealt with them initially and often saw them through to their conclusion, or carefully brought someone else in—whether from the pastoral team or outside it (often an elder or his wife)—with the consent of the person who needed help. The systematic visitation of the unwell and those confined to their homes was delegated to the assistant and the deaconess. They visited some on a weekly basis, some

191

on a monthly, and others on a bimonthly or quarterly frequency. In the Edinburgh situation, we divided the city into north and south, and they took it in turns each month to do one half of the city. The understanding was that they would alert me whenever they felt I should call on any of those whom they regularly visited. In hospital visiting, once I had made the initial visit when an operation was imminent or there was serious illness, we then took it in turns, always ensuring at least a weekly visit, and more in the case of serious illness.

The assistant's job was to feel a particular responsibility for the student and young people's work, and the deaconess for all the womenfolk in the church, especially the single women. We met each Monday lunchtime to eat together, to review the previous week's pastoral work, to anticipate the new week's tasks, and to pray together for all the people we had mentioned in our discussion, as well as for one another. On the first Monday of the month we met early in the morning (8:00 A.M.) and surveyed the month's work, and had two or three sessions of prayer with no set time to conclude.

In working as a team, there has to be mutual trust and care. It proved right to have a balance between a regular weekly meeting that was kept within a strict time limit and a meeting when there was no such restriction. It meant that any matter of moment that came up at the weekly meeting that was not adequately dealt with or thought through would not be left like that long because of the monthly opportunity of going into it in greater depth. Although working as a team, one person has to be clearly the leader, especially as some team members will be new and probably inexperienced. The team leader must encourage honesty with one another and mutual caring. He in particular must be sensitive to the needs of the team members—both spiritually and physically—because they may well overstretch themselves or become emotionally exhausted through their involvement in other people's lives. As team leader, he can instruct them to have pauses and breaks that they would not take themselves, and that probably he would not give himself. But that is a price of good leadership.

The second sphere of pastoral delegation was within the eldership. The membership was more or less equally divided up between the elders, and they were provided with a constantly updated list of the names and addresses of those in their pastoral group. My first concern was that they should pray for the members of their pastoral group on a daily basis so that each person or family was remembered weekly before God in this way. Nothing better serves to keep people on our hearts, and to create sensitivity to the Spirit's promptings of concern, than intercession. From time to time I referred to this desirable practice, and tried to encourage new elders in this as they were appointed.

Fundamental to encouraging others to share in pastoral concern is avoiding constantly lecturing them on what they ought to be doing. It is better to assume their pastoral involvement by passing on information relating to the people for whom they care. Whenever possible, I, or a member of the pastoral team, passed the news on immediately to an elder when someone in his group went into the hospital. If a crisis came to light, and it was not breaking a confidence, then that would be communicated similarly. I made a point of not asking elders to visit or take action when such information was conveyed, but they invariably did, with increasing effectiveness.

A useful development of pastoral groupings was the meeting of all the members of the church fellowship in their pastoral groups for prayer every four months. Church members were encouraged to let their elders know if they could not be present. By this means three times a year a spiritually and pastorally alert elder was prompted to make visits or contact with those who did not attend and whose absence he did not understand. Once a year each elder was provided with a new list of the members of his group, and asked to indicate on it any spiritual or pastoral need that he felt the pastoral team should be aware of, and to which they should be giving their attention. This was an important annual double check that we were visiting all the shut-ins, for example, as invariably each year new people needed to be added to the list. It also made much easier and more efficient the annual review of the membership when we considered the need for church discipline or removal from the church roll. The more effectively pastoral care is exercised throughout the year, the less such discipline is required.

The third sphere of pastoral delegation was by means of those responsible for areas of the church's corporate life. In our church situation in Edinburgh, we had a variety of groups: the young people's meeting, the women's morning fellowship, the young wives, Group 35 (those between 25 and 45), Group 45 (those 45 and over), the student committee, and so on. Where they had a committee —and all but one did—each was encouraged to divide its membership among the committee members for prayer. Some did this well, and others not so well. But the encouragement was there, and it generated a spirit of caring. I met with each committee once a year, aiming to encourage them in this, and to underline the readiness of the pastoral team to help in situations of need to which they felt they should alert us.

A fourth sphere—with numerous applications—was the deliberate encouragement of individuals to undertake pastoral responsibility for people they were equipped to help. Those who are older and more or less permanently shut-in require more than the monthly visit that perhaps the pastoral team can reasonably manage. Most of the elderly in our society tend to be womenfolk, and so the deaconess nurtured a group of women who each adopted one or two older women to visit regularly. I followed a similar pattern in entrusting the care of new Christians to individuals who not only kept a watchful eye on them, but also did their best to integrate them into the life of the church fellowship.

AB At Parkside we find ourselves constantly adapting to the changing size and structure of our congregation. Our attempts at dividing the congregation into elders' groups along geographical lines have, for a variety of reasons up until this point, been unsuccessful. We have not concluded that such an approach will never work, and we continue to seek to find meaningful ways to "get our arms around" the congregation. The elders are at the forefront of interviewing individuals for membership. They also take the lead in teaching our membership class as well as our pre-baptism class. Along with members of the pastoral team they share in the leadership of various aspects of pastoral care.

It remains customary for churches to be subdivided on the basis of age. While this is, to some extent, unavoidable and even in certain instances desirable, we have tried not to allow age to be the determining factor in establishing small groups. In order to help us shepherd a congregation that is divided between three morning services, we encourage the participation of each member in a life group. Some of these meet on Sundays and others during the week throughout the city. They exist to develop leadership, provide biblical instruction, foster fellowship, and encourage evangelism. One of our pastoral team has oversight of the leaders and teachers of these groups. However, since not all of our members are involved at this level, this structure does not allow us to care for the whole body. This is one of the areas in which even after twenty years I feel my alien status and find myself relying on my colleagues to develop models that are effective in this culture.

Each situation requires its own pastoral organization and structures for pastoral care. Charles Simeon organized the pastoral side of his parish work in the late eighteenth and early nineteenth century in Cambridge through a "Visiting Society." He described the work of the body in a sermon preached at one of its anniversaries:

> Its design is to find out the modest and industrious poor in a time of sickness, and to administer to them relief for their bodies, and at the same time instruction for their souls. He divided the parish into areas and appointed a man and a woman church member to be responsible for the homes in their particular district. These two would keep on the look out for cases of distress and special need, and be authorised to give them assistance at their discretion. Once a month the visitors would meet together under the chairmanship of Simeon himself, and report on what they had been able to do, and be advised in cases of special difficulty.[3]

Simeon kept these district visitors going for fifty years—no small achievement. Such was the work of a genuine pastor and teacher.

Although our purpose in this and the previous chapter has been to stress the importance of pastoral work, we must never forget that it is not quantity that counts, but quality. We must not be in such a hurry to do that we forget to be. Our own spiritual freshness determines the usefulness of our pastoral ministry. Because there is always more pastoral work to be done, we may fall into the trap of dashing here and there to the detriment of our personal walk with God and our duties to our own families. Our relationship to God must be guarded at all costs.

Even so, the work of a pastor is an anxious one. Like Paul we will know what it is to be "harassed at every turn—conflicts on the outside, fears within" (2 Corinthians 7:5), to be "struck down, but not destroyed" (2 Corinthians 4:9), to struggle on behalf of believers (Colossians 2:1), and to "face daily the pressure of . . . concern for all the churches" (2 Corinthians 11:28). But there is no work to be compared with it, for none shares the Good Shepherd's fellowship or joy more than those who care properly for the sheep and put themselves at their disposal.

CHAPTER 10

THE CONDUCT OF WORSHIP

Few privileges are greater than leading Christians in their worship of God. It may be from a pulpit or a platform; it may be to a large congregation or a house group. We often shrink beforehand at the awesome responsibility, and yet find great joy in fulfilling it.

PRACTICAL PRELIMINARIES

It is always worthwhile checking beforehand the physical layout of meeting places we are unfamilar with, preferably before people arrive. More often than not a service is conducted from a pulpit; sometimes it may be from a platform or a table. We check first that a hymnbook or songbook is there, and open it at the first hymn or song. Or in the case where the words are projected onto screens, we ensure that the slides have been prepared and that the technician operating the computer is alert to the task. It causes an unnecessary distraction if we announce what we are going to sing and then have to look for a copy of the words.

We also make certain that there is a glass of water. We may not always require to use it, but it is reassuring to have it if an unexpected tickle in the throat develops or if we have a cold that brings a cough with it. Better to have the water there than for—as it has been known to happen—some well-meaning person to get up out of his or her seat and come to you with a cup snatched hastily from the church kitchen, causing considerable disturbance.

If a service is conducted from a pulpit, we ensure it is at the right height, if it is adjustable.

DP I am rather short, and I have learned to do this through being uncomfortable because of the height of the desk. The occasion I remember most vividly was when a University Christian Union evangelistic service followed close upon the conclusion of the church's evening service, and there was little time for the changeover of the two congregations. To avoid being conspicuous by going into the pulpit while lots of people were flowing into the building, I did not check the pulpit's height. When I went into it to begin the service I discovered to my horror that I could scarcely see over the top of the reading desk in the pulpit—the person who had preached at the earlier service must have been at least six feet tall! In my panic, instead of working out how to lower it, I announced the first hymn and precariously balanced myself on two hassocks throughout the service. It certainly stopped me moving about as I spoke!

The desk height is obviously important if you are short, but it is equally relevant if you are tall, in that if the desk is too low, you will be inclined to stoop, and your voice will be lost to many. People will seldom comment on this, and you may get into the bad habit of bending over the pulpit or reading desk. As a matter of courtesy, we should ensure that visitors who minister for us have an opportunity to view the physical setting beforehand so that they can be made as comfortable as possible in it.

These things checked, we like to sit for a few minutes or so, sometimes in the pulpit, in order to pray briefly for those who will soon gather. It is easy to be so caught up with our own part in a meeting or service, because we are burdened with a sense of our responsibility, that we forget the people to whom we are to minister: To pause to pray for them helps to get our service into perspective. We want them to come hungry for God and to go away satisfied. We want everyone to sense God's presence and to see the glory of Christ.

The second most helpful preliminary is the opportunity to pray with others before a meeting's commencement. If we had to isolate a single factor that makes us feel most at ease before a service— and especially when we are preaching in unfamiliar surroundings— it is prayer fellowship beforehand. Sometimes we may be left entirely on our own until just a minute or two before a service, or a few spiritual leaders may gather in a somewhat haphazard way and engage in small talk. Neither is helpful. Better by far when all the spiritual leaders, who are not otherwise on duty, meet together to pray for the worship and preaching that is to follow. They should be encouraged to see this as the best support they can give to those whose responsibility it is to minister.

It is not unrealistic for leaders to arrive half an hour or twenty-five minutes beforehand, and for there to be a quarter of an hour of corporate prayer. This then leaves a helpful pause for those leading the service to be quiet before its commencement. Habit has so much to do with the church practice in matters like this, and our initiative may be needed to change it for the better. It is worthwhile raising the subject in a meeting of the spiritual leadership, or, if we are leading a service, to say to those who have gathered before-hand, "Let's make the best use of our time by praying together." If the priority of undershepherds is prayer and the ministry of the Word, corporate prayer at such times must be their privileged responsibility as no one else's.

PUNCTUALITY, BEARING, AND VOICE

Meetings and services should begin punctually. If we announce a time for a service, and we expect people to make an effort to get there on time, it is courteous to honor their effort by beginning at the arranged time. If we do not, we arrive at a situation where most people reason, "There's no point in getting there on time; we always begin late." This can be off-putting for the stranger or visitor who invariably arrives in good time, and who feels self-conscious for apparently being early. As church leaders we must set the pattern. Ideally we should be sitting in our place, ready to begin, a few moments before time. People should be able to check their watches by our punctuality. Once people know that meetings begin punctually, they respond accordingly.

We appreciate sharing the leadership of services with others, and when doing so we have been aware of the different ways in which people may climb a pulpit's steps or make their way onto the plat-form: Some almost run into it; others climb the steps two at a time; and others, although young, climb the steps as if they were ninety-nine! No doubt the manner and pace with which we approach the place from which we will preach says something about how we view our task. Our bearing unconsciously reflects our attitudes. Clearly we should be ourselves in such matters, but always with a keen sense of our awesome responsibility on the one hand and a sense of eagerness to fulfill it on the other. It is good to say to ourselves as we enter a pulpit or come to a platform, "I believe in the Holy Spirit," or "I can do everything through Him who gives me strength"—or some equivalent statement of our confidence in His help.

We may sometimes wonder if the common habit of pausing for prayer before standing up to begin, especially if we have already had prayer beforehand, is merely a piece of unthinking ritual. It can be, but it ought not to be the case. We can never remind ourselves too often of our dependence upon God, and it is good that others should recognize this truth by such habits. From time to time it may be good to suggest to the congregation, "Let's spend a moment in silent prayer together as we seek God's presence and the Holy Spirit's help."

Dress is a very personal matter. In certain traditions the wearing of a surplice or gown means that dress is largely taken care of, but for others of us it is not. The way we dress should reflect our sense of privilege at being Jesus Christ's representatives. Although He does not look upon outward appearance but upon our hearts, we know that the world at large expects important occasions to be handled with dignity, and rightly or wrongly, they may come to conclusions about our respect for God by the way we dress. We should be clean, smart, and yet unspectacular in our appearance and clothing when we are in the public eye, so that we do not draw attention away from the worship of God and careful listening to His Word to ourselves.

AB I have raised the hackles of some by introducing a policy of no facial hair for members of my pastoral team. The reason is quite simple: To ensure that we are "clean, smart and unspectacular." It is the only way that I can ensure that we will be saved from a variety of handlebar moustaches, goatees, and bushy beards in which birds might safely nest. The fact that this would have excluded Spurgeon and many others from our pastoral team causes me no loss of sleep! This paragraph will be an eye-opener to many readers who have long since ceased to give any consideration to such matters. Dressing down has become so prevalent that it probably never crosses the minds of many that we are conveying something by our mode of dress.

⁂

We should aim at naturalness in the manner in which we speak in public. The voice we use in the pulpit should be the same voice we use out of it. We ourselves may be unaware of any difference. It is wise to ask someone whose honesty we can rely upon to tell us if our voice and its whole tone differ in public speech from how they are in private. This may be especially the case in public prayer. We may not notice it readily in ourselves, but if we reflect upon our listening to others we will be aware in some cases of a definite "leading others in prayer" voice. There will always be some difference between our voice in conversation and our voice raised and projected in order to make what we say clearly heard, but it is the artificial or assumed voice we must avoid—the ecclesiastical tone that can be so easily caricatured.

Some voices are easier to listen to than others. What we say may be as well prepared and worthwhile as what someone else says, but not so effectively conveyed because of our voice. Having said this, we recognize the sovereignty of God the Holy Spirit who can use us in spite of all our weaknesses. But where we can help ourselves to be better communicators, then obviously we should. If our voice tends to be monotonous, one aid is to change the pace at which we speak. A voice, no matter how attractive, if it never changes its pace soon makes what it says seem boring.

The best way to change pace is to be guided by our material. If dealing with narrative, we should let the narrative influence our speed of speech—where things happen quickly, then we should tell them more quickly. If there is an element of excitement, our voice should reflect it. But all our material is open to this approach. If a matter is urgent, then we may help convey this to our hearers by increasing the pace at which we speak. If it is solemn, then we may slow down our pace, providing we do not stay slow too long. If the theme is joy, then we may reflect that joy in our voice and sense of excitement. The most common fault is dropping the voice, so that words and sentences are not heard by all, and this becomes a great disincentive to attentive hearing.

SOME CONSTITUENT
PARTS OF PUBLIC WORSHIP

Church traditions influence the inclusion, prominence, or lack of prominence we give to the different parts of public worship. Those who claim they have no pattern follow some pattern, even if it is that of no pattern at all! There has been a reaction, some of it justifiable, to what is derogatorily known as a "hymn-prayer" sandwich. We shrink from using such a phrase, because by it we may confuse form with formality, and be judgmental when really we ought to be discerning God's presence among His people. What matters is not whether a hymn happens to both follow and precede a prayer, but whether or not those who worship are doing so in spirit and in truth.

A completely unstructured form of public worship is no more guaranteed to be guided by the Holy Spirit than a structured one. Whatever tradition we belong to, and whatever convictions we have, the crucial issue is that our worship, in all its parts, should be acceptable to God rather than to us, and therefore in spirit and in truth (John 4:23–24).

The Invitation to Worship

Many worship services begin with "an invitation to worship" or "a call to worship" through the reading of a verse or two of Scripture. We warm to this, providing, as always, that it is not simply unthinking routine. Few if any of God's people will feel that they have prepared themselves as much as they would have wished for worshipping God and hearing His Word. Many will come with pre-occupations and anxieties that they cannot easily shake off. The purpose of the opening sentences of a service is to focus attention upon God Himself—either upon all that He is, and wants to be to us, or upon what He requires of us as we approach Him. These verses need to be chosen thoughtfully. The more important we appreciate them to be, the more likely it is that God the Holy Spirit will graciously use them for the ends we have in view. We may choose a verse that is appropriate to the opening praise we are about to sing, or to the theme of the service as it proceeds and culminates in the preaching of the Word. We may choose a verse upon which our opening prayer of praise and worship can be based.

We would recommend collecting suitable verses—perhaps a hundred or more—so that a different choice may be made for every service throughout a year—with the list being added to as appropriate verses are discovered. There needs to be variety in the verses we use so that we sometimes take God's people by surprise in using unfamiliar verses that provoke thought on that account. Using a small loose-leaf book both for our preaching notes and our notes for the conduct of a service, we have the verse for the beginning of the service typed out on a single sheet for the front page. We will not always use it, since in the time of prayer before the service another verse may be quoted or come to mind that takes precedence. To change that verse may be vitally important for some unknown person in the congregation.

DP One evening after the time of prayer in the vestry I looked again at the verse I had chosen for the service. Having a few minutes to spare I quietly read the Scriptures and found another verse staring me in the face that seemed especially meaningful, and so I decided to use it.

Later that evening when I was home the phone rang. The person would not give his name. "Can you tell me, please, why you began the service with those words this evening?" I told him, and then asked, "Why?" He explained that years before God had used that verse to speak to him, and having wandered away from God, and coming to church apparently by chance, he had been arrested by God as the first words he heard were this verse of Scripture. He knew it was more than a coincidence.

Hymns, Psalms, and Spiritual Songs

The choice of hymns, psalms, and spiritual songs is usually left to whoever is leading worship and then preaching. That is appropriate, since a service should be regarded as an entity, and the Holy Spirit uses praise and preaching to complement each other in focusing upon aspects of God's character, Jesus Christ's glory, and particular truth He wants God's people to understand. Where the leadership of the service is shared, there should be prayerful consultation so that there are reasons behind what is sung at different stages.

Usually the opening hymn, psalm, or song should be one of worship and praise, so that people are helped from the beginning to be aware of God and to be exercising their souls in their unique capacity of appreciating God Himself. The current trend in praise, which begins with our thoughts and feelings, needs to be challenged for the good of the congregation and for the sake of God's glory.

The singing before the preaching of the Word should prepare God's people to listen to Him and express their submission and delight in His will. The closing hymn should apply the Word of God that has been taught and preached, whether in praise, thanksgiving, or obedience. If possible, other hymns and songs should relate to the theme that the ministry of the Word is to follow or to the known needs of the congregation.

Those who assist in services from time to time may be inclined to choose their favorite hymns, psalms, and songs, but we should avoid doing this by exploring thoroughly the whole of a book, so far as we feel the hymns and songs are appropriate. The simplest method is to keep one copy of each for writing in the dates upon which we sing the different hymns and songs. This should not rule out repeating something soon after it has been used if especially apt, but it should preclude unhelpful repetition when other less-sung hymns and songs are equally appropriate. As we set about our sermon preparation, we jot down any thoughts that occur about suitable hymns, psalms, or songs. We usually find we have more than we need, and we then make our selection in the light of which of them have not been recently sung.

If hymn numbers are announced it helps if we give the number twice rather than just once, since within every fellowship some are hard of hearing, and if we are in a place for the first time people will be unaccustomed to our voice. Following upon the announcement of the number, the first line or two should be read in a meaningful way. It adds little to a service to announce a hymn number and to say, "How sweet the name . . ." but it says a lot to Christians when we read the sentence "How sweet the name of Jesus sounds in a believer's ear." It becomes tedious if the whole of the first verse of every hymn and song is read. What is always helpful is reading out the first words in a manner that makes complete sense: If to make sense the whole verse needs to be read, that is acceptable, but it will be the exception. If something we sing is chosen because of the words of a verse other than the first, we may help the congregation to benefit from it by drawing attention to that verse rather than reading out words from its first verse.

We should never forget that no matter how much we might wish it otherwise, we are the natural focus of people's visual attention. When we announce a hymn, psalm, or song, we should set a good example of entering wholeheartedly into whatever is sung, concentrating upon the words, and recognizing that if we mean what we sing we are talking first to God, and then to one another to encourage and to stimulate spiritual growth. An indication of shallow worship is using singing as an excuse for other things, whether it is to slip in late or to leave early, or to put on the coffee for whatever is going to follow the service. When singing is spiritual, it is as important an exercise as prayer—and for the most part it *is* prayer, only sung rather than spoken.

The Public Reading of Scripture

Paul's instruction to Timothy holds good: "Devote yourself to the public reading of Scripture, to preaching and to teaching" (1 Timothy 4:13). Our experience may not be typical, but we are sometimes aware as we travel around that people do not feel this to be important. We have been in meetings where no provision has been made for it, and it has simply been assumed that the preacher will announce his text and preach without any previous reading of the Bible book in which his text or passage is found. Although we would not advocate its practice, since any habit may become routine, we have been glad to worship with God's people in different parts of the world where everyone stands for the reading of the Bible. It draws attention to its importance and the privilege of possessing it.

The public reading of Scripture is a part of a service where others can be easily brought in to contribute. But in doing so, we should not fail them or the congregation by neglecting to give simple yet important instruction. Where in the Bible the reading is from should, like the hymn numbers, be announced plainly and repeated, since not all will catch it the first time. A slight pause should follow so that people may be able to find the place themselves if they wish to follow the reading, a practice to be commended. If the reading is from a version different from that which the majority use, it is a matter of courtesy that this should be announced so that people are not confused.

Public readers of Scripture should be helped to read a passage through carefully beforehand and to understand what it is all about, so that in the public reading the proper sense is given. They should be encouraged to read with dignity and with enthusiasm. It is helpful to discuss what people should say at the conclusion of the reading, since well-known words like "The Lord bless to us the reading of His holy Word, and to His name be glory and praise" may lose their force because they are so familiar. Sometimes it may be appropriate to say nothing.

We would always plan to ask those who are going to read the Scriptures to join the elders or spiritual leadership for their time of prayer before a service. Prayer can then be offered together that God will use the public reading of His Word to speak to His people and to prepare them for instruction from it.

We should rebuke ourselves and correct our attitude if we ever feel we are only asking someone to read the Scriptures. An incident described in the biography of Bishop Taylor Smith illustrates this. During his training for the ministry, he was sent to assist in a mission at an Islington church. "He said that he was so nervous that before the service he spent an hour in prayer seeking God's aid in the duties he would be called upon to perform. When he got to the church he found that all that he was required to do was to read the lessons! On the following Wednesday, however, the vicar wrote to him to the effect that during the reading of the second lesson (it happened to be Romans viii) his church-warden (a man who had been a church-warden for years) was converted."[1]

Announcements or Notices

Notices or announcements form part of practically every coming together of God's people, whether under the name of notices or announcements. An alternative is to put them into written form and place them in people's hands as they arrive, but invariably people want some emphasized or others may have been forgotten for inclusion. A gracious ruthlessness is required of whoever gives them out to keep them within bounds, and that person needs the support of discerning folk if the object is to be achieved of avoiding unnecessary distraction.

While they can be given at the start of a service so that they are over with, they do not provide the best way to begin a time of worship and waiting upon God. If they are put at the end of the service, they may distract from what has been said. Put in the middle they can interrupt the flow of a service. However, people do need to know what is going on, and provision must be made for this.

Providing the week's basic program is in everyone's hands, and whoever gives the announcements simply draws attention to changes or special events, the notices become more spiritually beneficial if they relate more to the circumstances of individuals within the fellowship than to regular organized functions. Everyone knows that the young people meet on Wednesday, and the young wives on Tuesday; but few may know about the member going into the hospital, or the family spending their last Sunday in the fellowship before moving because of a change of job, or the couple who have just gotten engaged, or the missionary members who have arrived safely back in Africa after their furlough. As churches grow, it becomes more difficult for each member to know every other member, and even more difficult to be acquainted with their needs in order to pray for them intelligently. But announcements that are alive to the present circumstances of the membership do much to foster that family spirit that is so essential and becoming to a church—and people listen to notices like this!

Public Prayer

Preparing ourselves to lead publicly in prayer is as important as preaching, and is much more revealing of our spiritual freshness.

To avoid the snare of just saying words rather than genuinely praying requires watchfulness.

Our own conviction is that the first prayer should usually be an expression of worship, a confession of need, and a desire for God's presence. Other elements may be included, and those already mentioned do not need to be always present or in a particular order. But, remembering that we were created originally for God, and re-created by Him in Christ for His praise, this high privilege of appreciating God and worshipping Him should be a primary element.

Nothing warms God's people's hearts more than being led in heartfelt praise and worship of God through His Son, Jesus Christ. Inevitably some—if not all—will be aware of their unworthiness and sinfulness in varying degrees. A few will feel themselves such desperate failures that they will find it hard to believe that God will receive them. Bearing them and ourselves in mind, we should consciously approach God's throne as a throne of grace, and enter into His promises of forgiveness. If this is not done at the commencement of a service, some may struggle throughout it to be aware of their acceptance by God and the relevance to them of all that is said and done. While God's presence with us does not depend upon our feelings, the greatest blessing God can give His people is the awareness that He is with them. Our privilege is to express the longings of God's people after that experience.

The second prayer in a service tends to be one of intercession, and that is entirely right. Unworthy as we may often feel to pray for ourselves, it is our duty always to be praying for others, beginning with those in authority over us (1 Timothy 2:1–4). The power of public prayer is when it really is corporate prayer, when the prayer of the one leading becomes the prayer of all, to which they add their secret, and preferably audible, "Amen."

Intelligent involvement in public prayer is aided immeasurably if we intimate subjects or people beforehand for whom we are going to pray, perhaps giving the briefest snatches of news or information that explain how and why we should pray for them. If the notices or announcements precede the intercessory prayer, and include up-to-date news of the fellowship, some of the intercession naturally flows from that. Prayer becomes more meaningful and specific when it is anchored to individuals and real situations.

DP One experience of this lives with me. Early on in my ministry while on holiday I went to a well-known church with an equally well-known minister. Although we arrived early, we could not get into the main church sanctuary but had to sit in an overflow hall, and I never caught sight of the preacher. It was before the days of closed-circuit television, and so we could hear but not see.

What I remember most was the manner in which the minister preceded his intercessory prayer by mentioning the distressing circumstances of someone in the fellowship who had asked for the congregation's prayers. In a few sentences he described how he believed we should pray. Although I had never met the person, I found myself identifying with that individual with feeling and sympathy as the minister prayed, and I sensed the whole congregation's similar involvement. That prayer alone benefited me and gave me a delightful awareness of belonging to God's family.

Variety in the matters and subjects for which we pray is vital. Our praying in public must not be limited to immediate and urgent needs, but should include spiritual priorities like the growth of the fruit of the Spirit, practical holiness and evangelism, and moral priorities such as justice, righteousness, and social concern.

DP My own practice has been to build up 104 envelopes—two for each week of the year—in which I place outline prayers on hundreds of subjects, usually jottings from Scripture relating to them. Some have arisen from my preparation for preaching on certain subjects, and others in the course of my reading. I carefully choose four for each period of intercessory prayer. They will be entirely different from the four chosen the previous week. I never feel bound to use them once I have selected them, as some other subject may come to the fore before the service begins. But if not, then I am helped by the preparation I have already made. If in the course of the week a passage of Scripture forces itself upon my attention, I will often jot down the kind of prayer it calls forth, so that I may preserve it while it is fresh, and use it the following Sunday if it comes to me with the same force, as is often the case. Such a discipline helps to avoid getting into a rut in the language we use, with our prayers becoming predictable and ceasing to have the essential ring of truth and reality. Although not our primary purpose, our public prayers should teach people to pray, and how to pray.

AB While not adopting the 104-envelope approach, I nevertheless have endeavored to reach the goal of freshness, clarity, and reality by my own circuitous route. As I mentioned earlier I am continually helped by reading the prayers of godly men and women and learning from them how to approach God with bold humility.

To appear critical of the language we use in public prayer is a delicate issue. God looks upon our hearts, and what our hearts feel is more important than the verbal expression of our feelings and desires. But that having been said, we must ensure that the language of our prayers is as helpful to people as possible, and that it does not get in the way.

If we lead in extemporary prayer only occasionally, our language is not as important as it is when we regularly do so. There are obvious snares to avoid. We must be consistent in the manner in which we address God, whether we use "You" and "Yours" or "Thou" and "Thine." We should use the kind of language we are convinced is right for us, but it is unhelpful if we continually switch between the two as if we have not made up our mind which is appropriate.

Old-fashioned language and clichés should be avoided. Have you noticed how often in public prayer we may say "this day" or "this night" rather than "today" or "tonight"? And what of that repetitive word "just"? "We just want to ask . . ." Similarly, we may keep on saying within our prayer, "We pray . . ." when it is obvious that we are praying!

It is particularly unhelpful to pray about God rather than praying to Him. For example, having begun to address God in prayer, someone may say, "We pray that God will be honored, and that His voice will be heard." Now that is not prayer to God but words addressed to the congregation. If we are truly aware that we are talking to God, we will say, "May You be honored, and may Your voice be heard," and we do not need to preface that request with the words "We pray that . . ." since we are praying! This habit of suddenly not addressing our prayers to God is one that some fall into without being aware of it, and perhaps no one has the courage to mention it, with the consequence that it becomes a lifelong habit.

Each part of a service or coming together of God's people should be a means of grace. Every part may bring God's Word to those who wait upon Him—through what is sung, prayed, read, said, taught, and preached. It is an exciting exercise to prepare for a service throughout the whole of the preceding week. A Bible reading may provide suitable words with which to give an invitation to worship or prompt the kind of desires that should be expressed in prayer.

A letter from a missionary or a newsflash about the country in which he works may fuel intelligent prayer. A pastoral visit to someone unemployed will prompt intercession for all who are unemployed and will bring forth prayers of earnest assent from those who have unemployed friends.

The best way to prepare for any share we may have in the leadership of God's people in worship, prayer, and teaching is to prepare ourselves and to give priority to our private walk with God. The members of the congregation Robert Murray M'Cheyne served were stirred to comment upon their awareness that in ministering to them he had come straight from the presence of God.

CHAPTER 11

THE RESPONSIBILITY
TO LEAD

Shepherds of Christ's flock are to lead His flock. Leadership is a responsibility entrusted to all who shepherd and teach His people. Too often the leadership aspect of our responsibilities has been played down, with unhappy consequences. A report commissioned by the Church of England in the twentieth century, entitled *Towards the Conversion of England,* drew attention in its first pages to its conclusion concerning leadership: "Conditions . . . vary from parish to parish: the determining factor being, apparently, the personality of the incumbent. More particularly is this the case in villages, where a spiritual leader can often make an astonishing difference."[1] Although much has changed since then, the strategic necessity for leadership has not. The Church of Jesus Christ does not progress beyond the spiritual progress of its leaders.

Every team has its captain, or equivalent. Although each member is equally important, someone has to lead. Without a captain, a team loses direction and discipline; without a leader or conductor an orchestra forfeits coordination and harmony. So it is with

God's people. The three years our Lord Jesus Christ was with His disciples, He was their leader. As soon as He ascended to heaven, Peter became the obvious leader of the apostles. He and his fellow apostles then appointed leaders in all the churches they planted. The apostle Paul made it plain to Titus that things were not in order in a church without proper leadership being established (Titus 1:5). Without good leadership, chaos so easily follows. Most unsolved problems in church life can be traced back to defective leadership.

LEADERSHIP—BOTH A GIFT AND A CALLING

Leadership, like other gifts of the Spirit, is for the edifying of the body of Christ. It is not presumptuous, therefore, to feel the desire to lead if we are called to it. The two words that sum up our function in the body—shepherds and teachers—both imply the leadership function. A shepherd's task is to lead his sheep, whether into green pastures or to safety when danger threatens. At every moment he is to be ready to take initiative for the sheep's good. A teacher's responsibility is to lead by the instruction he provides. Christian teachers are directive in their approach because their task is not to put forward their own ideas but "the very words of God" (1 Peter 4:11).

Leadership in the church should always be shared—that is one reason that the apostolic pattern was to appoint a plurality of elders rather than a solitary elder in all the churches (Acts 14:23). But leaders too need to recognize one of their number as leader. This is an inbuilt principle of life, and we should not despise it. Husband and wife are equal, but leadership naturally rests with the husband. Children are equal in a family, but the oldest is looked to first when a crisis occurs. In some situations there may be one elder or spiritual leader who is actually called "the pastor," who will be expected to lead his fellow leaders; and in others there will be a team ministry. But in every team there has to be a leader.

Even if the leaders try to avoid calling one of their number the team leader, someone will inevitably come to the fore, or will be regarded by the church fellowship as the leader among the leaders. It is better that the leaders should choose their "team leader" rather than simply let it happen. The latter may lead to misunderstandings and difficulties in relationships. One answer is to distinguish the different functions and responsibilities of the leaders, but even so a chairman or coordinator is required if they are to function effectively. To try to avoid leadership, and a leader among leaders, is to avoid not only a fact of life but a spiritual principle.

The New Testament sets a high value upon leadership. A generally accepted truth of the early Church—perhaps even a proverb —related to it: "Here is a trustworthy saying: If anyone sets his heart on being an overseer, he desires a noble task" (1 Timothy 3:1). This saying may have been submitted to Paul for his comment, and he responded by commending it as good and acceptable. Paul's exhortation in Romans 12 that if an individual's gift is leadership he should "govern diligently" (verse 8) implies the temptation to shrink sometimes from the exercise of leadership because of its demanding nature.

We must not be afraid of leadership as if it were somehow or other not really Christian to want to lead. Christian leadership models itself upon our Lord Jesus Christ. One of the paradoxes of His ministry was that although He was so obviously the leader, He was conspicuously the servant. He illustrated and underlined this truth when He washed the disciples' feet (John 13). We are spiritually effective as leaders as we follow His example. Although leaders, we are first and foremost servants. Genuine Christian leadership is not status-oriented. It is helpful to think of shepherding and teaching as functions rather than offices. While Paul knew Timothy to be a shepherd and teacher, he deliberately referred to him as a servant of whom a particular pattern of conduct was required: "The Lord's servant must not quarrel; instead, he must be kind to everyone, able to teach, not resentful" (2 Timothy 2:24).

Christian leadership, modeled upon Christ's, is leadership by example. "Being examples to the flock" is where Peter lays the stress in writing to the church leaders of Asia Minor (1 Peter 5:3). This is the opposite of lording it over people, and of telling them what they should do, without first leading the way by personal example.

Our example as leaders must begin with our own families and homes, for if we fall down there we fail to provide the most telling example of godliness (1 Timothy 3:4, 12). Christian leadership, unlike leadership in some other spheres, demands humility (Acts 20:19) and the kind of gentleness that characterizes mothers and fathers with their children (1 Thessalonians 2:7, 11). Our Lord's example in these respects wrote itself upon the minds of His disciples (cf. John 13:12–17; 1 Peter 5:5). Christian leaders ought to be able to say: "Whatever you have learned or received or heard from me, or seen in me—put it into practice" (Philippians 4:9) and "Follow my example, as I follow the example of Christ" (1 Corinthians 11:1).

THE PRACTICE OF LEADERSHIP

Leadership skills need developing, like all gifts and abilities. They grow by exercise, and particularly by our willingness to learn from Scripture, from the example and instruction of others, and from our mistakes. We lead all the time—and for the most part unconsciously—by our character. This happens in every sphere.

For a while we could not make out what had happened to the atmosphere in a bank. To begin with the staff seemed happy and cooperative, but their interest in their customers and their general helpfulness visibly diminished. We then discovered that a new manager had taken over, who proved somewhat discourteous and offhand with his customers. Our hunch was that this unconsciously rubbed itself off onto his staff. We have noticed how an enthusiastic and generous-spirited restaurant proprietor finds his own attitudes reflected in the warm and energetic approach of his staff. So it is in a church fellowship. If we do not look for praise from people, but from God, so will our people (1 Thessalonians 2:6). If we are undemanding of those whom we serve, but rather show we are prepared to be completely spent in serving people (2 Corinthians 12:14–15), others will follow. If we lead without partiality and favoritism (1 Timothy 5:21), many will see its wisdom.

When tempted to be disappointed at the attitudes of those for whom we have responsibility, we must be prepared to ask ourselves if they mirror at all our own unconscious attitudes. Admittedly, it takes time for people to follow an example, and that example must be utterly consistent, but its importance must not be minimized or ignored.

We lead by our capacity to make decisions. As leaders, we cannot avoid decision making, whether in the personal exercise of our duties or when we meet with others to discern the mind of Christ. Some find decision making difficult and are regular waverers; but leaders must not be. The leader must not be a person who says yes and no at the same time. When he says either yes or no, he must mean what he says, having carefully thought out his response (2 Corinthians 1:17). This may mean we defer giving an immediate answer when asked for our opinion or guidance, in order to pray and think the matter, through. God's Spirit may give an immediate insight into the matter; but He is equally likely to provide it as we wait upon God so that we grasp the reasons behind the insight that will be useful in the future. We must know our own mind, and how we believe God would have us think on important matters.

If we find ourselves hesitant in decision making—and we have in mind only those situations where we are plainly called to make decisions—we must take ourselves in hand. First, we must establish all the issues that need to be weighed. One satisfactory way of doing this is to write them down. Then we must determine which factors have priority or can be discarded. As we do this, sharing both the process and our conclusions with God in prayer, we will find proper convictions developing.

We lead by our drive and enthusiasm. We are not suggesting

that leaders should put on a false show of enthusiasm. Such quickly wears thin and will undermine confidence. Having decided that a course of action is right—and only then—we must show our whole-hearted commitment to it. It is too easy to drift into an evangelistic program or another new church program without genuine conviction. It is not surprising that we then lack drive and that our enthusiasm rings hollow. Better to be completely honest at the start about our hesitance than to engage in halfhearted enterprises.

Leaders must lead and not be led by their desire to please those who want the church to undertake activities of which the leadership is not completely assured. True enthusiasm comes from being filled with the Spirit, and as we strive to do that to which we know God has called us, in conscious dependence upon Him, we will then be able to convey our excitement to others and carry them with us. But successful drive and enthusiasm means only doing the things we are convinced are God's will for His people.

We lead by our readiness to accept responsibility. Some naturally shirk it since it is contrary to their nature and temperament. But leaders do not shrink from it—they thrive on it! That is not to say that they do not feel its weight, but they rise to its challenges and automatically think of ways of achieving their assignments. One responsibility usually leads to another. As we prove ourselves in one sphere, we invariably find it equips us for another.

We lead by our ability to convey a vision. Leaders must be forward looking. Although others within a church fellowship may be quite content with things as they are, leaders must be constantly seeking God's way forward. As leaders pray together, and particularly as they are confronted with practical or spiritual needs, their response will often be a new initiative—it may be a building extension, requiring large capital expenditure, or it may be a new evangelistic enterprise. Part of their spiritual leadership at this stage will be to think the whole project through in exhaustive detail, so that they may convey it to the church fellowship with such conviction that the church will be united in wanting to put it into action.

We lead by knowing what has to be done, when it should be done, and how it should be done. It is not enough simply to be ideas people, although that is part of leadership. Spiritual leaders should have an overall picture of the spiritual state of the church fellowship and its immediate and long-term priorities. Placing on the agenda of every meeting of spiritual leaders the question, "What is the spiritual state of the fellowship?" provokes thought and highlights shortcomings. Leadership is seen then in asking, "How do we meet this need? How and when should we implement our convictions? Who among us in the fellowship should be involved? Who will set these plans into motion?" We should plan with wisdom and act firmly and decisively. The cultivation of a right sense of timing is part of wise leadership since "there is a time for everything, and a season for every activity under heaven: . . . a time to tear down and a time to build" (Ecclesiastes 3:1, 3). To rush into a project at the wrong time may jeopardize eventual progress and ruin a necessary initiative.

We lead by the exercise of faith and the proper optimism it produces. All Christians exercise faith, and some more than others. Christian leaders will be given a particular capacity to trust God so that they may lead God's people forward into new obedience and enterprise. Pretended faith offends both God and His people, and we should never profess a confidence we do not possess. Those whom we lead have a right to expect us to lead by the faith God graciously gives us. The active practice of faith cannot be separated from large views of our Lord Jesus Christ, and leaders should provoke one another, and then God's people in general, to an ever-greater appreciation of the person of Christ. The writer to the Hebrews links leadership with the example of faith when he urges his readers: "Remember your leaders, who spoke the word of God to you. Consider the outcome of their way of life and imitate their faith" (13:7). Hopefully God's people will not have to wait until we have died to imitate our faith!

We lead by keeping our head in all situations (2 Timothy 4:5).

All church fellowships go through periods of difficulty. Various assaults of Satan, or practical issues like depleted numbers through the movement of population or the redevelopment of an area, will prompt some to imagine that everything is going wrong, and they will panic. Such reactions put spiritual leaders under pressure, and they will not be immune from imagining the worst possible consequences and seeing all kinds of potential dangers. But spiritual leaders must not overreact. Rather they must fix their sights on what is right rather than what seems expedient. They must aim to steer a straight course, whatever is happening around them. Difficulties—like storms—pass. The church—like a ship in a storm—has passed through such before and survived. The only real danger is in abandoning the ship when there is no need to do so.

We lead by recognizing that there are occasions when we must positively exert ourselves to lead. When people panic, we must be quick to give reassurance and provide good reasons for not doing so. When the church flounders in its mission, we must stir ourselves up to show the way in which she may remedy failures. Much leadership is low-key and almost unconsciously exercised, but there are vital moments when we need to say to ourselves, "God's people require leadership at this point, and I must clearly provide it because it is to this that God has called me." There will also be occasions when we will need to exert ourselves in our leadership of those who share leadership with us.

AREAS OF LEADERSHIP

We should lead through teaching. Aptness to teach is essential to leadership (1 Timothy 3:2). Our teaching function enables us to exercise constant leadership, a leadership of which people may be scarcely aware at times. If we expound and apply the Scriptures, we urge God's people, beginning with ourselves, to live lives worthy of God who has called us into His kingdom (1 Thessalonians 2:12).

DP I can recall times when the regular and systematic teaching of the Scriptures has been the best and most effective means of leadership. In a period of debate and confusion concerning spiritual gifts, it was timely and rewarding to study the whole of 1 Corinthians, and to see the discussion of spiritual gifts in their context, and not least the context of love in 1 Corinthians 13. We were faced at one stage with a mammoth building redevelopment, which was going to prove extremely costly and demanding of our faith. The best preparation was a study of the book of Ezra, and that quickened faith and obedience.

Our leadership in teaching is not to be limited to our public ministry, but is to extend to all the situations in which leadership may be required. When an issue has been raised in a church meeting, it may be appropriate to say, "Before we discuss this topic further, let's remind ourselves of the principles the Bible says we should apply to this subject." In a pastoral visit, we may sense that people have lost their way in a matter about which the Scriptures are clear. Without embarrassment we must be quick to suggest, "Let's look at what the Scriptures say about it." If we do not take such initiative, it is unlikely that others will.

We should lead through our conduct of corporate worship. The encouragement of others to share in its conduct should always be at the initiative of the appointed undershepherds and under their direction. We lead by taking great care about our own example in leading worship, whether in the choice and expression of praise to God, the offering of prayer, or the reading of Scripture. The kind of preparation we give to it—and not least the spiritual preparation—soon reflects itself in the attitude and behavior of others.

When we first ask individuals to assist, we serve them and others best by providing clear guidelines as to the proper approach to their assigned task. We do well to suggest that we will not hesitate to mention afterward anything that it will be good for them to bear in mind when they have another opportunity. The purpose of all spiritual gifts is the edifying of the whole body, and never the selfish enjoyment a person may have in exercising a gift: Whoever leads the worship of God's people, therefore, must not function according to his personal preferences but by what he knows will benefit all the members of the body.

As undershepherds, we must lead in constantly reminding the flock that worship is not confined to the expression of praise through singing, or even praise and prayer, but rather it is the offering of ourselves to God in daily obedience (Romans 12:1), and that only then is our more public worship acceptable to God.

There is much for which to thank God in the Church's renewed appreciation of worship, although discernment is needed here as elsewhere. It is not always easy to recognize what is merely a matter of personal taste—and capable, therefore, of being changed—and what is fundamental to worship and should, therefore, be unaltered. We should encourage people to test every contribution by its God-centeredness and its ability to edify, and for all to learn to see debatable issues from other people's point of view. In our own conduct of worship, we may engage in an educative process by explaining sometimes the reasons for our choice of hymns and songs, and by indicating the principles the Scriptures establish about spiritual worship. The most vital truth we must convey is that what is important is not how acceptable our worship is to ourselves or to others, but how acceptable it is to God—a priority sometimes forgotten.

We should lead through the importance we attach to prayer. The apostles set an example to the early Church and us in their determination to delegate administrative responsibilities in order to give themselves to prayer (Acts 6:4). The busyness that characterizes the typical undershepherd and teacher threatens prayerfulness and at the same time indicates its priority. Only God and we ourselves know the place we give to private prayer. We have considered that earlier, and its vital importance cannot be overstated. The source of our failures is most often there. But having established the priority of prayer in secret—which is part of our hidden leadership of God's people—we are to give the lead through prayer in other ways. It is not just a good habit to precede and conclude an interview or a committee meeting with prayer. By such means we carefully remind ourselves of our dependence upon God and His wisdom. We lift conversation out of the realm of mere talking into the realm of being in God's presence and discerning His will.

As often as church leaders meet for "business," they should meet for prayer. Prayer is their business. It is possible to link the two activities by dividing a meeting into two, with one half for prayer and the other for business. But so often the business takes over. A separate evening reserved for prayer ensures its proper priority. Whatever the agenda, it is good to spend time in prayer at the beginning of every meeting for business.

Reflecting over many elders' and deacons' meetings, we are convinced that the more time we gladly devoted to prayer, the less time we needed to spend over our business. Any endeavor to cut down on prayer at the beginning, because of the pressure of getting on with the matters before us, served only to make the business more difficult to complete. It is not surprising that such should be the case. Whether in a general church meeting or a leaders' meeting, when a difficult matter is under discussion, and perhaps there is the possibility of its getting out of hand, we do well to call for a pause to devote time to prayer there and then before proceeding further. Prayer not only sweetens attitudes, but it brings the guidance asked for.

We should lead through pastoral initiatives. It is unwise simply to wait until pastoral needs are brought before us; we must try as leaders to anticipate them. For example, all parents begin with no experience of parenthood. The instruction of new parents is an obvious provision that needs to be made, perhaps on an annual or twice-yearly basis.

When we become aware of differences between Christians or between a husband and wife, we must not hesitate to take action, remembering that God has called us to be their undershepherds. Some of these situations are extremely difficult to approach, but their difficulty underlines their importance and the satisfaction of seeing their proper resolution. The longer they are left unattended, the more likely it is that they will be unresolved. George Whitefield wrote in his diary on Friday, January 20, 1738, "Spent all the morning in composing a sermon. Happily composed a difference between a soldier and his wife, who were one of the four couples I married when first I came on board. The man had resolved to leave her, but upon my reminding him of his marriage vow, and entreating him with love, he immediately took to her again. What may not a minister do through Christ when his flock love him?" Our initiative may be to ask someone else to make a pastoral visit or to follow up a call we have made.

Sometimes our difficult leadership task may be to take initiative in church discipline. Church discipline is neither popular nor a common practice in the church, and this is to be regretted. Its absence indicates that people have lost sight of the love and tenderness that is always to be behind it and of its necessity if those who err are to be restored. If church leaders are not clear about church discipline and how it should be exercised, then church members will certainly not. Church discipline can be set in motion properly only when the procedure for it has been established beforehand and explained to the church fellowship. If it is merely put together at the time, it is likely to be drawn up hastily and to be misunderstood. Wise leadership prepares beforehand.

We should lead by evangelistic concern and endeavor. A church fellowship should be outward looking rather than inward. To care for the flock is not enough; those other sheep whom the Chief

Shepherd wants added to it are to be sought and found. Evange-lism should be on the agenda of every regular meeting of spiritual overseers, whether to review what is being done or to respond to new opportunities for outreach. They should lead from the front by striving to set an example in personal evangelism and by involving themselves in all church outreach endeavors.

> **DP** An example may help. I do not find door-to-door visi-tation easy in prospect, although once I engage in it I en-joy it. Our regular monthly visitation of homes near the church was on the same evening as our church prayer meeting so that prayer could be focused upon the visits as they were made, and then reported upon. To encourage people to join the visitation team, I realized that I needed to be a member myself. This meant that if it was my turn to lead the prayer meeting, I asked someone else to do it. It also gave me an opportunity to fellowship with another church member in making the visit, and to get the feel of the neighborhood and the response to our visits. Review-ing that work, far more people joined in with enthusiasm when the elders personally involved themselves in it than when they did not.

If we lead others in public prayer, we have the opportunity of praying thoughtfully and intelligently for those who are still with-out Christ and of crying to God for His help in fulfilling our re-sponsibility to them. This is all part of our leadership of the flock.

We should lead by wise and able chairmanship. Chairmanship inevitably falls to undershepherds. Where a Christian fellowship calls one person to be "the pastor" or "the minister" it tends to be his task. It does not have to be the case, as others may be more gifted for it. But it is understandable that because a pastor is someone whom God's people trust—they would not have recognized his call otherwise—they should consider him an obvious person.

A pastor's responsibility for chairing meetings—especially of those who share leadership with him—is somewhat different from ordinary chairmanship. Usually the task of a good chairman is to order the discussion of others, to keep people to the point, and to ensure that everyone who wants or ought to contribute does so. Ideally he keeps himself and his own ideas out of the picture as much as possible. This remains an ideal for a pastor, but there is a difference. Although being the chairman, he remains a pastor, and a leader among leaders. In chairing the meeting he is keenly involved in all the matters discussed and has a pastoral concern for the usefulness of the meeting and the direction it should take. He will fail in his leadership if pastoral goals are not attained. He will have convictions about most of the matters under discussion, and if others do not raise them, he must not hesitate to raise them himself—but he will be wise to see if others do so first so that the initiative is preferably not always his. He must thoroughly prepare himself for the meeting beforehand in a way that anyone not chairing the meeting will seldom if ever do.

The success of elders' and deacons' meetings depends a great deal on our prior preparation, both in prayer and thought. A balance needs to be struck between being thoroughly prepared and going to the meeting with everything so cut and dried that there appears to be little point in discussion!

DP My own plan was to begin by writing down on a separate piece of paper each subject that I thought would be raised or that appeared on the agenda. If the composition of the agenda was left to me, I then juggled my pieces of paper around so that I had the topics in an order of priority. It is easy for important matters to be left to the end of a meeting, and then for there to be a mad rush to deal with them with too little time. Determining the priority order helped to avoid this, and it sometimes meant suggesting alterations in the draft agenda if prepared by the secretary. On each slip of paper, I then jotted down aspects of each subject that I felt ought to be discussed or at least mentioned if meaningful and intelligent decisions were to be made. That meant that when we came to some topics, I might begin our discussion by saying, "Having thought about this a little, I feel we ought to discuss the following aspects of the subject . . ." I might develop this by questions such as: "Does anyone have any views or convictions about it? Would someone like to start our discussion?" At the bottom of each sheet of paper, I wrote down my own convictions concerning the way in which the discussion should probably go. But I never began with them, and sometimes I did not need to mention them, either because others did, or because my mind was changed by what was said. It is particularly helpful to prepare in this way for a meeting when we anticipate a subject may be a touchy one or possibly divisive. We can then think beforehand of the appropriate Christian approach, and the emphasis to place at the beginning on the spirit in which the discussion must be carried out.

There is a world of difference between going to a leaders' meeting with our mind made up and knowing our own mind. It is doubtful if we should ever go with our mind made up, for that presupposes we will reject whatever else is suggested. Knowing our own mind means being clear as to our convictions and why we hold them. We may then share them coherently in a discussion, and at the same time we are willing to adjust our opinions and alter our convictions as fresh light is shed upon the subject through what others say.

THE RELATIONSHIP OF
LEADERS TO EACH OTHER

Leadership must be shared. Some have departed from this principle with disastrous consequences. A principal reason for shared leadership is that it keeps us under the discipline of others. If God's people need to be under discipline, so too do their leaders (cf. Acts 20:30). A leader among leaders must ensure that he is himself under the pastoral care of one or more of the other leaders. He is then in a position to feel a special pastoral responsibility for all who share leadership with him—it is his responsibility as no one else's.

We must try to know our fellow leaders well and not least on a spiritual and personal basis for mutual encouragement. We may often be surprised to discover that those who are so ready to discuss the personal and intimate problems of others may be slow to speak to one another of their own. When spiritual leaders pray together, it is valuable, on a frequent but irregular basis, to devote part of the time to sharing personal needs. Frank opening of the heart between leaders can be a tremendous encouragement and a means of lifting burdens from those who spend most of their time giving encouragement but not receiving it. Prayer, after such sharing, warms the heart and binds people together. If our fellow leaders are reluctant initially to share their personal and family needs, then we should take the initiative and do so, and this will help them to follow suit. Such openness to one another is yet another safeguard against the perils of professionalism to which we have made frequent reference.

As a general rule it is good to share as much as we can with our fellow leaders of the knowledge we have of the life and concerns of the church and its members. The only restriction is where to do so would be breaking a confidence. If in the course of our pastoral work we become aware that a crisis may be imminent or learn of some need for church discipline, the earlier we can share it with our fellow leaders the better, so that it does not take anyone by surprise and in order to marshal prayer for God's gracious deliverance.

Sometimes in conversation with a church member, it may be appropriate to say, "I would appreciate it if you would allow me to share this with the elders for their prayerful interest." Sometimes we may feel it necessary to say, "Although you have shared this with me, it is really a matter for the elders, and I am duty bound to share it with them." If we are to practice this kind of honest communication, it is of fundamental importance that the elders—or whatever title the leaders are called—maintain complete confidentiality. This is a principle we need to refer to frequently—first, because people sometimes forget its importance, and, second, because there are always fresh additions to the leadership.

This principle of confidentiality in all matters discussed by those in leadership needs to be firmly established. It ought not to be necessary to do it, but experience shows it is. If confidentiality is not practiced, the elders will not be prepared to share openly with one another about a domestic need or a problem at work. If confidentiality is not preserved, church members will hesitate to share personal matters with their undershepherds.

It is natural for a man to want to talk to his wife about matters of concern, but he must discipline himself to observe the principle of not revealing any details of confidential pastoral discussions in which he has been involved. There are exceptions, but the general rule is important. The kind of exception we think of is where husband and wife share in the pastoral care of a couple, or where a wife may be involved in the counseling of a woman in her husband's pastoral group. In such circumstances he would be right to share with his wife—with his fellow leaders' approval—the convictions they have about such a person who has been the subject of their conversation.

The best general pattern is for the spiritual oversight to share with the whole church fellowship all that may be shared of their convictions and decisions, and for other matters, and especially those relating to individuals, to remain absolutely confidential. It is to a husband and wife's credit when a church member approaches an undershepherd's wife to raise a subject that has been "leaked" from a leaders' meeting and she can honestly say, "I don't know anything about it. My husband respects the principle of confidentiality."

We must always strive after unanimity in meetings with our fellow leaders. There are a few occasions when unanimity may not be possible. Sad situations occur where someone does not respond spiritually to a situation but emotionally and personally; or where a leader loses out spiritually and perhaps does not appreciate what has happened. Or the subject under discussion may be a secondary matter where the application of right principles may allow different conclusions. Nevertheless unanimity should consistently be our goal. To gloss over disharmony is perilous. It is like putting a coat of paint over damp woodwork; the immediate appearance may look all right, but the dampness will reveal itself eventually, doing damage to all that has been done.

The moment disharmony appears, and the temperature of a meeting rises, the best approach is to suggest pausing together while two or three lead in prayer, seeking God's guidance and the invaluable gift of unity. It may be good to ask someone who feels strongly about the issue in hand to be one of those who pray. Then, rather than pressing for an immediate vote or a solution, there may be wisdom in waiting for unanimity, perhaps suggesting leaving the subject until the next meeting, with all covenanting to pray about it daily until then. The subsequent joy of agreement is great! If unanimity cannot be arrived at, but the consensus clearly points in one direction, before acting upon that consensus, it is helpful to be unanimous in agreeing that the decision will not be a cause of division but a demonstration of what it means to accept one another and to respect each other's convictions. Then whatever decision is arrived at, it may and should be presented as the decision of all. Although we may be able to say to our brothers, "That decision is not one I would have taken myself," believing in corporate guidance, and recognizing that we do not see everything perfectly, whatever is decided corporately, we will implement as our decision and chosen course of action. To depart from this principle encourages disunity, and God's people are puzzled by the failure of their leaders to strive after unity.

The leadership's spiritual unity is the clue to the spiritual unity of the flock. It is always our responsibility to lead people away from contention and to point them in the direction of unity.

DP As a pastor, I have had to chair the meetings of those in spiritual leadership. While not everyone may agree with my practice, I have aimed at being on equal terms of friendship with all, but not cultivating particular friendship with any. The explanation is that I have been in situations where I have known people's reactions to be predictable on the grounds of friendship. If we have a special relationship with a colleague in leadership, we may be tempted to take sides with him in a debate out of sheer loyalty, rather than out of conviction. Now that need not be the case, but it is a snare worthwhile taking steps to avoid.

The danger of discussing leadership is that we may feel ourselves to be too important! There is a difference between being important—as each person's function is in the body of Christ, including that of leaders—and feeling important. We should avoid spiritual elitism, majoring on demonstrating in every way possible that as leaders we are servants. Any competence we have comes from God (2 Corinthians 3:5), and we know that "neither he who plants nor he who waters is anything, but only God, who makes things grow" (1 Corinthians 3:7).

CHAPTER 12

DELEGATION

Delegation is an essential extension of effective leadership, and it demands separate consideration. Leadership may be defined as the ability to give rise to other leaders, but it is also the ability to develop other people's maximum potential for their own works of service in the body of Christ. This goal can be achieved only through delegation. The title "overseers" given to shepherds and teachers implies that we are to superintend certain tasks rather than to accomplish them ourselves. The qualification for elders that they should be able to teach (1 Timothy 3:2) may include not only the ability to teach Christian doctrine and conduct, but also the passing on of information and skills so that people achieve the works of service God has foreordained for them.

Delegation is part of our public recognition that the ministry is that of the whole church. While we have high views of our calling as shepherds and teachers—or "ministers" as we will often be called—the unhelpful concepts of "clergy" and "laity" should be discarded. This way of thinking has focused so many aspects of min-

istry upon one individual, creating the "one-man ministry." Too
many things tend to be expected of the conventional pastor. One
means of avoiding this snare is a proper emphasis upon shared leadership, and establishing that "the minister" is but an elder among
elders, although called to be the "presiding elder."

A further way of avoiding this snare is to practice delegation
of responsibilities as part of our recognition that ministry is the work
of the whole church, with every member finding his or her rightful place. Basic to this practice is the conviction that the Lord Jesus, the Head of the Church, provides adequate gifts for His
Church, and for each visible expression of it in the local church.
Those gifts may not always be quickly apparent, but as delegation
is practiced they are brought to light and developed. If delegation
does not happen, then they may lie hidden. Proper delegation elim-
inates pastoral elitism.

OLD BUT TIMELY LESSONS

No passage in the Bible has greater relevance to delegation than
the advice Moses' father-in-law, Jethro, gave on his visit to his
daughter and son-in-law when he "heard of everything God had
done for Moses and for his people Israel, and how the LORD had
brought Israel out of Egypt" (Exodus 18:1). His assessment of
Moses' situation will be a profitable reference point in this chapter.

> *Moses took his seat to serve as judge for the people, and they stood
> around him from morning till evening. When his father-in-law saw
> all that Moses was doing for the people, he said, "What is this you are
> doing for the people? Why do you alone sit as judge, while all these
> people stand around you from morning till evening?"*
>
> *Moses answered him, "Because the people come to me to seek God's
> will. Whenever they have a dispute, it is brought to me, and I decide
> between the parties and inform them of God's decrees and laws."*
>
> *Moses' father-in-law replied, "What you are doing is not good. You*

and these people who come to you will only wear yourselves out. The work is too heavy for you; you cannot handle it alone. Listen now to me and I will give you some advice, and may God be with you. You must be the people's representative before God and bring their disputes to him. Teach them the decrees and laws, and show them the way to live and the duties they are to perform. But select capable men from all the people—men who fear God, trustworthy men from all the people—men who fear God, trustworthy men who hate dishonest gain—and appoint them as officials over thousands, hundreds, fifties and tens. Have them serve as judges for the people at all times, but have them bring every difficult case to you; the simple cases they can decide themselves. That will make your load lighter, because they will share it with you. If you do this and God so commands, you will be able to stand the strain, and all these people will go home satisfied."

Moses listened to his father-in-law and did everything he said. He chose capable men from all Israel and made them leaders of the people, officials over thousands, hundreds, fifties and tens. They served as judges for the people at all times. The difficult cases they brought to Moses, but the simple ones they decided themselves. (Exodus 18:13–26)

THE SAD CONSEQUENCES
OF NO DELEGATION

Like the work of administering justice for the people, the work of shepherding and teaching the flock is too heavy for us to do single-handed, much as we may try. If we do not delegate, we do tasks needlessly on our own, and we place strain not only on ourselves but also upon others. Jethro's observation upon seeing Moses' situation was discerning (Exodus 18:14). If we try to do too much ourselves, without bringing others in to help, we end up with many undercared for, and with everyone feeling that we have not really given them sufficient time. Jethro recognized that delay in getting things done, even if the person in charge is doing his best, breeds discontent.

Without delegation, we run ourselves into the ground and experience what is sometimes described as "burnout." We wear ourselves out, and paradoxically wear out those who would love to help but whom we have caused to stand by helplessly because of our unwillingness to shift some of the load onto their willing shoulders. As a result they are discouraged, and the life of the church fellowship gets into a dreadful rut or grinds slowly and almost imperceptibly to a halt. God is not glorified by pastoral burnout. He is not a hard taskmaster who expects us to do everything on our own. Rather He always has on hand those He has prepared to share our work so that we may not be overwhelmed and lose our sense of vision and direction.

Part of leadership responsibility is to undertake new tasks and to carry forward fresh initiatives to the point where they can be handed over to others. However, if we do not delegate, we have little or no time to consider development and progress, and we place ourselves on the treadmill of being pushed on by the pressures of busyness through immediate tasks labelled "urgent" rather than being free to consider the really important tasks of leadership. We give the sad impression to onlookers that we feel ourselves to be indispensable. Worse still, we become a hindrance to the growth of the church, although we would probably protest that all our work has its growth in view. David Watson drew from personal experience when he wrote:

> The vicar or minister is usually the bottleneck, if not the cork, of
> his church; nothing can go in or out except through him. No meet-
> ings can be made without his counsel and approval. I know of
> some parishes where the laity cannot even meet for Bible study
> and prayer unless the vicar is present. This bottleneck concept of
> ministry makes growth and maturity virtually impossible. Members
> are unable to develop into the God-given ministry they could well
> experience because, in structure and practice, there is room for
> only one minister. It is no doubt because of this that the fire of the

Spirit has resulted in the bottle exploding into numerous house fellowships or house churches where there is room for growth and for the sharing of ministry. Unless there are new wineskins for the new wine, some bursting out is inevitable.[1]

It is no commendation of our leadership if everything collapses when we are not there or when the time comes for us to leave. Like Moses we need to listen to those who objectively observe the truth about our situation and offer advice. It took considerable humility on Moses' part to do it, but the rewards were rich not only for him, but more important still for God's people. Behind Jethro's voice Moses discerned God's, and we too need to recognize that God may speak to us through the comments—and criticisms—of others.

Reluctance to Delegate

There are always reasons behind failures to delegate, and we need to identify them in order to cure them. Some are not easy to admit, such as our fear that delegating responsibility may give someone else prominence and perhaps push us out of the public eye. We may fear that we will be displaced in people's affections. There may even be the fear that the person concerned may eventually prove to do the job better than we do it ourselves, and thus prompt people to feel we could have done better. Or behind our slowness to delegate may be sheer possessiveness. We need to recognize the evil of these and similar attitudes. We are to rejoice in the usefulness God gives to others, not to be jealous of it. We must not see the Church as our kingdom, but as Christ's. If we engage in His work successfully, we must decrease in it, and He must increase—and since delegation furthers that great goal, it is a priority.

A less unworthy reason for failure to delegate may be our fear that the task may not be done well. Some people are afraid to trust others. We may be overconscientious and concerned lest when we hand a task over the person who does it may not do it efficiently. If pride on our part is behind that concern, then we must recognize it and put it to death. If our fear is justified, we must major on giving the person all the help we can, with built-in safeguards to ensure that if problems develop, they can be handled without undue difficulty. It may well be that we can do a task better than the person to whom we entrust it, but how else will he or she learn if we do not provide the opportunity? It is by learning that he or she will not only cope, but even end up doing it better than we could have.

The Benefits of Delegation

Wise division of labor helps efficiency. Adam Smith describes in his *Wealth of Nations* the division of labor he observed in the manufacture of metal pins for industry: "One man draws out the wire, another straights it, a third cuts it, a fourth points it, a fifth grinds it at the top for receiving the head; to make the head requires two or three distinct operations; to put it on, is a peculiar business, to whiten the pins is another; it is even a trade by itself to put them into the paper. . . ."[2] John Galbraith comments: "Ten men dividing the labour, Smith calculated, could make 48,000 pins a day, 4800 apiece. One man doing all the operations would make maybe one, maybe twenty."[3] Obviously we cannot apply industrial principles lock, stock, and barrel to the service of people. But by trying to do everything—as some of us may foolishly attempt—we slow down the total efficiency of the body of Christ; whereas if we share the tasks, and do the ones we are especially called to do, in harmony with those to whom we delegate, we increase our spiritual efficiency and benefit the church. When God-honoring delegation is practiced, people are satisfied because they are properly cared for, and everything is done decently and in order. Jethro encouraged Moses to recognize that, and the principle remains true.

Delegation eases the burden of responsibilities and enables us to know greater joy in what we do because we are not under such great pressure. It is possible to be proud of the amount of work that we do and our numerous responsibilities, but they may not be to our credit at all if others ought to be involved. When others share the load, besides being better able to stand the strain of our proper tasks, fresh ideas and life are brought to well-established activities. A new person may be like a breath of fresh air, just as we probably were when we first put our hand to the task.

By delegation we ensure a succession; and new gifts, including those of leadership, will emerge. Delegation not only helps us, but it also benefits those who are then privileged to find greater involvement in the work of the body of Christ. God, who has given us our abilities, has given equal abilities to others. Most of us owe our own spiritual development in service to people who trusted us —and the evidences they perceived of God's Spirit at work in us— enough to entrust us with responsibility.

A criminal aspect of the failure to delegate is that other people's potential for responsibility and leadership may remain untapped and undeveloped. How immeasurably poorer the whole Church of Christ might have been if Barnabas had not recognized the potential in the apostle Paul and encouraged him in service to the point where Paul became more prominent than himself, and without any feeling of jealousy. Proper delegation encourages spiritual growth in others, and as we practice it conscientiously we fulfill our duty as shepherds and teachers to fit every Christian for the work of the ministry (Ephesians 4:12).

AREAS OF DELEGATION

Where there is a pastoral team, that is where delegation begins. A reason that there must be a leader among leaders is that every team needs its work to be coordinated and for someone to be recognized as the initiator in delegation. So as not to be vague and indefinite, it is better that we should write in terms of the team situations with which we are familiar.

DP The team situation I knew was that of a young assistant, a lady worker, a secretary, and latterly a second assistant. The young assistant was usually someone straight from theological or Bible college, and a gentleman's agreement existed that he should stay for at least two years. The first year the young assistant found his feet and felt his way. By the second year he was much more sure of himself—in the right sense—and able to take increased responsibility. The assistantship was as valuable to him as to the church, and the church was always encouraged to see the employment of assistants as one of its contributions to the whole body of Christ in that it provided the practical experience a young man ought to have before being called to a more demanding sphere of leadership. The second assistant was an older man, and the intention was that he should continue for a longer and open-ended period, the same kind of arrangement as for the lady worker/deaconess. The secretary was an important member of the team, because so much spiritual administration is involved in the care of God's people, and she was able to coordinate this on behalf of the whole team, to be the person always available during the day in the office to take telephone calls when team members were out visiting, and to keep in touch with new needs and crises.

Within this kind of team, as any other, there had to be a chain of command and carefully defined areas of delegation. My primary task as pastor was to coordinate our combined work and to recognize that it was important to give time to the team members, both as a group and individually as required. Team or staff meetings, with everyone present, were the best general pattern in that, although individual members' responsibilities might be under discussion, it was important that team members should regard each other's work as their shared prayer responsibility. Nothing unites a team more closely than the ability to pray together and to pray for each other intelligently and in relation to specific assignments.

Whenever a new person joined the team, I took time to outline his or her responsibilities—having kept a note of how I had done it before, and updating those notes as necessary—and going over in detail the way each individual task should be tackled. I tried to make a point of doing three things at that first meeting: first, fixing a date—perhaps a fortnight or a month ahead—to review how things had been going; second, encouraging the person to be in touch immediately if there was something he or she could not understand or felt out of depth in; and, third, stressing the importance of striving after complete honesty and frankness with one another and other members of the team.

The chain of command was simple and obvious enough. When I was not present at a staff meeting the older assistant was in the chair. When we did not have an older assistant, the task fell to the young assistant, not because he was necessarily the best qualified, but in order to provide him with this experience as part of his training. But if ever I felt there might be any doubt as to who was to act in my place, I mentioned it at a staff meeting beforehand so that there was no possibility of misunderstanding. Careful and detailed communication is essential to good relationships.

The breakdown of responsibilities was uncomplicated. The young assistant was responsible first for the young people and the student work. Because of his age, it was good for him to major on establishing a rapport with all the young marrieds, especially if he himself was married.

The deaconess felt herself responsible for the overall pastoral care of the womenfolk in the church, but especially the unmarried and those whom it would not be easy or appropriate for male members of the team to visit or counsel. The young assistant and the deaconess took equal shares in the visitation of the older members of the fellowship, many of whom could seldom get out to church. This was to relieve the responsibilities upon the deaconess, as the majority of the older members were female, as is so often the case. It meant that she had time then to devote to other women. The older assistant's task was to assist me first and foremost in pastoral work, and especially in the crises that arise almost daily, and to undertake systematic visitation of church families, with their encouragement and integration in view.

The members of the pastoral team, in turn, were encouraged to delegate. The younger assistant chaired a student committee so that others might share in the pastoral care of students. The deaconess formed around her a group of women who adopted one or more of the elderly womenfolk and visited them regularly in liaison with her.

Each team member made brief notes regarding the people he or she visited or met during the week, and all gave me the list on a Sunday in preparation for our Monday staff meeting. Comments were necessary only where there was anything they thought I should know or where prayer was needed. It also prompted discussion about how to meet pastoral situations, and this helped us all to grow in spiritual sensitivity.

AB Here at Parkside we are a "work in progress." Over the years as the size and structure of the congregation has changed I have been learning how to adapt both my expectations (of myself as well as others) and my mode of operating.

After serving as an assistant to Derek I pastored a church on my own for six years. During my final year I had an assistant and secretarial help on a couple of mornings a week. If I had remained there, I would have tried to develop the ministry along the lines detailed above.

In coming to Parkside I inherited a youth pastor, a pastor of discipleship, a music director who was a woman, and two secretaries in the office. It very quickly became apparent that the pattern of delegation that I had brought across the ocean could not be superimposed upon the structure here. For the next ten years I tried my best, but with only marginal success.

It took all that time for me and my fellow elders to realize that I needed significant help in this area. When a church is smaller and more manageable, then it is easier to "muddle through," but before too long the deficiencies will be hard to disguise.

Over a period of a few months I met with three of our elders to think and pray about how we might do better at delegation and developing ministry at Parkside. These discussions were prayerful, honest, and challenging. They caused me to recognize places where I was either inefficient or perhaps incompetent, or maybe both! I would in passing recommend this kind of process to other pastors who may be facing a similar challenge. The "solution" adopted by too many churches is simply for pastor and people to part company. This seldom solves the problem and usually sends the pastor somewhere else to "muddle through" until he reaches the same impasse as before.

Our solution was to invite one of our elders, who at that time was a partner with an accounting firm, to join our pastoral team as "director of ministry." This involved a very significant delegation on my part. Essentially what I did was give Jeff the oversight of the other members of the pastoral team and ask him to help me in the overall direction of ministry.

This is a subtle, crucial, necessary balancing act, which is fraught with danger and should probably not be attempted in most cases. The only analogy that comes close to describing the nature of this relationship is that of marriage, indeed of a good marriage. For example, if we can think for a moment of the other members of the pastoral team as children (only for the sake of the analogy), then when the father is absent, the mother's role is not to establish a whole new set of guidelines for family living, but to uphold the principles that Dad has established and to do so with an infectious enthusiasm. In the same way, in the father's absence the mother does not bemoan the fact that she is alone but instead prays with and for the children and encourages them to look forward to his return.

In the goodness of God and on account of the peculiar graciousness of my colleague, this has proved to be not just a "working model" but the key to developing ministry at Parkside. Jeff makes and keeps lists, and I tend not to. He interprets my ramblings and either gives structure to my hopes and dreams or helps me to see just how unwise or unrealistic they are.

We are like copilots who, having filed their flight plan, seek to follow it together. Operating in this way I do not evade my duty or give up a rightful sense of "control." As the first officer he defers to me as captain, not in a spirit of unwilling submission or superficial acquiescence but having prayerfully, honestly, and persuasively made his position clear.

This one act of delegation establishes a pattern right

through the pastoral team and allows us tremendous freedom in preparing God's people for "works of service, so that the body of Christ may be built up" (Ephesians 4:12).

❧

Whenever we work in a team, it is inevitable that there will be fairly frequent personnel changes. Since membership in a team is usually God's preparation for greater responsibility elsewhere, we should never begrudge giving time to explaining thoroughly to a new member of the team how to go about his or her work. We mentioned earlier Dr. Alexander Whyte, who exercised such an effective ministry in Edinburgh.

> A series of letters . . . show how thoroughly Dr. Whyte trained those who worked under him. The first letter tells that Dr. Whyte had been going over the congregational roll with the Session-clerk . . . and asks his new assistant to obtain from the clerk the names of members in three districts. It concludes: "Then dine here, say on Friday night, and bring your book; and I will give you some private jottings to guide you in your first visits to the people." Further instructions follow in a letter from Balmacara: "This is my first letter from this place; and I write it because I left so much of my work in your hands. Take from two or three hours five days a week among the sick, etc, and your own other visiting; and be good enough to send me as full a report as you can of whom you have seen, and how they all are. Let me have your report once a week, or so. All my men have done this when I was from home. But Mr. Davidson beat them all in the business-like way he kept his book and kept me up in everything. I felt as if I visited every afternoon when I read his diary."[4]

We have thoroughly enjoyed working in a team, and especially on account of the fellowship that is its natural by-product. The one who is the leader of the team must feel pastorally responsible for the other members and be quick to notice any failure of communication between team members or lack of harmony. Sometimes the answer may be to say when everyone is present, "Is there any problem or difficulty we ought to be discussing?" so that we provide an opportunity for the unknown issue to surface. Or we may do better to speak to someone privately and ask, "Is there something wrong?" But whatever course we take, we should not pretend that all is well when we know it is not. The sooner action is taken the less harm is done, no matter how much we may naturally shrink from dealing with a problem. All teams experience difficulties at times. Properly handled they strengthen the team, rather than weaken it.

The next obvious area of delegation is within the spiritual leadership of the church. Leaders may be called by the New Testament name "elders," but the title they bear is not the important thing, but their function. If we emphasize—as we ought—the parity of elders (including as an elder anyone who may be termed the minister or pastor), we go a long way toward correcting the failure of elders to appreciate and perform their proper responsibilities in pastoral care and spiritual government. Our own conviction is that if we believe in the parity of elders, and the pastor as one of the elders, then elders should be ordained in exactly the same way as "ministers" or "pastors."

The leading elder—or pastor—must not do the whole work of the eldership, and yet that is what sometimes happens. An effective way of delegating pastoral work is to divide up a fellowship's membership between the elders, with each elder having a group, except any full-time members of the pastoral team. The reason for the latter exception is that the principal duty of the leading elder or pastor must be to care for the elders and their families. The other members of the pastoral team, not having pastoral groups of their own, are able to stand in for elders when illness or absence necessitates. In addition, just as the elders and their families need pastoral care, so, too, do the members of the pastoral team, and by not having pastoral groups, they can themselves be under the care of an elder by belonging to his group.

The spiritual leadership may usefully delegate responsibilities for interviewing and counseling among themselves, or to those outside their number with special gifts.

DP Initially I felt I ought to be involved in interviews of prospective church members or those seeking baptism. I tied myself into knots trying to fit in all these interviews, until I recognized that others were perfectly capable of functioning without my presence. One elder was given responsibility for arranging membership interviews and appropriate elders to attend, and another the task of interviewing, with two colleagues, those seeking baptism.

AB From the beginning I have encouraged the elders to take the lead in the membership process. They take turns teaching the three-week membership class and also the preparation-for-baptism class. They conduct the interviews for membership, and in our meetings we hear their report and review the membership application forms. In this way we all participate in the process.

A group of couples can be given responsibility for a homemakers' group for those about to be married, as complementary instruction to the preparation we give. The instruction of new Christians, and membership talks for those coming into church fellowship, are best entrusted to those who can see these tasks as their principal teaching responsibility and give their whole energies to them. Although there would seem to be wisdom in the presiding elder or pastor/minister chairing the principal meetings of the church leadership, he does not need to chair subcommittees.

DP When I first went to my second pastoral charge I found that I was expected to be present at every church committee, and more often than not chair them when I was present. This meant that everything seemed to hinge upon my presence, and it also filled my time with committees. Consulting with the elders and deacons, I determined to chair only the elders' and deacons' meetings, and to attend no other meetings on a regular basis unless my involvement was really necessary. The evangelism committee was the one committee I felt I ought to attend whenever possible, but under the chairmanship of another elder.

AB I have adopted the same pattern, and have tried hard to make clear that in doing so I am not seeking to evade responsibility but to ensure that I do not become a roadblock in developing ministry. It is important that the pastor's presence is not seen to be the key to effectiveness. Nothing has given me greater encouragement than to discover just how well everything went when I was absent for some six months on sabbatical.

Delegation of responsibility among the spiritual leadership of a church must always be done corporately by that leadership, and not simply at the initiative of an individual elder or the leading or presiding elder. The elders may well choose to give the task of delegating responsibility in some area to one of their number and say, "We leave it to you to do, and you don't need to confer with us." But if that has not been said, then decisions regarding delegation should be corporate. No one should be asked to exercise pastoral care, to teach or preach, or to share in the leadership of meetings or of worship without the spiritual leadership being happy together about it, because these important issues have been entrusted to them, both by God and His people. There is safety in corporate wisdom and guidance. To think we know better sows the seeds of disaster and disharmony.

PRINCIPLES OF SUCCESSFUL DELEGATION

Before delegating responsibility, we must identify our own principal tasks. In delegating we are not shifting these off ourselves, but we are handing over those other tasks that stop us properly fulfilling our primary work. As shepherds and teachers, our priorities are prayer and teaching, in the context of the pastoral care of God's people.

Wherever delegation of other responsibilities is feasible we should practice it. If a job we are doing is not our first priority, and someone else is free and able to do it, we should aim to pass it on. Delegation is not an easy way out of responsibility—far from it! When we delegate we have the initial duty of keeping a watchful eye upon those who need to feel that they have the full responsibility but who nevertheless may need us to hover in the background to assist in the early stages.

The first principle of delegation is to test potential. As soon as people come into church fellowship, it is good to provide opportunities by which they may be gently put to the test to reveal gifts and abilities.

DP With this objective in mind, I would argue for the appointment of deputies for every definable task, within reason. The church secretary should have an assistant, and perhaps more than one, according to how his duties may be devolved. Similarly with the church treasurer, with someone looking after regular expenses and another after smaller items like petty cash. If someone is responsible for church catering, that person can have an assistant. Even if the assistant does not become the ultimate successor, he or she will be equipped to fill other necessary positions, and along the way may display gifts that otherwise would have been missed.

A particular experience stands out in my mind. We were in the process of trying to relieve the church secretary of some of his duties that others could share. One such task was correspondence relating to the admission of new members and arranging membership interviews. A couple had recently joined the church, and we had little idea of their gifts. We asked if the husband would assist the secretary in this way. He not only did the job well, but we discovered that he and his wife went beyond all we could have hoped for in their care of people. Before people came to meet the elders for their membership interview, this couple invited them to their home for tea, and having gotten to know them, introduced them to as many church members as they could. I remember the assistant secretary's wife explaining how nervous one of the young women was about her forthcoming membership interview, and she offered to accompany her—a suggestion we readily took up. In a matter of months the assistant secretary handed over his job to someone else in order to become an elder. Through delegation we discovered undoubted gifts of pastoral care, and I doubt if we would have discerned those gifts as quickly had we not devolved responsibility in this simple way.

Although delegation should be entered upon readily, it should never be done haphazardly or carelessly. Moses carefully selected those who were to help him, guided by Jethro's apt instruction that they should be "capable men from all the people—men who fear God, trustworthy men who hate dishonest gain" (Exodus 18:21, cf. 25). Moral qualifications are as important as ability when we delegate spiritual responsibility. Although we may have doubt as to the exact nature of people's gifts, we should not be in any doubt about their Christian character and integrity.

We should also respect people's reluctance to undertake a job suggested to them. It may be a natural diffidence that needs to be overcome, but it may also be because they cannot cope with responsibility, and we may do harm to them and to others by putting wrongful pressure upon them. Discernment and graciousness are necessary here as everywhere.

A clear job description and careful instruction are essential in delegation. We need to sit down and carefully describe the task in view. If we are not clear, we can hardly expect the person we approach to be clear! Moses—following Jethro's advice—gave instructions that difficult cases were to be referred to himself (Exodus 18:22, cf. 26), and that delegation within delegation was to be carried out, so that once officials were appointed over thousands, then the same was to be done in hundreds, fifties, and tens (verse 21).

Once we have defined a task clearly in our own minds, and how we feel it should be tackled, we are in a position to sit down with the person concerned. Besides being unfair, it is both frightening and discouraging for someone to be given responsibility without guidance and positive direction. Our Lord gave considerable responsibility to His apostles, but He devoted three years beforehand to their careful instruction. Paul delegated pastoral care to men like Timothy and Titus, but he took time to train them, principally by having them as his companions and assistants, and then by keeping in touch with them by letter. Timothy, in turn, was told to remember Paul's instruction of him and to entrust it to "reliable men who will also be qualified to teach others" (2 Timothy 2:2).

When delegating new responsibilities, it is best not to rely upon memory, but rather to write down matters for discussion. Better still is the habit of having two copies, so that one can be handed to the other person, prefacing our time of sharing by saying, "So that we don't forget anything important, I've jotted down the things we ought to talk through together, and it will give us an agenda so that we make the best use of our time." It is good to establish the standards we feel should be aimed at, not to hesitate to talk about small details, and to show our awareness of the problems that may be experienced.

DP In the early days of my ministry, I used to visit the contacts we made in the neighborhood through people signing the church's visitors' book. There came a point when I was able to pass this on to someone else, who in turn brought together a team of people to do this vitally important work of showing friendship and being ready to talk to people about Jesus Christ. When I handed the job on, I explained my standard practice of always aiming to make a call the week following a person's visit. I expressed the hope that this would continue, because the sooner the visit the more caring it shows us to be. I usually met with the church members who did this visitation once a year before a church prayer meeting, and encouraged them in this, so that they realized that this requirement, passed on to them by the person to whom leadership in the work had been entrusted, was deliberate policy and not just his personal preference. If ever an immediate visit was impossible, they were to pass on the call to someone else in the team who could fit it in that week. Explaining what constitutes a task well done helps to set reasonable objectives before the person taking up responsibility.

Although often a lot of time has to be spent in the early stages of delegation, it is not only time well spent, but it saves time having to be spent in the future on mistakes and misunderstandings. It is also part of our unconscious training of others in how to hand on responsibility.

It is invaluable to build in safeguards and institute regular times for review. If a delegated task is one of considerable responsibility, it may be necessary to maintain an initial element of control, although always discreetly. Having discussed and prayed together about the new task, the final thing to do before parting is to make an appointment to review how things go, and to suggest that this should be done every three months to begin with, and then perhaps at longer intervals. We referred earlier to Charles Simeon's division of his parish into areas and his appointment of a man and woman church member to be responsible for the homes in their district. An obvious key to its success over the fifty years he sustained it was his monthly meeting with those who visited when they reported on what they had done, and he gave his advice on difficult cases. The dual elements of complete delegation and the possibility of control, where necessary, were present.

The development of house groups within churches makes

imperative the training and pastoral care of house group leaders as a vital key to the groups' usefulness. If high standards are not set from the beginning, the groups may be helpful for people getting to know one another, but not for instruction and pastoral care. They can even be times for the propagation of ignorance rather than of knowledge. Besides a straightforward job description, a group leader needs initial instruction and regular opportunities to meet together with other group leaders, so that he himself is under discipline and care and is stimulated to increasingly effective pastoral leadership.

AB In order to meet these objectives we have found it helpful to have a member of the pastoral team as the teacher of the teachers of our geographically based life groups. In this way we seek to ensure that each group not only is working on the same material but is receiving the same instruction.

Because honesty and frankness are so essential to integrity and success, we have usually said something like the following as we have delegated a task: "I want you to feel that you can always be honest with me about the suggestions I may make to you concerning the work you are beginning—and you will not hurt my feelings by disagreeing with me or suggesting better ways of doing it. At the same time I equally want to feel that I can be honest with you if I think the task can be done in some better way, or if ever anyone voices a criticism to me about the manner in which you are going about your responsibility. I promise I will never agree or side with them, but I will support you. At the same time I will talk to you as soon as possible so that if there are any grounds for just criticism we may put it right together." We must give firm support to those who undertake tasks at our instigation. We should be quick to commend progress and to encourage. If we do that, it will not be difficult to discuss problems or for the person concerned to accept our constructive comments.

No matter how hard delegation may sometimes be, it is a necessity. There are occasions when we need to take a calculated risk, providing we have introduced the necessary safeguards suggested. Whatever happens we should expect the best, and be confident not simply in the person's ability, but in God's ability and the working of His Spirit in that person's life. We will have some wonderful surprises, and they will be to God's praise and the lasting good of His people.

FAMILY
AND LEISURE

Family and leisure go naturally together. If these two priorities are neglected, disaster quickly follows. We relax most easily when we are at home and with our families, and we require leisure to do so. As undershepherds, we must give our families the care and attention we expect other husbands and fathers to give to theirs. More than that, we should be examples of what a husband and father should be like. We cannot faithfully expound the Scriptures without stressing the importance of the home. Those who listen to us have the right to expect us to practice what we preach.

New Testament qualifications for church leaders link spiritual usefulness in the home with spiritual effectiveness in the body of Christ. We cannot expect to help others if we are of little use to those closest to us. There is shame in caring for others and neglecting our own soul's needs; there is equal shame in neglecting the spiritual well-being of our families. An undershepherd must be his wife's undershepherd too, not in a professional or patronizing way, but because of his love for her. The best way to help our wives is to take care of our own relationship to God, so that we are in private exactly as we are in public.

The proof of godliness is our godliness in the home. This may seem an extremely high standard, and it is. But the home is the most strategic sphere of witness because it is there that we demonstrate how genuinely we do what we tell others to do. People rightly expect—whether Christians or not—that Christian ministers should be examples, and nothing is more important in human relationships than the family. If we neglect our families, we eventually undermine our entire pastoral and teaching ministry. Pastors' families are the objects of special attack by the enemy of souls; if he can ruin our home life, he mars our total usefulness.

IDENTIFYING THE PRESSURE POINTS

If we can identify the pressures upon an undershepherd's family life, we are in a better position to deal with them. The principal pressure for some arises from the home being the working base. Working from home, pastors talk with people in the home, and the home is the place to which people come in times of distress. If the pastor is not around, and his wife is present, then she has to step in to help where she can. This does not happen in the same way for doctors and lawyers and other professional men.

Rather than business lunches being the focus of hospitality, our home is. It is possible to shift our working base elsewhere, perhaps to a church office. But while that helps, it is not always ideal in that we cannot work normal office hours, and, if we try to do so, we find ourselves becoming remote from the people we want to serve. For our regular study times, we need to have all our books in one place, rather than two.

The danger inherent in our home being the working base is that we never get away from our work—it is too easy to feel that we must slip away from our family into the study to complete a pressing assignment. If we worked a nine-to-five day in an office, we would have left that work behind us and closed the door to it until the next morning. We may seldom clear our desk, and so there is always something demanding attention. To this is added the constant ringing of the telephone, so that in the middle of a family meal we may be called upon to discuss church business. As a consequence there is the temptation to be always talking church matters, something to be avoided if our families are present.

DP I learned an important lesson when, as a young minister, recently ordained, I preached in a church in the north of England. The pastor and his wife had a family whose children were in their early teens. I knew a little about the church and some of the difficulties through which it had been passing. As we sat around the lunch table on Sunday, I asked a question about these problems. Immediately I felt a gentle kick on my ankle. My hosts gave a noncommittal reply and quickly changed the subject. Later when the children were not around they explained a principle I have never forgotten, and have tried to follow. They made a point of never discussing before the children any matters of difficulty within the church, or anything that might be interpreted as criticism of individuals. They did not want their children to grow up with a jaundiced view of church life because of the inevitable problems with which pastors have to deal.

AB We have unconsciously done the same. Our children still make inquiries about church life, even though they are out of the home. Since they were never privy to personal details or difficult problems, they tend to ask only general questions. How was Sunday? Did you preach well? Is anything fun happening? What about Mr. X or Mr. Y? We never made them feel that they had to share any burdens or that they should be peculiarly concerned about church life. They never heard the designation "PKs" (pastor's kids) in our home and consequently did not grow up thinking in that weird way.

The invasion of a family's privacy cannot be helped, but we should do what we can to minimize it. One of the best ways to counter it is by encouraging ourselves—and then the family by our example—to see interruptions as opportunities for showing kindness and hospitality. We recognize that is easier said than done. But if we resent intrusions, then our family will. If we greet someone's arrival or the ringing of the telephone with a groan, the family will soon emulate us. But if we show genuine pleasure at seeing and hearing from people, and back that up by what we say in private, we will have done much to remove a sense of irritation. Practical actions are important, like not having the television in a room into which we bring people when they come to talk with us. The unexpected visitor whose arrival curtails a favorite television program is bound to cause disgruntlement to children. We can avoid such a circumstance.

Our children may grow up feeling that they are much more under people's scrutiny than other children. They may also be subject to being spoiled more by others—something they may not mind! Members of a congregation will take a great interest in our children, and that is natural enough, since it so often reflects their regard and concern for us. We should not be overly worried about this, providing we ensure our children are not pressured into doing things simply because they are the pastor's children. While people may sometimes make it difficult for us to be ordinary people because of the fuss they make of us, we must make it plain that both our children and we are ordinary. We must help our children to be themselves, and to balance that with the loyalty that all children should show their parents. If we are ourselves, then our children will be themselves. The problem is not so much what the congregation may think and feel about our children, but what we think they may be thinking!

Pastors and their wives are often supersensitive about whether or not their children should be compelled to go to church activities when they are young, because they do not want them to resent being minister's children or to feel hard done by because of seemingly more pressure placed upon them than upon other children. Acting on the principle that young children do not know what is best for them, our conviction is that we should be quite firm about their involvement in church services and with young people's activities until they are in their early teens, in the same way that we would expect other parents to be.

A good basic family philosophy is that families should enjoy doing things together: Some activities individual members may enjoy more than others, but learning to do what the majority want is part of the give-and-take of family life. If a younger member goes rather grudgingly with the family to a church event, it is important that the other members do not go grudgingly with that younger member to something he or she wants to do. We need to be sensitive and honest enough never to encourage a member of the family's involvement in an activity for our sake or because we feel noninvolvement reflects badly upon us. God often uses our families to keep us humble and aware of our daily need of His grace, and that is no bad thing.

Family prayers are no easier for a pastor and his wife to keep going than anyone else, and their practice must not be maintained simply because we feel it is especially expected of us. They are possible when our children are younger in a way they may not be when our children are all going off to school at different times and when evening meals are seldom eaten with everyone present.

DP I look back with particular joy to the period when the whole family could sit around the meal table and read the Scriptures and pray together. The missionaries from the church became household names to the children, and their furlough visits to the home were family highlights. But there came a time when I recognized that it created unnecessary problems and conflicts to organize our family of six to have profitable family prayers every day, especially when different schools and their activities meant that often we were not all together for a meal. What became more important and natural was to seize opportunities spontaneously, whenever everyone was present for a meal, to pause to pray for one another, and to do so regularly at a Sunday lunchtime when we were all together. The warmth and reality with which we thanked God for our church fellowship and prayed for it, together with our honesty in prayer when we had difficulties as a family in fulfilling all that the church expected, did much to unite the family in its desire to serve others without pretense.

AB By the time our children were leaving for school on three separate buses and participating in a multitude of after-school activities, I was feeling a complete failure as the one responsible for "family devotions." Bursts of enthusiasm were followed by periods of chronic inertia. While always praying together at meal times, we soon recognized the wisdom contained in the Hebrew *Shema*

(Deuteronomy 6:4–9). The things of God are to be upon our hearts. Our children can quickly tell whether this is the case. We are to make these things the natural focus of conversation while we are driving in the car or lying on their beds with them in the evening. My biggest regret is stopping too soon in saying their prayers with them before they turned in for the night. In their midteenage years, in wanting to protect their privacy, I did not pray with them at the end of the day as much as I should have done. It remains a great joy to be in their presence and to hear them pray.

If working from home is the principal area of potential difficulty, the unusual working hours of the typical pastor come close behind it. We may fail our families by allowing the sheer pressure of our duties to swamp us and carry us along on their momentum. It is for this reason alone that the delegation of responsibilities we have considered in the previous chapter is so important, and the deliberate policy of not sitting on so many committees that we are seldom home in the evening.

It is necessary to pause from time to time and to ask afresh, "When does my family need me most? How can I structure my day so that I fulfill my pastoral duties and give time to my family?" The question needs to be asked repeatedly, because family life changes. The best time to be available to the family when they are young is seldom the best time when they are older. Bedtime is especially significant when children are young, when a wife appreciates her husband's involvement in bathing the children, reading to them, and praying with them. When our children are small, discussions in the early evening with people coming straight from work are not the best arrangement. Yet they may be ideal when our children are older, so that we can then be around later in the evening to get close to them in their work and interests. Some may be able to set aside two hours with their families each evening; the minimum ought to be an hour that the children know belongs to them.

DP We cannot help being busy, but looking back over the years I recognize that often I have been too busy. The real problem is not busyness, but our making sure that however busy we are, we still have time for our families, and especially when they need us. They always need us around, and periods of acute need are far less likely to arise if we communicate meaningfully with them daily. So often I have responded wrongly to my family when they have wanted my attention with "I am busy" or "I must get on"—the latter is an expression I have tried to avoid since the family teased me so much because of it! Our duty to God and His people will seldom conflict with our duty to our family. That does not mean that we may not sometimes have to decline doing what a member of the family wants at one particular moment—that is true in any family. But God's will is never that we should be so busy that we neglect those closest to us.

AB In my early days at Parkside one of my elders took me aside and offered me wise counsel and granted me great freedom in this area. As a physician he was concerned for my physical well-being, and as the son of a pastor he was aware of how easy it was to neglect one's family. Instead of suggesting that I work out a foolproof formula to prevent mistakes, he encouraged me to acknowledge that I would often get it wrong. Then he suggested that I should feel free to take time to redress the balance by taking a special day or couple of days to spend with Susan and the children. As I began to travel more I relied upon this mechanism. The children knew that upon my return we would seek to make up for lost time. We have happy memories of those catch-up days.

Our view of our pressure points will be completely jaundiced if we do not counter them by drawing attention to the rich compensations of our calling for our families. Because we are responsible for the division of our time, we are able to be with our children when they are young for their bedtime in a way that few who daily commute to work are able. Admittedly, we then have to go out most evenings, but that is much preferable to regularly coming home so late that our children are already in bed. If we work from our homes we have daytime opportunities to be with our wives, if only to eat lunch together—something few other husbands can do. We and our families are more prayed for than any other members of our church fellowship, and a value cannot be put on those prayers. Our children benefit immeasurably by the unconscious Christian influence of the numerous and interesting visitors who enjoy our home's hospitality. Focusing upon meeting the challenges to the undershepherd's family must be seen in the perspective of the unique benefits it enjoys.

THE SPECIAL PRESSURES THAT MAY BE UPON A PASTOR'S WIFE

The area in which the greatest watchfulness needs to be exercised is the care and protection of our wives from undue pressures on account of the nature of our work. Although they may sometimes appear to be in the background, they are to the fore in their contribution to our usefulness. Charles Simeon arranged annual summer house parties for clergy and their wives as early as 1796, including sessions for the wives as well as the ministers, and he was well ahead of his time in this. He playfully referred to them as "Ministresses, half-Ministers, often the most important half in your husband's parishes."[1]

More is required of our wives than wives of men in other callings and professions. They cannot be separated from our work as other wives can be from their husbands' employment. Some wives may have little idea what their husband's work involves. But not so our wives; they not only marry us, but they marry our job as well, since they live in the middle of it.

In the UK, where we live is frequently our office as well as our home. When we are at home, we are more often than not working in our study. Our wives will be called upon to make innumerable cups of coffee or tea, and to offer impromptu hospitality. Lonely people and those whom some would regard as misfits of society tend to gravitate toward a pastor and his wife, and they must be welcomed. It was for that reason that we came to the conclusion—perhaps not always appreciated by some—that we should offer hospitality principally to those who could not normally return it: students, those away from home, and those living on their own.

In this context a pastor's wife will be more aware than anyone of how much her husband needs to safeguard his mornings for study, and when she is at home she will try to deal with calls that are not really urgent. That is no easy task. People who call unexpectedly at the door or who ring up may not be keen to divulge the reason for wanting to speak to the pastor, and a wife needs considerable tact and discernment to know whether to put them straight through or to suggest that some other time would be better. If she discerns that it is clearly a nonurgent call, it is not unreasonable for her to say, "My husband is in the middle of preparing for Sunday. Would it possible for him to phone you, or for you to call him at the end of the morning?" If there is doubt about the urgency of a call, it should be treated as urgent. That avoids the heartache of sad mistakes.

DP Scroungers who come to the door sometimes provide a burden to a wife, and all the more so when we are away from home. Most are men, and some can be disagreeable and even threatening if disappointed. I initially fell into the trap, as many have, of giving money. This is seldom if ever wise. Having listened to countless stories of need from scroungers, and checking out their stories where possible, I have not found one to be wholly true. But I am always fearful lest I should not help the one that is genuine! We learned to give help by gifts other than money, and principally by the provision of food. It is wise to make plain to scroungers that if they return—and they usually do—it will be food that they will receive rather than money, and that we are instructing our wives and families to give help only if we are there. If they then come when we are out, they must expect to be disappointed.

AB Derek's observations here offer the average American pastor a bird's-eye view of a slice of life that many have never seen. Certainly those of us who are lost in the suburbs know little of these circumstances. However, my friends with churches in the inner city can identify fully with these pictures.

Financial pressures tend to be felt most by a wife. Our own time is so filled with our work's demands that we may push such practical concerns from the forefront of our minds. But our wives are in and out of shops most days of the week, aware of increasing prices often unmatched by increased income, and conscious of the demands of growing families. Some pastors receive realistic and generous salaries, but many do not. One of the ironies of life is that when a family's demands are the greatest the income tends to be the lowest, and vice versa. It sounds glib to say that finance must not become a major factor in our thinking, but it is not stated lightly. God uses all sorts of disciplines to perfect our characters and to strengthen our faith in Him—and financial dependence upon Him may be one.

Whatever our income, if we believe ourselves to be in the place He has chosen, we must strive after contentment. That does not mean that we should not be honest if asked by those who determine our salary whether or not our income is adequate. We have felt it inappropriate to take any initiative in ever mentioning increases in salary for fear of being misunderstood. Looking back we are thankful that was the case, since if our needs were not met by one means they were by another. The best principle is to expect nothing from God's people, so that we are never disappointed —for disappointment breeds grudges—and then we will be surprised by unexpected thoughtfulness and generosity. While God's people have a duty laid on them by Scripture to support their undershepherds, we are not the people to remind them. We may and must trust God to raise up others to do that, if it is appropriate.

When financial pressures are upon us, it is vital to talk matters through with our wives, and to strive after complete honesty, so that money never becomes a source of disharmony. A difficult balance needs to be struck. On the one hand, we want to live within our means, and not try to keep up with others—including those who share leadership with us who may be salaried through secular employment. On the other hand, we do not want to draw attention to our circumstances by living as though in poverty. If people become aware of our financial limitations and give us gifts, it can be hurtful to our pride, and we may resent being the supposed objects of charity. Many of the problems related to living in a parsonage or a church house are linked with finance.

DP It was only when we obtained a small holiday flat of our own, having been in the ministry about twenty years, that I appreciated the difference it made to have a home of our own, and the sense of freedom it gave not to have to ask permission or to wait until a committee came to a decision about anything needing to be done.

Both from a church's point of view and a pastor's, there is much to be said for his being in a position to own his own house. But that can bring further pressures if a salary is inadequate.

The answer for some has been for the wife to go out to work, and this is especially tempting if she has a professional qualification guaranteeing even well-paid part-time employment.

DP My personal preference is against this possibility where it can be avoided, for two reasons. First, it can undermine the marriage relationship. Since so much of a pastor's work takes place during the evenings, if his wife is out at work during the day, they are going to see little of each other—a sure recipe for disaster. The tempting question will then raise its head, "Some of these pressures would not exist if we were not in spiritual leadership in a church; perhaps there is alternative work we could do?" With both a job and a home—and perhaps a family—to care for, a wife is going to be hard pushed to give the hospitality her husband's calling so frequently demands. Second, while a wife is at work, there will be unexpected female callers through a variety of emergencies, which can make her husband more vulnerable than he would be if she were there.

AB In Scotland we lived in a house that was owned by the church. As a result any suggestions for improvement became agenda items for the church meeting. On one memorable occasion I had suggested that we might make better use of the bathroom by repositioning the tub. Doing so meant installing a smaller bathtub. On the evening this was discussed I left the room to grant freedom of deliberation. I must confess that I stepped out of my vestry at one point and listened behind the door to see what progress if any was being made. I discovered that a great debate was taking place over the length of the tub. Their concern was simple. It was obvious that their present pastor could fit into a smaller tub, but what would happen if their next pastor was "a big, tall man." I do not miss those days. The elders at Parkside not only suggested that we purchase our own home, but they made it possible for us to do so. I find it helps me to live in the "real world" of mortgage payments and property taxes, and I would always suggest this pattern whenever possible.

A pastor's wife may have to battle with the high expectations people have of her as a pastor's wife, of her husband, and even of her children. Although she is not salaried by the church as her husband may be, church members may often treat her as if she were. Since a pastor is called to teach and preach, a church fellowship may make the unhelpful and unfounded assumption that his wife is qualified and willing to do similar service in other areas of church life. The assumption may be right, but some wives are put into an intolerable straitjacket by such expectations. The pressures then often lead to tensions within the marriage, marring both partners' spiritual effectiveness.

There should be a clear understanding from the beginning—as early as preliminary interviews with regard to a possible call to pastoral responsibility—that the husband's call does not mean that his wife should automatically lead the women's or young wives' meeting or undertake similar tasks. Her principal contribution is her support of her husband and the care of her family. At the same time she must be free to develop and use her gifts like any other woman in the church. We must make this point on her behalf, rather than her having to do so. If she then later has the conviction that she should accept an invitation to leadership, that is fine, because it is not something she has been pressured into doing, or that she does simply because she is the undershepherd's wife. William Wand, one-time Bishop of London, described how his wife seemed to strike the right balance when he was in charge of a parish:

> She was clever enough not to appear to take the lead in anything and refused the chairmanship of various parochial organizations. But she attended their meetings and took a serious part in their activities. When they gradually discovered that at most practical things she was at least as good as they if not better, they realised that her refusal to take the formal lead was due not to slackness but to good feeling, and they admired her accordingly. She became

as much a part of the people's lives as I was, and I know she was as happy in that knowledge as I.[2]

Loneliness, the temptation to jealousy, and the burden of confidentiality are three problems wives face about which we need to be sensitive. Loneliness takes several forms. There is the loneliness occasioned by our frequent absences in the evening, since that is when most pastoral work is done. If we have families, we are not in a position to take it in turns with our wives to attend church activities, since we may be responsible for leading them.

It is imperative that we establish the principle from the beginning of using regular babysitters or family minders. There is value in using the same favorite person the family all appreciates, so that it develops a special relationship with someone as an adopted "auntie" or "grandmother." Single folk are ideal, and it is a service for the Lord and not simply for us.

A greater problem still is the sense of isolation a pastor's wife's position brings. She may find it difficult to develop special friendships with other women within the church because of the danger of apparent favoritism, which might hinder good relationships with others. If she develops a friendship with some members, they may become possessive of it, and talk about it with pride to others, so that barriers are erected. She will always have to watch the manner in which she speaks about many subjects—especially those relating to church business—since most will imagine, quite unfairly, that she speaks on behalf of her husband.

To make friends outside the church fellowship, or with other pastors' wives, is particularly helpful, but not always easy. Our wives need friends as all do, and we should pray specifically that God will raise up one or two friends, whether within or outside the church fellowship, who will be a special encouragement to her. If they are within the church, God can give them understanding to be discreet and thoughtful.

A wife may be tempted to be jealous of those who seem to have too great a claim upon her husband's time, especially when the person demanding his time is a woman. A wife may be working away at the ironing or other household chores, longing for her husband's company, while he sits in front of the fire in the lounge drinking coffee and speaking to someone. At the end of the discussion he comes out all smiles, with satisfaction at having done his job, while his wife feels like throwing something at him! Sensitivity is required on both sides. A wife must appreciate that her husband's calling demands he gives time to people, whoever they may be. A husband must keep his conversations within proper bounds, and especially with those women whom either he or his wife discerns seek his time because of satisfaction in his company. This requires honesty between husband and wife and the acceptance of just criticism on both sides, but it is vital.

The more we can know people together, the better—particularly when women come to see us. While we may seldom say to a man, "May I share with my wife what you have shared with me, so that we may pray together for you?" we try to do this consistently, as mentioned earlier, when any woman seeks our advice or counsel, unless obviously inappropriate. If she declines, then we will not do so. But ninety-nine times out of a hundred the response is a glad affirmative. That means that our wives are involved, and that our discussions are not a secret. Small things like this are important, and they mean that the person we have seen has a relationship with both husband and wife, rather than with the husband alone.

The burden of confidentiality can be considerable. People share anxieties and sins with a pastor and his wife as with few others. Nosy and inquisitive people will quiz us—and particularly our wives—about church business and people. As pastors the pressures of people's troubles will weigh us down sometimes, and it may be unfair to off-load them upon our wives, even though they are willing to share them. When we can share, without breaking confidentiality, it is good to do so, unless we feel it will unfairly burden.

The confidentiality we expect of our fellow elders concerning elders' business we must follow ourselves. But what we would be happy for them to share, we may share. It is good to be able to practice the kind of honesty in which we can say to our wives, "If I do not tell you something, it is so that if asked by someone who is inquisitive you will be able to say honestly, 'I don't know.'" If telling everything possible is our practice, there will be no resentment when we do not, but understanding and gratitude.

A wife's most important contribution to her husband's usefulness is her ability to be his best critic. Our wives may be relied upon to be honest with us as no one else, whether we want to know how our teaching came across or the rightness of an immediate response to a crisis or a decision that must be made. It may not always be easy to accept what our wives say because of its honesty, but it is the one judgment we can entirely trust because of the love behind it.

SAFEGUARDING THE MARRIAGE

We support one another as husbands and wives in these practical and beneficial ways only as our marriages are loving and harmonious. When Robert Rainy, a Scottish minister and scholar, was criticized and misunderstood, someone said to him, "I don't understand how you are so calm and serene." He replied, "Well, you know, I'm very happy at home."[3] The love that is to characterize our entire ministry must begin in the home. Soon after his marriage, Dr. William Sangster said to his wife, "I can't be a good husband and a good minister. I'm going to be a good minister." His son comments,

> It all depends, of course, what you mean by a "good husband." If it means a man who dries up as his wife washes the pots, or a handyman about the house, or even a man who takes his wife out for an occasional treat, then my father was the worst of all husbands. But if a "good husband" is a man who loves his wife absolutely, expresses that love daily, asks her aid in all he does, and dedicates himself to

a cause which he believes is greater than both of them, then my father was as good a husband as he was a minister.[4]

Dr. Sangster's dedication in his book *He Is Able* says, "To Margaret, my wife, with whom it is as easy to keep in love as to fall in love." Years later *Reader's Digest* quoted this dedication as "the perfect compliment." So it is likely that Dr. Sangster would have spoken differently later on in life, since there does not have to be a conflict between being a good husband and a good minister; the two roles should be mutually supportive. But a pastor's genuine declaring of his love to his wife, and demonstrating it, are fundamentally important.

The key safeguard of our marriages is ensuring we have time to pray and relax together. Realism and honesty are necessary in shared prayer. When we have young children, opportunities for praying together at the beginning of the day are hard to find, and the difficulties may be no less when the family grows up and all its members are at various stages at school and involved in different activities. But to pray together more than anything else keeps the lines of communication open, besides being the best stimulus and encouragement to mutual spiritual watchfulness and our walk with God. The one time in the day when the family is normally quiet is when we go to bed.

DP Over the years we have always prayed briefly together at the close of the day. Even if I have come home late and my wife is already in bed, we have committed ourselves, our family, and urgent needs to God. Then at least once a week—usually on my day off—we have had an extended time of prayer, sharing our quiet time.

AB We also end the day by praying together for family, friends, and the burdens of the day. Depending on how the day begins, we may read and pray together then, but we do not have a consistent pattern of activity. In the past this has been partly a result of how much traveling I have done. Now that my wife is able to join me, we no longer have that excuse and we are able to enjoy not just praying *for* each other but *with* each other.

The best way to safeguard a regular time together is to have a day off each week. Vital as it is for renewal and refreshment for the benefit of our daily work, it is equally vital for the well-being of our relationship to our wives and families. Our day off needs to be fixed in such a way that everyone in the church knows when it is. In the British context it is easier if the church secretary or someone like him draws attention to the avoiding of needless phone calls and interruptions on that day than if we do it ourselves. When such a suggestion is given, we obviously want it to be clear that we are always available in emergencies, and that people are not to hesitate to get in touch with us when such arise, whatever day of the week it is. If the church secretary makes the first point, we are then well able to balance it by making the second. In the States the means of communicating with the congregation may be different, but the objective is the same.

DP In determining my day off, I chose the day in the week when there were no church meetings requiring my involvement: In London it was Thursday and in Edinburgh Tuesday.

Our wives and children must be able to feel that our day off—or "sabbath," for that is what it is—is their day, and to this end we must hedge it about with as many barriers as possible so that it is wholly theirs.

DP Personally this has meant that I have always refused to speak at meetings on my day off except when away from home for a series of meetings. I have refused to attend committees or to have extra elders' or deacons' meetings on a Tuesday.

If once we break the principle unnecessarily, it is like a breach in a dam. When our day off is broken into by a funeral or an emergency, we should try to take time off in lieu. In practice this is extremely difficult because our program for other days in the week will already be made up of unalterable events. But we must not feel guilty in thinking that we ought to have time off in lieu, and taking it when possible, as much for our family's good as our own.

In addition to our day off, we ought to plan to spend at least one other evening a week at home.

DP I found that I could seldom do more than this, but it helped to have a rule of thumb, so that in arranging counseling, committees, visits, and the like, in addition to the evening of my day off, I tried to be at home one other evening—in my case, usually a Friday or a Saturday.

Saturday was important when our children were of school age, and I aimed to finish all preparation by midday Saturday, so as to spend the rest of the day with the family, or just to be around if they did not particularly need my involvement with them—something increasingly the case as our children were in their teens! To be around is important nevertheless.

We can get into an unhealthy state of mind in which we are afraid of being caught doing nothing in case people think we are slacking. So often I have felt guilty at relaxing because I have gotten out of the habit of doing so. Stephen Verney, an Anglican clergyman, relates how this truth came home to him through something that happened when he had been working flat out for six years as vicar on a new housing estate. "I went for a walk with my wife and children, pushing the pram; and one of my parishioners looked over his garden hedge in astonishment, 'That's the best thing you've done for me in six years,' he said."[5]

AB I also take Tuesday as a day off. My reason for doing so initially was driven by family concerns. When our children were tiny we became members of an athletic club that gave us access to a super swimming pool. Since the club was closed on Mondays, it would not be possible for me to enjoy it with the children unless I had a day other than Monday as my free day. So I opted for Tuesday. The fact that most private golf clubs are also closed on Mondays may have played a part in my thinking too!

I have been fortunate here in not having the weekly round of evening activities that many of my colleagues face. To be home on only one evening a week is an alarming prospect and is less and less the norm, not because of unwilling pastors but because our congregations are not as willing or able to engage in so many midweek activities. It is important that we are constantly assessing what is profitable and necessary and what is just a routine left over from another era.

RELAXATION AND LEISURE

To have time with our wives and families is at the heart of our relaxation and leisure. But there are other dimensions of which to take care. Within the bounds of giving priority to our wives and families, physical exercise is an important constituent of our day off. If it is not possible then, it is justifiable to take an hour or two each week to do something that is physically demanding and entirely different from our daily work.

DP My reaction has been to think myself too busy to take that hour or so off. But experience has also taught me that having made the effort to do so, I return to my work with my mind as well as my body renewed. While godliness has the greatest value, "physical training is of some value" nevertheless (1 Timothy 4:8), and our emphasis upon the former must not lead to the neglect of the latter. I owe a debt to one of my retired elders. When I first came to Edinburgh, he observed that I was getting little exercise, since practically all visitation involved using a car because of the distances involved. He suggested I learn to play golf. I gave assent to the idea, not expecting anything much to happen. Within a couple of days he arrived on my doorstep with a half-set of clubs for me to purchase, which he had obtained cheaply through an advertisement. The next Tuesday afternoon at two o'clock I was at the municipal golf course, and he expected me to meet him there every Tuesday unless I rang him to the contrary. I never became much of a golfer, but I profited from the exercise and the total change it provided.

AB It should be obvious by now that Derek's work rate was significant! While there are times when I feel it is impossible for me to take time out for exercise or recreation, that does not happen very often. Finding a balance in this is not easy, but we must try. In the early days before change and decay began to take their toll, I played in an indoor soccer league. This put me in an environment that was totally unlike anything else I experienced during the week. It not only allowed me to do something I loved, but it also put me in the company of many non-Christians and provided me with opportunity for witness. I find too that golf is a great way to meet and encourage people while thoroughly testing one's sanctification. Some pastors have taken the pursuit of leisure to a wrongful extreme, but probably most need to "pick up the pace."

Dr. F. W. Boreham found his relaxation in cricket. He wrote,

I have devoted so much time to the game for three reasons. (1) I love it. (2) I find it the most perfect holiday. If I go to the beach or the bush my mind runs on sermons and articles; if I go to cricket, I forget everything but runs and wickets. And (3) I have found it good to form a set of delightful friendships outside the circles in which I habitually move. I review quite impenitently the hundreds of long and leisurely days that I have spent at cricket.[6]

We all need something of interest, totally distinct from our work, to which we can turn our minds for rest and relaxation. When our minds are full at the end of the day with people's needs, it is extremely difficult to turn them away from these things, even though we seek to cast the burden of them upon God. To have something totally different in which we are interested, to which we may turn our minds, is a major help.

DP For me it has been to think of a do-it-yourself job in which I am engaged, or photography or stamp collecting. Dr. Boreham found that in times of insomnia, from which he frequently suffered, nothing helped him more to cope with it, and then to get to sleep, than to follow in his mind's eye memorable matches he had watched.

The pressures of contemporary life demand we give attention and priority to holidays and vacations that fulfill their purpose of renewal and refreshment. A major part of the enjoyment of a vacation is the pleasure and relaxation there is in planning it.

DP We must plan our holidays within our means, and as a rule of thumb I have felt it right to spend a twelfth of my yearly salary on our month's family holiday, when circumstances have not dictated otherwise. It is foolish to skimp on our annual holiday if skimping means it is not going to accomplish its purposes. The growing pattern of churches is to give a winter week's holiday as well as a month in the summer, and this is to be commended. Having experimented in breaking up my month's summer holiday, I concluded that it was best to take the whole month together. It always took me more than a week to unwind and to feel that I was on holiday, and then by the beginning of the fourth week I was just rearing to be back in harness—a healthy sign. Furthermore, I seldom relax if I realize that in a day or so I must be preparing for preaching, since my mind is both consciously and unconsciously thinking about it. If I broke the month up, this kind of intrusion happened more frequently in the holiday.

AB This section illustrates the difference between the British/European approach to holidays and the average American vacation schedule. The American pattern seems to be to take shorter breaks more frequently. Whatever our pattern may be, it is important that it accomplishes the objective of a complete break from the routine activity of pastoral ministry. My personal preference is to take the four-week vacation, but after twenty years I find myself more and more influenced by my environment. We do well to pay particular attention to the hopes and dreams of our wives and children when we seek to determine our approach.

An assistant of Dr. Alexander Whyte's "said that the only advice he remembered receiving from Dr. Whyte was to take good holidays," to which "the old man replied with a smile, 'Well, sir, and if you have followed my advice, have you or your congregation ever seen reason to regret it?'"[7]

When planning our time for our family and relaxation, we probably begin by asking, "What time should I give to my work?" Far from advocating slackness, we would suggest we would do better to ask ourselves, "What time should I give to prayer, to my family, and to relaxation?" Having established these fixed times, we should give the remainder to work. That may be a better way around, for most undershepherds tend to be workaholics.

CHAPTER 14

PERILS TEMPERED
BY PRIVILEGES

In the course of a meeting of ministers when the difficulties of the ministry were under discussion, and the temptations to flee from them were honestly expressed, one minister confessed that on really bad days the only light in the tunnel was the light of a train to take him away! No worthwhile task in any sphere is achieved without obstacles, and so they must be overcome. Unique difficulties associated with the ministry constantly beset us. They need to be balanced by the unique privileges and compensations of the ministry, but when its trials are acute it is easy to lose sight of them.

A VARIETY OF DUTIES

Paul instructed Timothy, "Discharge all the duties of your ministry" (2 Timothy 4:5). Significantly he did not spell out a definitive list; their variety is one of the joys of the ministry, and yet also one of its difficulties. In one week we may counsel a couple who are about to get married, and then spend hours trying to keep another couple together whose marriage is breaking up. We may visit a couple rejoicing in the gift of a child, and moments afterwards go to a family where tragic bereavement has taken place. That same day we may have to speak at a school assembly or Christian union, and then chair an elders' or deacons' meeting. As soon as we get home, we may find someone waiting for us in the depths of despair because of failure or depression. The mail will have brought letters to reply to and urgent testimonials to be written.

Many other daily permutations could be suggested, and, in addition, there is our all-important task of preparing for teaching and preaching and fulfilling these functions efficiently and profitably. Pastoral pressures so easily push out sermon preparation. We get the balance right in these things only by determining our priorities and sticking to them as rigidly as we can, without feeling a failure if we cannot always do so. If we keep our mornings free for study and preparation—apart from pastoral emergencies—we will keep on top of that priority task. If we reckon on devoting most afternoons to pastoral work, with one or two set times for talking with people, either at church or at home, we will keep most of our pastoral work within bounds. Particular discipline is necessary to avoid too many outside commitments. To limit ourselves to one extra meeting a week—like a school assembly or a Christian union—is probably wise.

COMPLEX SOCIAL AND MORAL PROBLEMS

The variety of our duties is compounded by the complexities of so many contemporary social and moral problems, and especially those related to marriage. It would be possible to spend most, if not all, of our time in marriage counseling. If we really get to grips with the needs of society, we are going to have to help people whose background is not dissimilar from that of the Corinthians (1 Corinthians 6:9–11). But we must beware of being sidetracked from our primary task of teaching the Word of God, and not least to such people. If teaching is our calling, we should ensure that others who are not teachers but who have pastoral gifts should undertake the one-to-one care such people require. We may exhaust ourselves counseling people whom really we should have handed on to others, with the consequence that we neglect our primary task.

DP Early on in my ministry, I found myself dealing with a number of people who were depressed. My reaction was to enroll for a course I saw advertised for counseling people with mental illness. I shared my intention with a man who was a spiritual father to me. He immediately rebuked me and said that if I did this, I would soon find more and more people coming to me for such help, and I would be diverted from my primary calling to teach and preach God's Word and to care for people spiritually. His advice was timely. Naturally we want to help people who are depressed, but if it is obvious that it is not just spiritual help that they need, we must be quick to introduce them to someone else who can better assist them. We must not fall into the snare of feeling ourselves to be experts in every area of life.

AB In seeking to respond to the variety of people and problems we face, we have encouraged a number of our own people to attend training in biblical counseling. As a result, in any given week a significant number of individuals are being helped. Instead of all of this falling to the pastoral team we are able to share the load.

When the Reverend Alexander Fraser was inducted in Aberdeen, he told his new congregation, "The ministry is a serious business and I will have no time or strength for side issues. I will concentrate on the real work of the ministry. . . . Even if I am to be considered narrow, I would rather be narrow in the sense that a mill lade is—narrow and deep with some driving force and achieving something—than broad and shallow."

KEEPING PEOPLE TOGETHER

Holding people together is frequently a difficult task. While Christians are united in the fundamentals of the gospel, there are so many secondary matters over which people will have opposite views. People's backgrounds will dictate varying convictions or prejudices. All may agree that evangelism is vital, but there may be sharp reactions to certain forms of evangelism and the methods employed. Words and phrases like Calvinism and Arminianism, or the sovereignty of God and free will, may immediately raise people's hackles; or convictions concerning church government and the place of elders and deacons may threaten to divide people. Terms like *charismatic* and *reformed* tend to produce caricatures, and people take sides without thinking through individual issues as they arise.

As undershepherds we not only have to understand all these and other issues, but our task is to hold people together. We, above all, must be moderate in our expression of our views on these subjects. We are not suggesting we should be wishy-washy or hide our convictions, but we should be outstanding for conveying our convictions without heat or animosity. At the same time, we should teach and demonstrate that secondary matters should never be allowed to divide Christians, and that watchfulness against the enemy is called for whenever they are discussed. As far as possible we should avoid labels that tend to divide. We should take the lead by always asking first, "What do the Scriptures say?" If they are not dogmatic, then we should not be.

There are always controversial matters that, wrongly handled, have the ability to divide the church. Wise pastors do not hedge the issues, but they go out of their way to handle them honorably and spiritually. In the first century both circumcision and slavery held potential for controversy within the church. Paul did not fudge the issues, but he gave positive direction to those who were troubled by them (1 Corinthians 7:17–24). We must aim to do the same with the topics that trouble God's people now.

MISCONCEPTIONS ABOUT A PASTOR'S CALLING

A difficulty we are often aware of in the ministry arises from the misconceptions people have of our task. At one extreme some may think we only work on a Sunday, and at the other we may be expected to be able to do everything that needs to be done in the church. We may be expected to be an evangelist as well as a pastor, whereas the two gifts are quite distinct. There is a difference between being gifted as an evangelist and doing the work of an evangelist (2 Timothy 4:5), but people in general may not be aware of it. Here, as elsewhere, we find extremes: People may have too high a view of the minister's importance or too low. People may consider that the whole success of the church's endeavors is tied up with his performance, and they look to him rather like football supporters look to a football coach—if the team does not win, then he ought to be replaced.

DP In the first church I served, we had a shrewd caretaker, who recognized the inevitable honeymoon period most pastors experience with a church, prompting him to tell me one day, "In the first year, they idolize you; the second, they criticize you; and in the third they ostracize you." I am glad that he was not proved right, but there is a necessary warning within those words against worrying about people's conceptions of us and our task.

AB The quarreling and boasting in the Corinthian church emerged in part from confusion about the role and significance of the church's leaders. In my experience this uncertainty remains a feature in many of our churches. Clericalism puts the pastor on a pedestal, and anticlericalism seeks to knock him off. We are wise to steer clear of the pedestals.

We cannot correct misconceptions at a stroke. If correction is to be achieved, it is best done when our systematic exposition of the Scriptures arrives at passages where a correct view of the ministry is conveyed. To do it otherwise is open to misunderstanding. At the same time we must be clear in our own minds what our primary tasks are and stick to them whatever people may think or say. Time will prove the wisdom of this and provide the best instruction for God's people. Preaching on 1 Corinthians 4:1, Charles Simeon began, "The ministers of Christ are generally unduly exalted or undeservedly depreciated, by those around them; but they should discharge their duties with fidelity, without any regard to the opinions of men, and approve themselves to him who will judge them righteously in the last day."

OPPOSITION AND THE SPIRITUAL BATTLE

One of the most difficult situations to face is opposition from God's people. We ought not to be surprised that it happens, since Satan is the accuser of the brethren. Our very endeavor to achieve balance, and to hold people together, may at times mean that few people are pleased with us, because we refuse to take sides. We may be misunderstood and maligned, especially by those who do not appreciate the adherence we give to God's will through obedience to the Scriptures rather than to any labeled position or tradition. People may turn from us and desert us when we most need them.

Our consolations are real: First, we follow in the footsteps of our Master; and, second, walking in His footsteps we will find that He never leaves us without the assurance of His presence when we most require it—an assurance that will give us the strength to hold fast to what is right (cf. 2 Timothy 4:16–18). As Charles Simeon said when misrepresented, "My enemy, whatever evil he says of me, does not reduce me so low as he would if he knew all concerning me that God does." These and similar difficulties are all part of the spiritual battle in which we are necessarily involved.

In his letters to Timothy, the young man called to be a shepherd and teacher, Paul uses most forcibly the language of battle: "Fight the good fight" (1 Timothy 1:18); "Fight the good fight of the faith" (1 Timothy 6:12); "Endure hardship with us like a good soldier of Christ Jesus" (2 Timothy 2:3). We must not flinch from the necessary battle that there is in the care of souls and the winning of the lost. Our principal recourse must be to put on as deliberately as we can the whole armor of God (Ephesians 6:10–18), for wearing each piece we shall be able to stand successfully against every assault. Wearing the armor, we shall be able to take up the two weapons with confidence. No weapon in our hands is more powerful than the Scriptures, and no resource greater than prayer. As John Newton said to a young minister much aware of the battle, "Above all things, be sure not to be enticed or terrified from the privilege of a throne of grace," for the devil would want to rob us of it.

TRIALS

Trials are a necessary part of the ministry; not that we should look for them, but we should not be surprised by them (cf. 2 Corinthians 6:3–10). They can be divided into three principal groups. The first are those of a general nature such as the common difficulties of life: suffering, accidents, dangers, and sadnesses from which we are not exempt as God's servants. God uses them in order to make us better equipped to help and comfort others. Martin Luther declared trials and temptations to be a minister's best teachers.

The second group are trials inflicted by others through their too high expectations and demands, or misrepresentation or misunderstanding, or simply the unceasing demands of people to be cared for, with the consequence that we never feel our work is done.

The third group are self-inflicted for the sake of the work, in our constant availability to people, our refusal to work set hours, the loneliness of avoiding special friendships so as to serve the whole flock, the burden sometimes of leadership and of maintaining confidentiality, and our denying ourselves the luxury of self-pity when the going is tough.

Few if any of us anticipated beforehand how great the difficulties of the ministry were going to be. "The ministry of the gospel," John Newton wrote, "like the book which the Apostle John ate, is a bitter sweet; but the sweetness is tasted first, the bitterness is usually known afterwards, when we are so far engaged that there is no going back." No trials are wasted in God's economy. Spiritual graces such as purity, understanding, patience, kindness, and sincere love shine out by the Spirit's power all the more powerfully against the background of our trials (cf. 2 Corinthians 6:6).

Our greatest difficulty is when we feel that the trials implicit in our ministry detrimentally affect our families. We can accept suffering in our service for ourselves, but we are unhappy about that which troubles those whom we love. That is a reasonable attitude, and we may have the confidence that the well-being of our family and the well-being of God's people are never in conflict in God's will and purpose. When some right course of action appears costly to our families as well as to us, we will prove God's faithfulness— He is never in our debt.

The trials of the ministry require two virtues in particular: patience and self-control. As well as enduring hardship like soldiers, we need to be patient like farmers and self-controlled like athletes (2 Timothy 2:4–6). When others lose their patience or their tempers, we must not (1 Thessalonians 5:14). When it seems that Christians are unwilling to face up to necessary change, we must be prepared to be patient with them, and to teach the new generation of Christians we see established to test everything by Scripture, rather than by practice, tradition, or custom. A major benefit of longer rather than shorter ministries is that they provide the opportunity for the exercise of patience, and in particular the patient sowing of God's Word, to bring about the change and progress He purposes.

LAZINESS

Perils go hand in hand with difficulties. We mention laziness first not because it is the most likely peril, but because it would be foolish to ignore it. Most of our work is unseen, whether it is private prayer, preparation for preaching, or visitation. Working on our own, we work to our own timetable. We determine when we start work each day and how much time we apportion to each responsibility. Laziness, slackness, and failure to discipline ourselves in the use of our time lead to our being unbusinesslike and unreliable. Some are naturally better organizers than others, but a degree of organization is necessary for efficiency. Behind the apology "I'm no organizer," there may be a streak of laziness to be corrected. We need to be sitting at our desks as punctually as anyone in an office, and to organize our calls as systematically and carefully as a doctor on his rounds.

In a postcard to a friend in the ministry, Dr. Alexander Whyte wrote, "Nothing will make up for a bad pastorate. The blood of Christ itself does not speak peace to my conscience in respect of a bad pastorate. Set every invitation and opportunity aside in the interest of a good conscience toward the homes of your people."[1] "All would be well," said Samuel Rutherford, "if I were free of old challenges of guiltiness, and for neglect in my calling, and for speaking too little for my Well-Beloved's crown, honour and kingdom."

DISCOURAGEMENT

Discouragement is a most subtle peril. Involved so much with people and their spiritual progress, people may give us tremendous joy and great sorrow. The very people who have given the greatest joy may give the greatest sorrow. While Paul could write, "Now we really live, since you are standing firm in the Lord" (1 Thessalonians 3:8), he knew the opposite emotion when believers wavered and went backward. God's people have a unique capacity to sweeten or spoil our days, to thrill us or to cast us into the depths of depression. One moment we may feel that there is no other place to be but where we are, and the next we wish we could be anywhere else. People may listen carefully to what we say as we faithfully declare the truths of the gospel, and then choose to turn away. "Have I now become your enemy," Paul wrote to the Galatians (4:16), "by telling you the truth?" We may feel acutely the absence of those who have decided not to come anymore because they have found the cost of discipleship too great.

VULNERABILITY TO CRITICISM

Discouragement may arise from our particular vulnerability to criticism. When the team plays well, everyone congratulates the team; but when it plays badly, everyone blames the captain or coach. It is inevitable that people express their criticisms to us as to no one else, and before we know where we are we may become preoccupied with them, forgetting all the good things that are equally important. A few critical individuals may blind us to the support of a great crowd of others and cause us to lose our balance. If criticisms are voiced when we feel a particular sense of failure or lack of success, we will be all the more discouraged and filled with self-doubt. "A survey among 300 United Methodist pastors in Minnesota in USA found that 'while they all enjoyed their work . . . a majority were also afflicted with self-doubt and loneliness.'"[2] Doubt is a root cause of anxiety and discouragement.

However discouragement comes, we must learn to talk to ourselves as David does in Psalms 42 and 43. If we are discouraged because of people's turning away from God's truth that we have taught, we must remind ourselves that our natural desire to stand well in the affections and regard of those we shepherd must never mean that we compromise the truth or hold back saying all we know ought to be said. We may trust God's Spirit to witness to their consciences that what we have said is true (2 Corinthians 4:2). If we are discouraged because of self-doubt and awareness of failure, we should remind ourselves that it is "through God's mercy we have this ministry" (2 Corinthians 4:1), and that we did not call ourselves, but God called us. With that confidence we may then fan into flame the gift of God that is in us through our being set apart for the ministry (2 Timothy 1:6), knowing that God has not given us a spirit of fear, but of power, and of love, and of self-discipline (2 Timothy 1:7).

If criticisms are just, we should be thankful and act upon them as part of God's gracious discipline. If they are unjust, we should commit our cause to God who judges justly, even as our Savior did (1 Peter 2:21–23), thanking God for the privilege of walking in His Son's footsteps and for the knowledge that He knows the truth about us (1 Corinthians 4:1–5). True to the Lord, and true to our conscience, we may leave the outcome to Him.

OVER-INVOLVEMENT WITH
PEOPLE'S TROUBLES, STRESS, AND BURNOUT

Because we so regularly have people coming to us with problems, we can become too problem-conscious, so that our teaching and preaching become problem-oriented, rather than concentrating on the clear exposition of the whole of Scripture, which has unique ability to provide spiritual answers to people's problems without our knowing them or the answers God will give to them through the preaching of His Word. The benefit of knowing our people and their difficulties well is that our teaching is anchored in reality. That does not mean that every time we teach we deliberately address the battles they fight. The best answer we can give so often is a clear view of Jesus Christ and the resources He provides.

Some of the sad circumstances into which we enter will frequently live with us, and as we go to bed at night, we may find our mind returning to them and reviewing all we have said and how we might have dealt with them more effectively. There will be occasions when we genuinely weep with people, and we cannot simply turn off our feelings when we leave them and return home. Paul knew the daily pressure of his concern for all the churches, so that he could write, "Who is weak, and I do not feel weak? Who is led into sin, and I do not inwardly burn?" (2 Corinthians 11:29). Committed to sharing people's deepest concerns, we must school ourselves to cast the care of them constantly upon God, and to keep on doing so no matter how inclined we may be to carry them.

There is the added peril that in helping people we may become emotionally involved, and this argues particularly against regular in-depth counseling with someone of the opposite sex. Similarly, in trying to help others in their temptations, we may be tempted ourselves, as the New Testament warns us: "If someone is caught in sin, you who are spiritual should restore him gently. But watch yourself, or you also may be tempted" (Galatians 6:1). Sins and temptations are discussed with us about which we could wish we had never heard and which Satan may use as an unexpected means of assault. We should beware of any subtle pleasure in people's sharing their sins and temptations, and we should put a restraint upon their doing so when no good purpose is served.

Stress comes in a variety of forms. We mentioned earlier the possibility of financial stress, and this is accentuated when the church fellowship itself is under pressure to meet its financial commitment to us. Where the latter is the case, the contemporary equivalent of Paul's tent-making ministry is a worthy expedient, when feasible, providing our motivation is not material gain but the relieving of the church of what is perhaps an unfair burden. Stress comes through the open-ended nature of our work and our essential commitment to people. People may stress us. We probably underestimate what is taken out of us in pastoral work. We may find ourselves working fourteen or more hours a day, seven days a week. We get into what seems an endless treadmill of weekly preparation, mixed with crises, with little time to breathe.

Our wives will probably be aware first of the stress under which we work, and if we are not careful it will rub off onto them. Our sleep pattern may be influenced by it, so that sleeping less well, we become increasingly tired. We then find ourselves working harder, and the more we ruthlessly push ourselves the less efficient we become. The stress factor may be accentuated by the winds of change that constantly come upon the church, especially through issues like charismatic renewal, forms of worship, and increased participation by people in worship and ministry, which unwisely handled may divide rather than unite God's people. We may not have the time we would wish to think through our own understanding on such matters. While members of the congregation seem able to opt out of responsibility, we know we cannot. It is not surprising that what is commonly described as "burnout" then takes place.

A degree of stress is not bad for us, and some is inevitable in all caring professions. As pastors we must never give up on God's people: We must be willing to bear a great deal, and then to bear a great deal more. This is part of our filling up in our flesh "what is still lacking in regard to Christ's afflictions" (Colossians 1:24). But some stress is self-imposed, and it is to that we must give our attention. Talking things through with another pastor, especially if he is more experienced, can be invaluable. To sit down quietly, in an attitude of prayer, in order to write down our present priorities and what we ought to do to meet them may reveal areas where we have gotten our responsibilities out of balance. If we have been neglecting our day off, and time for physical and mental relaxation, then we must remedy the situation immediately. If we have been too busy to take in as well as to give out spiritually, we must take ourselves to task.

Spurgeon told the story of Old Nat,

> who had a large wood pile besides him, and he sawed very hard to make that pile smaller. His saw wanted sharpening and resetting, and it was dreadful work to make it go at all. An honest neighbour stepped up to him, and said, "Nat, why don't you get that saw sharpened? You want to get that put to rights, and then you could do a deal more than you are now doing." "Now then," replied Nat, "don't you come bothering here. I have quite enough to do to saw that pile of wood, without stopping to sharpen my saw."

We may feel too busy to go to ministers' conferences, whereas they may be God's provision to take us out of our situation to see it with a God-given perspective.

※

DP Looking back I regret two things in this regard: first, that I did not regularly attend at least one ministers' conference each year; and, second, that I did not have a regular sabbatical. In thirty years in pastoral charge, I had two, and on both occasions they were significant times of refueling and retooling, as much to the church's benefit as my own.

AB I have tried to learn from Derek's sense of regret. I have found that the privilege of speaking at ministers' conferences, where there were other speakers whose expositions and company I have enjoyed, has helped to maintain a sense of spiritual equilibrium as well as to recharge my battery.

AN OCCASIONAL DESIRE TO ESCAPE

The grass always looks greener in someone else's field. But we would not be long in another person's situation without finding similar battles, discouragements, and difficulties. When acute pressures are on us and discouragement covers us like a heavy blanket, the one thought we may have is of escape. There have been times when we have secretly longed to be somewhere else, and yet have known that is not the answer. Godly pastor as he was, Thomas Boston once complained that he was "staked in Ettrick." Isaac Watts entered into correspondence with a young man who assisted an older minister in a new chapel in Southampton. After some eighteen months he was unhappy and he wrote to Watts as he contemplated moving. Watts replied:

> Your last is now before me with all the long details of discouragements. . . . I own many of them to be just . . . if we look merely to appearances. But I have a few things to offer which will in some measure, I hope, reconcile your thoughts to a long continuance

among them. 1. Consider how great things God has done . . . in Southampton by your means. . . . 2. There are some persons in whom God has begun a good work . . . by your means. Oh, do not think of forsaking them! 3. There is scarce any people . . . who love their minister and honour and esteem him more than yours do you. . . . 4. Where is the man who is better qualified for carrying on God's work in the town than you are? 5. If you leave, whither will you go? The case is the same in many places as it is with you and much worse. 6. Consider whether this be not a temptation thrown in your way to discourage you in your work. 7. Let us remember that we are not engaged in a work that depends all upon reasonings, and prospects and probabilities, and present appearances, but upon the hand and Spirit of God. If He will work, who shall hinder? . . . Meditate on these things. Turn your thoughts to the objects which are more joyful, and the occasions you have for thankfulness. Praise and thanksgiving are springs to the soul and give it new activity.[3]

The young man followed Watts' advice, and evident success followed in the place he had been tempted to leave. A pastor shared how during a particularly difficult time in the seventh year of his first pastorate he was tempted to move elsewhere through an invitation extended to him. The main attraction was the possibility of leaving the difficulties behind him. He resisted, and testified that, looking back, he marveled at God's grace, because it was from then on that things changed and remarkable blessing came to the church. Difficulties are no ground for leaving God's people; they may simply underline the need God's people have for an undershepherd.

PRIDE AND ITS ATTENDANT PERILS

There are other perils in the ministry for which we have greater responsibility and that may be of our own making. The foremost peril here is pride. Ministering to others, whether in pastoral care or public teaching and preaching, tends to make us prominent and puts us in the public eye. We may easily slip into the snare of enjoying our work for the wrong reasons. Unconsciously we may give a false impression of superiority, and live for people's approval and applause, forgetting how ordinary we are.

John Newton described popularity in the ministry as walking on ice. We naturally and rightly want to be successful in God's service; but success may go to our heads, rather than humbling us and causing us to give heartfelt praise to God. William Burns found himself flattered when a woman told him that she was as blessed through his ministry as she had been under Robert Murray M'Cheyne's. He wrote in his diary that night, "I told her not to cast sparks from hell into my inflammable heart—to give thanks to God, and to beware of commending men."

John Thornton told Charles Simeon that there are three lessons which a minister has to learn: "1. Humility. 2. Humility. 3. Humility." Afterward Simeon wrote out twice in his private notebook in large letters, "Talk not about myself." We must never let ourselves or others forget that we are but "jars of clay" to show that all that is good is from God and not from us (2 Corinthians 4:7).

While Paul set the highest standards and example, he never failed to acknowledge that he was the worst of sinners (1 Timothy 1:15). Being regularly up front does not mean that we need always to be portraying a triumphant spirit. People will find us more approachable and helpful if we honestly acknowledge that we walk with a limp as they do. As often as it is natural, we must put ourselves and other Christian leaders in their proper place as Paul did: "What, after all, is Apollos? And what is Paul? Only servants, through whom you came to believe—as the Lord has assigned to each his task. I planted the seed, Apollos watered it, but God made it grow. So neither he who plants nor he who waters is anything, but only God, who makes things grow" (1 Corinthians 3:5–7).

There is always the danger of binding people to ourselves, rather than to our Lord Jesus Christ, and for their loyalty to be directed at us rather than at Him. This explains why Paul baptized few people, but left it to others (1 Corinthians 1:14–15). Without our wanting it to be the case, we may find people making an idol of us and exaggerating our importance. This does no good to them or to us. We need to remember two salutary truths. First, if they knew us as we know ourselves, they would never make so much of us—in fact, the opposite. Second, we find ourselves aware of the stars only when we cannot see the sun; we are preoccupied with men only when our minds are turned away from God. Although we cannot as shepherds and teachers keep ourselves in the background, we should try to make people forget us and remember our Master; we should always be saying in effect, by life and by lip, "Look at Christ! Look at Him!" If we do not do that, no matter how successful people feel us to be, we are failures. Experience also shows that idols never survive; something always happens to oust them from their wrongful place—God sees to that in His mysterious and sovereign manner.

Jealousy and worldliness in the ministry arise from pride. We can be jealous of other ministers who are in large churches or who are more obviously successful than we are. Philippians 1:15 illustrates how there can be an unspiritual rivalry between God's servants. With Paul's arrival on the scene, certain preachers lost their prominence and became jealous. Their reaction was to concentrate even more on being successful preachers, but with entirely wrong motives.

There is a worldliness that is unique to the ministry. It may be in the subtle snare of judging a call to a church by its size, its income, and its reputation, and of thinking of status and position in the body of Christ. Whenever we are aware of jealousy toward a fellow shepherd and teacher, we should include him daily in our prayers, striving to thank God for him, and crying for God's continuing blessing upon him. God will honor such a response, and make it real, so that jealousy is removed.

There is also the worldliness of a professional attitude to our work. The world at large regards the ministry as a profession, rather than the calling that it is. As people vie for positions in their profession, so we may fall into the snare of vying for positions in the church, whether within a denomination or being called to what may be regarded as a "prize" church.

If we are in God's will, we have no reason to envy anyone. God made us the people we are, and the gifts we have are in His sovereign power to give. Success in spiritual work is not synonymous with being in the public eye or even being regarded by God's people as successful. Success is finishing the work God has given us, and no one else, to do.

HURTING THE CHURCH

The greatest peril for shepherds and teachers is that while they have such a potential for good, they have equal potential for evil if they fail to fulfill their ministry. John Brown's prayer that "I may not tear God's Church, mangle His truths, betray His honour, or murder the souls of men" should be on our lips often. Richard Baxter gave eight reasons that ministers should examine themselves:

(1) You have heaven to win or lose yourselves. . . . A holy calling will not save an unholy man.
(2) You have sinful inclinations as well as others.
(3) [Ministers] have greater temptations than most men.
(4) The tempter will make his first and sharpest onset upon you. If you will be leaders against him, he will spare you no further than God restrains him.
(5) Many eyes are upon you, and therefore there will be many to observe your falls.
(6) Your sins are more aggravated than those of other men. They have more of hypocrisy in them, and are more detrimental to the cause of religion.

(7) The honour of your Lord and Master, and of His holy truth, doth lie more on you than other men.

(8) The souls of your hearers and the success of your labours do very much depend upon your self-examination.

When pastors turn aside from the Way, they cause many to stumble (Malachi 2:5–8). There can be nothing worse than seeing what a man has spent a lifetime building up suddenly destroyed in a moment by senseless failure. To be ruthless in the face of all temptations, and self-disciplined in all potential areas of failure, is not unnecessary for, as Paul says, "No, I beat my body and make it my slave so that after I have preached to others, I myself will not be disqualified for the prize" (1 Corinthians 9:27).

Privilege can seldom be enjoyed without corresponding responsibility, and shepherds and teachers will be judged more strictly than others (James 3:1). As shepherds we have responsibility for the sheep, and as teachers we must practice what we teach. As shepherds we must seek the other sheep that have to be brought into the fold, even as the Chief Shepherd did, and we must teach and preach faithfully the only gospel by which men and women can be saved. To be called to preach this gospel and to preach something else brings the greatest condemnation (Galatians 1:8). "Woe to me," Paul exclaimed, "if I do not preach the gospel!" (1 Corinthians 9:16). We must set ourselves to follow in Christ's footsteps— even to laying down our lives for the flock—and to preaching His gospel so that we exalt Him. If we feel out of our depth in the ministry, that is good, for we are. We are then in a position to depend upon God from whom competency to minister comes. A. W. Tozer formalized in later years a prayer he prayed before his ordination, in which he prayed at the end:

Though I am chosen of Thee and honoured by a high and holy calling, let me never forget that I am but a man of dust and ashes, a man with all the natural faults and passions that plague the race of men. I pray Thee, therefore, my Lord and Redeemer, save me from myself and from all the injuries I may do myself while trying to be a blessing to others. Fill me with Thy power by the Holy Spirit, and I will go in Thy strength and tell of Thy righteousness, even Thine only. I will spread abroad the message of redeeming love while my normal powers endure.[4]

PRIVILEGES AND COMPENSATIONS

We have considered the difficulties and perils of the ministry in order to be as realistic and as honest as possible, and so as to suggest positive approaches, remedies, and means of overcoming them. But the privileges far outweigh every difficulty and hardship. No privilege on earth can compete with being servants of the Lord Christ, entrusted with the care of His people and the stewardship of the gospel. When we see our ministry in its proper perspective, it is an extension of our Lord Jesus' ministry: He is our model, and His strength is our resource. Those who walk most in His footsteps know most of His fellowship. All valid ministry is an expression of His ministry to people.

As Satan strives to discourage us by disappointments, God will encourage us by the faithfulness of individual Christians and the love they express to us (Acts 28:15; 2 Timothy 1:16–18). Pastoral work brings rich compensations (1 Corinthians 15:31), and not least the joy of seeing our spiritual children go on in the faith and surpass our own progress. Flavel expressed this well, centuries ago:

> O brethren! who would not study and pray, spend and be spent, in the service of such a bountiful Master! Is it not worth all our labours and sufferings, to come with all those souls we instrumentally begat to Christ; and all that we edified, reduced, confirmed, and comforted in the way to heaven; and say, Lord, here am I, and the children thou hast given me? To hear one spiritual child say, Lord, this is the minister, by whom I believed; Another, this is he,

by whom I was edified, established and comforted. This is the man that resolved my doubts, quickened my dying affections, reduced my soul, when wandering from the truth! O blessed be thy name, that I ever saw his face, and heard his voice![5]

There are occasions, too personal and precious to share with others, when God graciously gives glimpses of what He has achieved through our ministry, and the hardships and difficulties are forgotten even as a mother forgets the travail when her child is safely born. But the best joys are in the future when we and our spiritual children will be gathered to our Lord Jesus Christ when He comes (1 Thessalonians 2:19). By God's mercy, we shall have many surprises that will be our glory and joy (1 Thessalonians 2:20). While the world may have despised what we have done, our Lord will not do so. Every endeavor in His name will be rewarded, and we shall discover that our labor in Him has not been in vain (1 Corinthians 15:58). No stress or pressure, no tear or groan that we have borne in His name will be overlooked. We will enter into the Chief Shepherd's joy, the joy that He set before Himself as He endured the Cross. Anything is worth enduring to share the Shepherd's joy!

NOTES

Chapter 1: The Call and the Calling

1. W. Y. Fullerton, *Life of F. B. Meyer* (London: Marshall, Morgan and Scott, 1929), 17.

2. Timothy Dudley Smith, *John Stott: The Making of a Leader* (Downers Grove, Ill.: InterVarsity, 1999), 87, 165.

3. Martyn Lloyd-Jones, *God's Ultimate Purpose: An Exposition of Ephesians 1:1–23* (Carlisle, Pa.: Banner of Truth, 1978), 92.

4. Alan Stibbs, *Expounding God's Word* (Downers Grove, Ill.: InterVarsity, 1970), 9–10.

5. P. Sangster, *Dr. Sangster* (London: Epworth, 1962), 76f.

Chapter 2: Life and Character

1. *Trail's Works,* Vol. 1, (Edinburgh: Banner of Trust Trust, 1975), 250.

2. Hugh Evans Hopkins, *Charles Simeon of Cambridge* (London: Hodder and Stoughton, 1977), 43f.

3. C. H. Spurgeon, *An All-Round Ministry* (Carlisle, Pa.: Banner of Truth, 1981), 3f. Scripture quotation is Hebrews 11:33–34 KJV.

Chapter 4: Prayer

1. Hugh Evans Hopkins, *Charles Simeon of Cambridge* (London: Hodder and Stoughton, 1977), 147.

2. Quoted by Dr. Martyn Lloyd-Jones in *The Puritans: Their Origins and Successors* (Carlisle, Pa.: Banner of Truth, 1987), 189f.

Chapter 6: Study

1. C. H. Spurgeon, *An All-Round Ministry* (Carlisle, Pa.: Banner of Truth, 1981), 133f.

2. A. Porritt, *John Henry Jowett* (London: Hodder and Stoughton, 1924), 146.

3. From *Power in Preaching,* quoted by Paul Sangster in *Dr. Sangster* (London: Epworth, 1962), 277f.

4. Iain Murray, *The Puritan Hope* (Carlisle, Pa.: Banner of Truth, 1975), 148.

5. Iain Murray, *The Life of Arthur W. Pink* (Carlisle, Pa.: Banner of Truth, 1982), 254.

Chapter 7: Preaching

1. Martyn Lloyd-Jones, *Preaching and Preachers* (Grand Rapids: Zondervan, 1972), 17.

2. A. Gammie, *Rev. John McNeill: His Life and Work* (London: Pickering and Inglis, 1934), 39.

3. John Shaw, *The Character of a Pastor According to God's Heart* (Morgan, Pa.: Soli Deo Gloria, 1992), 10.

4. Lloyd-Jones, *Preaching and Preachers,* 99.

Chapter 8: Pastoral Care

1. W. Wand, *Changeful Page* (London: Hodder and Stoughton, 1965), 98.

2. C. Warr, *The Glimmering Landscape* (London: Hodder and Stoughton, 1960), 117.

3. G. F. Barbour, *Alexander Whyte* (London: Hodder and Stoughton, 1925), 363f.

Chapter 9: Pastoral Care—The Practicalities

1. F. W. Boreham, *My Pilgrimage* (London: Epworth, 1940), 54f.

2. P. Sangster, *Dr. Sangster* (London: Epworth, 1962), 134f.

3. H. Hopkins, *Charles Simeon of Cambridge* (London: Hodder and Stoughton, 1977), 47f.

Chapter 10: The Conduct of Worship

1. E. L. Langston, *Bishop Taylor Smith* (London: Marshall, Morgan and Scott, 1939), 33.

Chapter 11: The Responsibility to Lead

1. Commissioned by the Church of England in the twentieth century, entitled *Towards the Conversion of England* (London, 1945), 3.

Chapter 12: Delegation

1. David Watson, *I Believe in the Church* (London: Hodder and Stoughton, 1978), 246.

2. Adam Smith, *Wealth of Nations,* Vol. 1, 8.

3. John Kenneth Galbraith, *The Age of Uncertainty* (London: London British Broadcasting Association, 1977), 23.

4. G. F. Barbour, *Alexander Whyte* (London: Hodder and Stoughton, 1925), 358.

Chapter 13: Family and Leisure

1. H. E. Hopkins, *Simeon of Cambridge* (London: Hodder and Stoughton, 1977), 120.

2. W. Wand, *Changeful Page* (London: Hodder and Stoughton, 1965), 97.

3. Quoted in John Carson, *Fraser of Tain* (Glasgow, 1966), 113.

4. P. Sangster, *Dr. Sangster* (London: Epworth,1962), 68.

5. S. Verney, *Fire in Coventry* (London: Hodder and Stoughton, 1964), 57.

6. F. W. Boreham, *My Pilgrimage* (London: Epworth, 1940), 16f.

7. Dr. G. H. Morrison in the *British Weekly,* 8 December 1910 (London).

Chapter 14: Perils Tempered by Privileges

1. G. F. Barbour, *Alexander Whyte* (London: Hodder and Stoughton, 1925), 528.

2. *Scottish Baptist,* October 1987 (Glasglow).

3. David G. Fountain, *Isaac Watts Remembered* (Worthing: Henry E. Walter, 1974), 81f.

4. "The Prayer of a Minor Prophet," *The Alliance Weekly,* May 1950.

5. *John Flavel: VI,* (Carlisle, Pa.: Banner of Truth, 1968), 579.

SINCE 1894, Moody Publishers has been dedicated to equip and motivate people to advance the cause of Christ by publishing evangelical Christian literature and other media for all ages, around the world. Because we are a ministry of the Moody Bible Institute of Chicago, a portion of the proceeds from the sale of this book go to train the next generation of Christian leaders.

If we may serve you in any way in your spiritual journey toward understanding Christ and the Christian life, please contact us at www.moodypublishers.com.

"All Scripture is God-breathed and is useful for teaching, rebuking, correcting and training in righteousness, so that the man of God may be thoroughly equipped for every good work."
—*2 TIMOTHY 3:16, 17*

MOODY
PUBLISHERS
THE NAME YOU CAN TRUST®

On Being a Pastor Team

Acquiring Editor
Greg Thornton

Copy Editor
Cheryl Dunlop

Back Cover Copy
Paige Drygas, The Livingstone Corporation

Cover Design
Smartt Guys Design

Cover Photos
David Smith

Interior Design
Ragont Design

Printing and Binding
Lake Book Manufacturing, Inc.

The typeface for the text of this book is
Fairfield LH